Transitional and Transformative Justice

This book engages the limits of transitional justice and, more specifically, the interface between transitional justice and the related concept of transformative justice. Challenging and developing the work of transitional justice scholars and practitioners, the book addresses both the limitations of existing mechanisms in contexts where they are currently applied, as well as the possibilities for using, or adapting, transitional justice mechanisms in contexts typically viewed as outside their usual remit. More specifically, chapters address shortcomings with regard to victim participation in transitional justice mechanisms in Cambodia; consider how the transformative justice framework might be mobilised to overcome limitations of standard approaches to transitional justice in addressing structural violence in post-conflict Colombia; and address how the concept of transformative justice could be used to address historical wrongs in post-apartheid South Africa and post-war Bosnia-Herzegovina. Further chapters explore the intersections of identity and culture with transitional and transformative justice, consider the role of elites in transitional and transformative justice, and put forward the case for applying a broader approach to historical truth-telling than is typical in transitional justice.

Dr Matthew Evans is a teaching fellow in law, politics and sociology at the School of Law, Politics and Sociology, University of Sussex, Brighton, UK, and visiting researcher in political studies at the School of Social Sciences, University of the Witwatersrand, Johannesburg, South Africa.

Part of the TRANSITIONAL JUSTICE series

Series editor:
Kieran McEvoy, Queen's University Belfast, UK

For information about the series and details of previous and forthcoming titles, see www.routledge.com/Transitional-Justice/book-series/TRANJ

Transitional and Transformative Justice

Critical and International Perspectives

Edited by
Matthew Evans

Routledge
Taylor & Francis Group
a GlassHouse book

First published 2019
by Routledge
2 Park Square, Milton Park, Abingdon, Oxon OX14 4RN

and by Routledge
52 Vanderbilt Avenue, New York, NY 10017

First issued in paperback 2020

A GlassHouse book

Routledge is an imprint of the Taylor & Francis Group, an informa business

British Library Cataloguing in Publication Data
A catalogue record for this book is available from the British Library

Library of Congress Cataloging-in-Publication Data
Names: Evans, Matthew, (Political scientist), editor.
Title: Transitional and transformative justice : critical and international perspectives / edited by Matthew Evans.
Description: Abingdon, Oxon [UK] ; New York, NY : Routledge, 2019. |
Series: Transitional justice | Includes bibliographical references and index.
Identifiers: LCCN 2018045125 | ISBN 9781138478510 (hbk)
Subjects: LCSH: Transitional justice. | Restorative justice. | Reparation (Criminal justice) | Political crimes and offenses.
Classification: LCC K5250 .T73 2019 | DDC 340/.115--dc23
LC record available at https://lccn.loc.gov/2018045125

ISBN 13: 978-0-367-66266-0 (pbk)
ISBN 13: 978-1-138-47851-0 (hbk)

Typeset in Galliard
by Taylor & Francis Books

Contents

Contributors

Cathy Bollaert is a PhD graduate from the Transitional Justice Institute at Ulster University. She has been involved in grass-roots reconciliation and peace-building initiatives located in South Africa, Sri Lanka, England and Northern Ireland. Her research focuses on the intersection between identity, culture and transitional justice.

Caterina Bonora is a lecturer at the Institute for European Studies, University of Bremen. She completed a PhD in Political Science at the Bremen International Graduate School of Social Sciences. Her research interests span the areas of human rights, civil society and global governance, the politics of gender and the post-Yugoslav space.

Matthew Evans teaches law, politics and sociology at the University of Sussex and is visiting researcher in political studies at the University of the Witwatersrand. Recent articles appear in *International Politics* and *Social and Legal Studies.* His first book is *Transformative Justice: Remedying Human Rights Violations Beyond Transition* (Routledge, 2018).

Paul Gready is the Director of the Centre for Applied Human Rights at the University of York and is co-editor of the *Journal of Human Rights Practice.* His most recent book is *From Transitional to Transformative Justice* (co-edited with Simon Robins, 2019).

Rachel Killean is a lecturer in law at Queen's University Belfast. Her research focuses on transitional justice, particularly international criminal justice and the role of victims within international criminal courts. Recent articles appear in the *International Criminal Law Review* and the *Journal of International Criminal Justice.* Her first book is *Victims, Atrocity and International Criminal Justice: Lessons from Cambodia* (Routledge, 2018).

Daniela Lai is a lecturer in international relations at London South Bank University. Her research focuses on the relationship between transitional justice and socioeconomic justice. She has recently published in the *Journal of Intervention and Statebuilding* and is a convenor of the British International Studies Association's South East Europe Working Group.

Pádraig McAuliffe has been Associate Head and senior lecturer at the University of Liverpool's School of Law and Social Justice since 2013. His research interests include rule of law, transitional justice and the historical institutionalism of human rights. His publications include *Transformative Transitional Justice and the Malleability of States* (2017).

Dáire McGill received his PhD from the Transitional Justice Institute at Ulster University in late 2018. His current research operationalises the transformative justice framework to create an analytical tool capable of identifying the transformative potential of initiatives implemented in transitional societies. He has recently published in the *State Crime Journal.*

Lars Waldorf is a reader at Dundee Law School. He has authored numerous publications on transitional justice, legal empowerment, and Rwanda, including three co-edited books, and is an associate editor at *The International Journal of Human Rights* and on the editorial board of the *Journal of Human Rights Practice.*

David Wilkins is an historian and teacher. He undertook his PhD at the Wilberforce Institute for the Study of Slavery and Emancipation, University of Hull and was a postdoctoral research fellow at the Wits School of Arts, University of the Witwatersrand (2014–2016). Recent articles appear in *Social and Legal Studies* and the *South African Historical Journal.*

Chapter summaries

1 Transitional justice and beyond: an introduction to critical, international and interdisciplinary debates – Matthew Evans

This chapter introduces and explores the key debates in which the book intervenes. Highlighting both the increasing acceptance of the implementation of transitional justice mechanisms following conflict and authoritarian rule, and increasing contestation and criticism of transitional justice in theory and practice, the chapter sets out the themes of the volume. Questions around both the limits of common transitional justice mechanisms such as criminal tribunals and truth commissions and the scope for applying lessons from transitional justice to a broader focus are explored. In particular, the chapter outlines debates over the space for the lived reality of affected communities and the participation of victims to be reflected in transitional justice mechanisms, the possible application of the emerging transformative justice framework and the interaction of transitional justice with intergenerational injustices. The chapter emphasises the need to engage critically and across national contexts in considering how periods of conflict and injustice can be understood and responded to.

2 Tackling structural violence through the transformative justice framework – Dáire McGill

Structural violence, acting to severely curtail and constrain the life chances of individuals and groups in society, is a major issue for transitional societies yet is often obscured by political, diplomatic and academic focus on more direct, visible and immediate forms of violence. This work begins by critically analysing the concept of structural violence, showing its principal components and effects, and its importance during a transitional period. Transformative justice is proposed as the appropriate framework through which this central issue can be addressed because of its focus on empowering local communities to challenge prevailing structures of economic, political and social power in society. However, while recognising the need for more ambitious agendas in transition, the chapter proposes that looking for synergies among different conceptualisations of transitional justice is a more fruitful and realistic avenue for positive change than a wholesale disavowal of previous scholarship. With this in mind, the chapter explores the links and influences of various 'adjectival justices' as a guide to theory and action oriented towards reducing structural violence. A transformative lens can enhance the suitability of existing transitional justice mechanisms for this purpose, as well as suggest additional initiatives that give a central role to local participation, social mobilisation, redistribution, and the promotion of economic, social and cultural rights.

3 Addressing historical wrongs in post-transition South Africa: what role for transformative justice? – Matthew Evans

This chapter asks what role the concept of transformative justice might have in addressing the effects of historical wrongs in post-transition South Africa. Transitional justice mechanisms have largely run their course in South Africa and have been evaluated as achieving varying degrees of success. However, South Africa remains divided by profound socioeconomic inequalities, many of which have their roots in historic structural conditions. The chapter asks whether it is analytically and practically useful to consider the shortcomings of transitional justice processes, and the need to address contemporary socioeconomic injustices, in terms of transformative justice. The value added by adopting transformative justice as a frame for understanding action as well as some of the risks and difficulties attached to translating the concept into practice are considered. The chapter argues for the utility of transformative justice as an analytical tool and for its possible utility in implicitly or explicitly shaping practice.

4 The transformative potential of post-war justice initiatives in Bosnia and Herzegovina – Daniela Lai and Caterina Bonora

This chapter investigates the transformative potential of civil society initiatives in post-war Bosnia and Herzegovina. The implementation of transitional justice in the former Yugoslav region heavily relied on retributive justice, through the work of the International Criminal Tribunal for the former Yugoslavia (ICTY), as well as of hybrid and domestic courts. As transitional justice became synonymous with war crimes trials, however, civil society initiatives tried to address other marginalised dimensions of the process of dealing with the past. This chapter explores how these bottom-up initiatives have contributed to developing alternative conceptions of justice in post-war Bosnia and Herzegovina and argues that, compared to the traditional transitional justice paradigm, transformative approaches better capture local understandings of post-war justice. By looking at the cases of the regional commission for the establishment of facts about war crimes and other serious violations of human rights (RECOM), the 2014 socioeconomic protests and the Women's Court in Sarajevo, it illustrates the transformative potential of social mobilisation around justice themes, as well as its limitations. In doing so, it takes into account the tension between grass-roots activism and professionalisation/institutionalisation, the challenges of overcoming ethnicity as an organising principle, and attempts to escape from the 'liberal transition' as the paradigmatic goal of transitional justice processes.

5 The problem of elites – Pádraig McAuliffe

While constructions of victims and perpetrators were reasonably straightforward to draw in the earlier 'truth versus/and accountability' era of transitional justice (though rarely uncomplicated), the explicitly distributive approaches we see in theorisations of transformative justice oriented towards equity in resources or redress of material discrepancies has yet to generate a similarly clear distinction between the subjects and objects of justice interventions. While victims can be understood as the indigent, the poor or those subject to horizontal inequalities, those domestic actors who bear responsibility for this state of affairs are somewhat amorphous. Initial conceptualisations as 'bystanders' and 'beneficiaries' profiting from conflict and authoritarianism (though not necessarily committing bodily integrity offences) have given way to less passive portrayals as elites proactively maintaining existing economic and political hierarchies at the national level over the interests of the many. Critics regard liberal discourses of transitional justice as empowering these elites at the expense of the most disempowered in society. However, the concept of elites remains deeply undertheorised in the transformative justice literature, problematically presented as a monolithic entity with a shared set of interests that operate in contradistinction to the victims of structural inequalities. If transformative approaches to transitional justice are to render structural inequalities legible, they need to better comprehend the interests of, and divisions between, national elites – conservatives and reformers, those who benefit from wartime profiteering and those who control natural resources, ***comprador bourgeoisies*** and patrimonial leaders, those who align with the post-conflict leadership and those who may not. Bearing in mind the reality that transformative justice must work, to some extent, within the parameters established by that which is being transformed, this chapter draws on literatures on development and peacebuilding to delineate who and what we mean by 'elites'. It argues that transformative justice is impossible without understanding how effective, accountable public authority evolves through a political process of bargaining by the state and organised groups in society with economic elites.

6 Culture: the missing link in transitional justice; an imperative for transformative justice – Cathy Bollaert

Transitional justice interventions have been coming under increasing criticism for their tendency to reproduce and impose Western approaches into non-Western contexts. Using the South African Truth and Reconciliation Commission as a case study, this chapter demonstrates how ontological disparities and different processes of meaning-making led to competing interpretations of its truth recovery process. It explores the relationship between culture and how transitional justice deals with the past and interprets key concepts such as reconciliation, accountability and nation-building. The chapter argues that when thinking about transitions in culturally diverse societies that may not share the same value system as those underpinning the human rights discourse consideration needs to be given to how culture impacts on protecting human rights and shapes intergroup relations. In its quest to challenge structural and economic inequalities, transformative justice needs to also challenge the cultural inequalities and their associated power relations in conflict.

7 Selective justice and constructions of victimhood at the Khmer Rouge Tribunal – Rachel Killean

This chapter explores how understandings of victimhood are shaped within transitional justice mechanisms, focusing on the example of the Extraordinary Chambers in the Courts of Cambodia (or Khmer Rouge Tribunal). Drawing on critical victimology in particular, the chapter considers the political and legal construction of victimhood by a range of heterogeneous elite actors, exploring how layers of exclusion can prevent victims from being recognised within official responses to international crime. By focusing on the actors involved in creating those layers of exclusion, the chapter contributes a thicker understanding of how transitional justice mechanisms select those victims 'worthy' of recognition. In particular, it explores how political compromise, jurisdictional limits, prosecutorial choices and procedural developments have shaped the construction of victimhood within the Khmer Rouge Tribunal.

8 Distant historical wrongs, truth telling and restorative justice: exploring schools and museums as potential vehicles for repairing historical wrongs – David Wilkins

Advocates of reparations for historical injustices such as slavery and colonialism argue that these historical injustices continue to cause harm in the present and need to be repaired. But how best can such intergenerational injustices be repaired? In seeking to address the national scars of more recent harms, theories of restorative justice have been increasingly utilised in processes of truth telling that seek to heal the emotional and relational harms of conflict, most famously in South Africa's Truth and Reconciliation Commission. Truth commissions emphasise the reparative power of listening to, and including within national narratives, the voices of victims whose opinions, perspectives and truths were previously excluded, suppressed and denigrated. Yet, with distant historical injustices, those who were victimised by the historical wrongdoing are dead, so how can the idea of truth telling be furthered? This chapter argues that schools and museums provide spaces in which previously biased and selective historical narratives can be revised and previously excluded voices can be empowered in a process of historical truth telling. This process is not straightforward nor will the reparative results be quickly manifest. It is vital that historical context is explored as this can aid understanding of history and legacies. Further, the process must prioritise inclusive dialogue and recognise debate as beneficial. These processes are central to repairing relationships, and schools and museums can potentially provide the safe, neutral spaces for such dialogue to occur.

Foreword

Paul Gready

The current global political context is an inauspicious one in which to talk about transformation. The tank in relation to hope and alternatives seems to be almost empty. But whether in relation to transitional justice, or broader economic and political questions, I would caution against responses which essentially say 'the system is broken, but it is the best one we have' or 'the system is broken, and modest reform is the best that we can hope for'. The bleakness of the political moment makes initiatives such as transformative justice more, not less, important – in that it barks along the borders of the status quo, 'prefigures' an alternative future, and is starting to provide more concrete guidance for those interested in doing transitional justice differently. This book makes an important contribution to this endeavour.

There is a struggle underway for the soul of transitional justice. It is still a relatively young field but with the fresh-faced enthusiasm and naïvety of youth now battered by experience. Impact assessments suggest that its core interventions have mixed or minimal real-world effects; when asked, local populations prioritise local needs and physical security over narrow forms of truth and justice. Ineffective and unwanted may be too harsh an assessment. Maybe. Current debates within transitional justice remind me of discussions in the 1990s about whether international nongovernmental organisations such as Human Rights Watch and Amnesty International should work seriously on socioeconomic rights. Some argued for caution (we should adapt the problem to our methods), while others championed greater ambition (we need to adapt our methods to address the problem). The battle between these two positions rages on, but now the debates are not about whether to address socioeconomic rights but what effects such work has had. I predict a similar contested trajectory for transitional justice, shifting between minimalist and maximalist agendas – and transformative justice will be part of a new wave of transitional justice activity.

This book usefully illustrates that part of the current change within, and challenge to, transitional justice involves a process of repositioning: as it becomes an ever-more interdisciplinary subject of study, and as it overlaps and intersects with related fields (security sector reform, peacebuilding, development, etc.). This process is essential to clarifying the evolving identity of the field. It will inevitably threaten some, as their turf is invaded by others or their specialist skill set is challenged or displaced. Transitional justice will become less pure and isolated, and more hybrid and networked.

Transformative justice itself has work to do. There is a need to more consistently go beyond critique to spell out clearly what alternative approaches might look like. Transformative reparations, and particularly transformative reparations for human rights violations affecting women, is one area where interesting initiatives are taking place. Obviously, reparations can only contribute to positive and progressive outcomes in this and other fields, but they can make an important material and symbolic statement about the kind of change needed.

This book includes scholars from different disciplines, working in different national settings, and with different perspectives on transitional and transformative justice. As such it frames a debate and makes a statement about the varied perspectives which characterise the field. By seriously analysing the limits of transitional justice, the possibility of reform and innovation within transitional justice, and the need to consider perspectives and approaches from outside transitional justice, the volume will be a useful resource for academics and practitioners alike.

1 Transitional justice and beyond

An introduction to critical, international and interdisciplinary debates

Matthew Evans

Introduction

Transitional justice is increasingly seen as a discipline in itself, with an industry developing around its promotion and implementation.[1] Indeed, transitional justice processes are promoted as a necessity in post-conflict and post-authoritarian contexts by international organisations, nongovernmental organisations and other actors. With this, transitional justice scholarship has also developed. Just as transitional justice has become increasingly mainstreamed in the discourse and practice of governmental and nongovernmental actors concerned with post-conflict and post-authoritarian states, criticism and contestation of transitional justice has increased.[2] Questions are raised regarding the efficacy and desirability of implementing the standard models of transitional justice. Can transitional justice provide space for the needs of victims to be expressed and addressed? Does transitional justice inherently serve the powerful, quell political dissent and facilitate neoliberalism? Can the legal and quasi-legal tools typically favoured in transitional justice processes addressing individual violations of civil and political rights (such as truth commissions, trials and amnesties) be reconciled with collective political and socioeconomic grievances underlying conflict? Transformative justice – conceived as an alternative to top-down, legalistic interpretations of transitional justice – has been proposed as a response to some of these questions. Nevertheless, as this concept emerges and is developed, further questions arise.[3] What exactly would transformation look like and what is or is not being transformed? Can existing transitional justice tools deliver transformative outcomes and, if not, what new (political, legal or economic) tools are required? Can (and should) transitional justice or transformative justice address historical wrongs rooted in the past prior to the immediate conflict or period of authoritarianism deemed to be ending? This book explores these questions, and others, arising

1 See, for example, Andrieu (2010); Mutua (2015); Gready (2011); Madlingozi (2010).
2 See, for example, Bell (2009); Branch (2014); *International Journal of Transitional Justice* (2015).
3 See, for example, Evans (2016, 2018a); Gready and Robins (2014); McAuliffe (2017); Brown and Ní Aoláin (2015).

from consideration of the space (or lack of space) for just outcomes to emerge from political and legal responses to conflict, authoritarian rule and past injustice.

The chapters which follow engage in theoretical and empirical discussion oriented around critical engagement with transitional and transformative justice practice across a range of national contexts and (inter)disciplinary perspectives. In this introductory chapter the key debates in which the book intervenes are outlined, and it is argued that critical, interdisciplinary and international engagement with these debates is necessary. First the chapter considers the limitations of transitional justice. Following this, possibilities within transitional justice are considered. Next, the chapter explores arguments for looking beyond transitional justice. Finally, conclusions are set out.

Limitations of transitional justice

A growing body of literature highlights the limitations, borders and – at times – failings of transitional justice. Indeed, the *International Journal of Transitional Justice*, the premier periodical in the field, recently published a special issue starkly asking whether transitional justice has a future.[4] It is a question worthy of serious consideration in light of the facts of the present. For example, South Africa, and especially the Truth and Reconciliation Commission (TRC), has often been put forward as the archetypal transitional justice success story. However, it is perhaps not surprising that, as the period since South Africa's transition to democracy moves from years to decades, questioning and criticism of post-apartheid transitional justice programmes have increased.[5] As the narrative of South Africa as an unambiguous success for transitional justice has fractured so too has the wider notion of transitional justice triumphalism.[6] Chapters in this book engage with these fractures and consider dilemmas surrounding a number of the possible limitations of transitional justice.

Chapters 2, 3, 4, 5 and 6 consider dilemmas associated with the limitations of the application of the standard transitional justice mechanisms and the assumptions which come with this. In Chapter 2, Dáire McGill argues that transitional justice mechanisms have failed to sufficiently recognise and engage in addressing structural violence. Particularly focusing on the impact of inequitable access to land in post-conflict Colombia, the chapter argues that transitional justice in its standard forms cannot effectively address key issues affecting post-conflict societies and, consequently, new approaches are necessary. Similarly, Chapter 3, by Matthew Evans, argues that the focus of transitional justice on relatively short time-bound interventions, as well as the specific foci of transitional justice mechanisms such as truth commissions and trials, mean that a number of historical injustices, particularly in relation to socioeconomic inequalities, have not been sufficiently

4 See *International Journal of Transitional Justice* (2015), especially Mutua (2015).

5 See, for example, Mamdani (2002); Madlingozi (2007); Gready (2011); Gibson (2011); Renner (2014).

6 See, for example, *International Journal of Transitional Justice* (2014, 2015).

addressed in post-transition South Africa. Whilst Chapter 2 puts forward the case for addressing the limitations of transitional justice in Colombia through incorporating the notion of transformative justice as a central component in transitional justice programmes, Chapter 3 takes a different approach. Here the argument for considering transformative justice as separate to – though overlapping with – transitional justice is put forward.

Chapter 4, by Daniela Lai and Caterina Bonora, addresses questions parallel and related to those raised in Chapters 2 and 3. Considering limitations of transitional justice in Bosnia and Herzegovina with regard to the selectivity and remoteness of formal, internationally endorsed mechanisms such as international criminal tribunals, Lai and Bonora assess the transformative potential of a number of alternative initiatives (Women's Courts, socioeconomic protests emerging since 2014 and the initiative for the establishment of a Regional Commission). These initiatives have emerged (to greater and lesser extents) from approaches which are more participatory and grass-roots oriented than established transitional justice mechanisms. Moreover, Lai and Bonora argue that the initiative with the greatest transformative potential (the socioeconomic protest movement) is that which least resembles the expected repertoire of mainstream transitional justice intervention.

Whilst Chapter 5, by Pádraig McAuliffe, draws upon some of the positions set out in Chapters 2, 3 and 4 (that transitional justice has tended to pay insufficient attention to the needs, interests and participation of affected communities, for instance), in the chapter McAuliffe shifts the focus – from criticism of the limitations of transitional justice *per se* to engagement with how these might be overcome. McAuliffe suggests that (in analysis and practice) insufficient attention is paid to the nature of elites in transitional societies. Arguing that elites are not a single, homogenous category on which blame can be placed for all of transitional justice's limitations and failures, McAuliffe suggests that for transformative approaches to be effective it is necessary to contend with empirical reality as much as normative aspiration. Consequently, McAuliffe argues, disaggregation of elites and examination of their interests, motivations and power is necessary to establish whether and how particular elite groups might play a role in transitional contexts, as well as the extent to which these roles might be necessary (or even desirable) for the pursuit of transformative outcomes.

In Chapter 6, Cathy Bollaert engages with limitations of transitional justice mechanisms less in terms of the degree to which they are able to address socioeconomic and structural issues (as in Chapters 2, 3 and 4), and more in relation to the ontological and epistemological assumptions which (frequently) accompany transitional justice programmes. Focusing particularly on South Africa, especially the TRC, this chapter argues that transitional justice mechanisms frequently fail to sufficiently account for and engage with the interaction between identity, culture and worldview and the effects these have upon mechanisms' effectiveness and the degree to which they are accepted by affected communities. The chapter criticises the dominance of Western actors and understandings in transitional justice and peacebuilding programmes. It is argued that transitional justice and peacebuilding programmes frequently fail to account for the possibility of diverse interpretation of the concepts with which they are concerned. This harms their efficacy in a number of ways. The chapter highlights, for instance, the different (and potentially contradictory) ways in which the concept of reconciliation has been interpreted in South Africa, including in the work of the TRC itself.[7] A lack of shared understanding (or, at least, of acknowledgement of different understandings) of concepts such as this damages the degree to which transitional justice programmes such as the TRC are able to deliver the outcomes they supposedly seek – or damages the degree to which these outcomes are accepted by all of the groups they are intended to serve.

Another, related, dilemma concerns the institutional design of transitional justice mechanisms. In Chapter 7, Rachel Killean considers this in terms of the dynamics of inclusion and exclusion of victims in the processes of Cambodia's prosecutions of Khmer Rouge-era crimes. Whilst she notes possibilities for innovation, contestation and progressive change within the transitional justice processes in place in Cambodia, institutional limitations are also evident. The chapter argues that, even as attempts were made to incorporate greater participation of victims in the trial process, a pushback occurred. In particular, the participation of victims, and the ways in which they wished to participate, were seen by the court as disruptive and were curtailed. Moreover, the reasoning put forward by the court for curtailing the participation of victims was due to the disruption this caused to the court functioning in the way it is expected to. Trials, it is suggested, cannot accommodate participation of victims in the ways that were first demanded. The goals of the court are not wholly aligned with those of the victims seeking to participate in proceedings. Trials are designed to prioritise the court's goals and to conform to the norms and expectations associated with the formal practice and performance of criminal law. The institutional framework within which criminal prosecutions exist arguably precludes the full realisation of victim participation, at least of the sort initially sought in Cambodia.

Possibilities within transitional justice

In response to some of the limitations of transitional justice – or, at least, the limitations of mainstream transitional justice programmes – scholarship and practice is increasingly turning towards critical reflection upon the standard models and mechanisms of transitional justice and towards considering the possibilities for innovation and adaptation within transitional justice. It is increasingly common for transitional justice mechanisms to be criticised for failing to sufficiently address socioeconomic rights issues and for failing to facilitate a sufficient degree of participation by victims and other affected communities.[8] This has, for instance, been tied to questions about the interaction between transitional justice and

7 On this issue in particular, see also Renner (2014); Evans (2018b).

8 See, for example, Robins (2013); Gready and Robins (2014); Evans (2016). For a critical discussion of whether transitional justice can realistically overcome these issues, see also Waldorf (2012).

development, and the extent to which transitional justice can (or ought to) contribute to addressing issues with which development is more usually concerned.[9] This book contributes to and further develops these discussions.

In Chapter 2, an argument for expanding and adapting transitional justice programmes to better address structural violence is put forward. McGill proposes a framework for considering transitional justice mechanisms in terms of their contribution to the diagnosis of issues which might be remedied through a transformative justice approach, the degree to which processes of implementation contribute to transformative justice, and the extent to which transformative outcomes result. McGill argues that the land restitution programme in Colombia is inherently limited and that despite the programme being well resourced it is not likely on its own to contribute significantly to transformative justice. McGill argues that the Peasant Reserve Zones, which have been set up both with and without official legal recognition, offer more transformative potential. It is argued that the limitations of established models of transitional justice ought to be analysed from the perspective of transformative justice and should be adapted and augmented in order to overcome these limitations. The chapter suggests that the inclusion of initiatives such as Peasant Reserve Zones within transitional justice programmes and the expansion of their implementation could be an effective means of addressing structural violence around rural land distribution in Colombia. Moreover, applying these principles to other transitional contexts might lead to a wider reformulation of transitional justice programmes in order to address existing shortcomings and, especially, to better address structural violence.

Chapter 4, likewise, considers how shortcomings of transitional justice with regard to addressing structural violence and socioeconomic rights issues might be overcome. However, it is questionable whether the more transformative initiatives Lai and Bonora identify are a part of (rather than complementing, following or providing an alternative to) transitional justice.

Chapter 5 focuses on what analytically (and, as a consequence, practically) is missing from critical accounts of transitional justice. By extension, the chapter considers what could (or *ought to*) be included within transitional justice in order to address both the concerns and weaknesses of critical approaches. McAuliffe suggests that engagement with the notion of elites (and their various composition, interests and activities), and the ways in which these have been understood in fields and disciplines parallel to transitional justice (such as peacebuilding), sheds light upon what is – and is not – possible (or necessary) in any given transitional justice context.

Furthermore, whilst Chapter 6 does highlight limitations which arise from standard (particularly Western) approaches to transitional justice, the chapter also points to the possibilities within transitional justice. The chapter draws on debates in peacebuilding over hybrid forms of peace, and in transitional justice over bespoke and bottom-up approaches. The chapter argues not only that it is

9 See, for example, de Greiff and Duthie (2009); *International Journal of Transitional Justice* (2008).

necessary to take account of ontological differences between contexts (especially between major traditions in Western and non-Western contexts), but also that it is possible to do this in devising and implementing transitional justice processes. Bollaert makes the case for centrally considering the core identities of transitional societies in the design and practice of transitional justice mechanisms. This requires moving away from the top-down imposition of pre-packaged, one-size-fits-all transitional justice programmes. Necessarily the kinds of mechanisms appropriate to or effective in one context will not be as well suited to another. Instead, building on initiatives gaining traction in the parallel (and to some extent overlapping) area of peacebuilding, transitional justice can and should take specific account of the interaction between identity, worldview and culture in developing bottom-up, locally specific processes appropriate to the context in which they are applied. Indeed, these contributions reflect and build upon those of McAuliffe in Chapter 5, responding as they do to similar questions. Given the observed limitations of (mainstream) transitional justice, and the criticisms which have been levelled at these, both chapters ask – and begin to provide possible answers to – the questions: what is missing from transitional justice and how could this be brought in?

Chapter 7 also points to possibilities for overcoming some of the limitations of established approaches to transitional justice. Though (as discussed above) it has not been possible to overcome all of the limitations of the transitional justice mechanisms put in place in Cambodia and pushback against increased participation by affected communities occurred throughout the process of accommodating victim participation in trials of Khmer Rouge, innovative potential also emerges. In the chapter, Killean notes that the attempts made to incorporate victims into the process of conducting criminal trials in Cambodia far exceed the degree to which victims have been incorporated in similar mechanisms in other transitional justice contexts. Moreover, the potential for civil society actors to contribute towards overcoming some of the shortcomings of transitional justice mechanisms is highlighted in the chapter. In particular, Killean points to important shifts in the degree to which sexual and gender-based violence during the conflict period was recognised and addressed by the mechanisms in place in Cambodia. Importantly, this indicates that ways of doing transitional justice are not set in stone, even after mechanisms have been designed and implemented. In at least some cases, it is possible to adapt and amend transitional justice programmes in order to better reflect the needs and desires of those affected by conflict and injustice. This serves – at least partially – to overcome limitations which come with particular institutional forms and, especially, with top-down imposition of particular mechanisms and narrowly defined mandates associated with these.

Beyond transitional justice

In addition to critical and heterodox perspectives within transitional justice having begun to gain some foothold in scholarly discourse, so too has a small, but growing, literature considering post-conflict and post-authoritarian justice from perspectives outside – or even against – transitional justice as it is usually understood.[10] Chapters in this book also consider responses to conflict and injustice which fall outside transitional justice or go beyond the borders of transitional justice. As noted above, even where there are possibilities within transitional justice, limitations are nevertheless evident. Furthermore, there are lessons which might be applied from transitional justice to contexts which fall beyond the remit of transitional justice itself. As well as this, insights from beyond transitional justice can also be applied, and add value to, transitional justice.

Chapter 3, like Chapter 2, is concerned with applying the concept of transformative justice. However, in contrast to Chapter 2, Chapter 3 focuses on understanding transformative justice as separate to (though overlapping with) transitional justice. The chapter explores the roles for transformative justice in practice to a greater extent than Chapter 2. Chapter 3 especially focuses on questions surrounding the possible value added by transformative justice to analysis of and advocacy in post-transition South Africa. Here it is important that the South African context is post-transitional. The chapter argues that despite transition (from apartheid to democracy) and transitional justice processes being over, there is nevertheless value added in thinking about and applying the notion of transformative justice. This goes beyond transitional justice both in the sense of looking to a broader timeframe than that of short-term transition and in the sense of considering concerns which are conceptually and practically beyond the remit of transitional justice. The chapter particularly considers the possible application of transformative justice as an analytical framework, as implicitly shaping practice and as an overt framework for advocacy and activism.

Chapter 4, likewise, considers transformative potential in advocacy and activism. Lai and Bonora consider the most potential for transformative justice to be manifested in initiatives which (of those surveyed in the chapter) are least similar to established transitional justice mechanisms. The chapter argues that to overcome the necessary limitations of transitional justice as applied to Bosnia and Herzegovina, grass-roots, participatory transformative initiatives are required. In exploring these, Lai and Bonora address dilemmas which build on those highlighted in Chapters 2 and 3.

Chapter 6 also makes the case for looking beyond transitional justice in attempts to understand and address conflict and divided societies. This chapter looks especially to peacebuilding as an alternative and additional disciplinary lens through which transitions out of conflict may be viewed. Chapter 5 also calls for insights from peacebuilding to be applied in order to reckon with responses to the existence and activities of different kinds of elites in transitional contexts. Inasmuch as transitional justice is inherently legalistic and both scholarship and practice have concentrated on a relatively narrow set of institutional mechanisms, Chapters 5 and 6 move beyond this. Bollaert, in particular, invites consideration of psychological and cultural aspects of identity and worldview in divided societies

10 See, for example, Madlingozi (2010); Palmer, Clark and Granville (2012); Branch (2014); Gready and Robins (2014); Evans (2018a, 2018b).

(see Chapter 6). In doing so, Bollaert proposes a broader, more nuanced and context-specific approach to addressing societal division than is typical in transitional justice.

Chapter 8, by David Wilkins, also looks beyond transitional justice but from a different perspective to the other chapters. Rather than considering what measures and approaches might be appropriate to addressing injustice in transitions out of conflict or authoritarianism (as in Chapters 2, 3, 4 and 6, for instance), Wilkins considers what might be learned from transitional justice in seeking to address injustices rooted in the deeper past. Considering the notions of truth telling and restorative justice, this chapter explores museums and schools as potential vehicles of historical repair. The chapter draws on lessons from transitional justice mechanisms, particularly truth commissions, and asks whether and to what extent the contributions these can make to transitional societies might be scaled up to address historical wrongs rooted in the deeper past. Wilkins asks, for instance, what can be learned from applying the different conceptions of truth (forensic, personal, social, healing) explored by the South African TRC (and subsequent truth commissions) to wider, less time-bound initiatives.[11] Considering the legacies of harms of transatlantic slavery, Wilkins argues that lessons from (but going beyond) transitional justice, and from transformative justice, can be applied in order for schools and museums to play a significant role in repairing the ongoing legacies of historical injustice.

Conclusion

By way of concluding this introduction, the following areas of focus are worthy of attention. This volume occupies a space in the growing critical literature on transitional justice and the emerging concept of transformative justice. Both the place of the volume within the wider literature and the place of the chapters within the book are as parts of a conversation. The chapters are in conversation with one another, and the book as a whole is in conversation with a wider community of scholarship and practice, including transitional justice advocates, critics, practitioners and theorists.

Critical questions are raised by the volume. What are the limitations of transitional justice? Can they be overcome, and, if so, how, and to what extent? Likewise, what are the possibilities for and within transitional justice? What can be learned from these beyond the established confines of the field, and how can transformative agendas be pursued or promoted following (recent, or more distant) periods of severe injustice? Neither the volume, nor the chapters within it are the final word on these questions. Nevertheless, these questions ought to be confronted. The chapters in this book go some way to proposing answers to these questions and, as such, significantly advance the conversation in which they – and the book as a whole – intervene.

11 On varieties of truth see, for example, Posel (1999, 2008).

The contribution made by this book is critical in both senses of the word – rigorous in the analysis and evaluation put forward, and crucial in addressing important issues of immediate and ongoing concern. The chapters collected here critically respond to assumptions of, and questions raised by, mainstream (and existing critical) transitional justice scholarship. In doing so, necessary debates for scholarship and practice are opened up and developed. These debates span a variety of disciplinary and geographical contexts. The contributions to this book include multidisciplinary and interdisciplinary work across social sciences, humanities and legal studies, examining European, African, Asian, Latin American and transnational case studies. This broad scope and these varied approaches represent just some of the possible elements required to gain a holistic understanding of the themes and issues with which this book grapples. Too often research and scholarship addressing conflict, injustice, and responses to these, has reflected a limited repertoire of narrow disciplinary approaches and sites of attention. Whilst this book cannot wholly redress the balance, the contribution it makes through its constituent chapters is significant, as is the invitation (perhaps provocation) it provides to respond to, develop, add to and build upon the arguments put forward.

References

Andrieu, Kora. (2010) 'Transitional Justice: A New Discipline in Human Rights'. *Online Encyclopedia of Mass Violence*, 18 January, www.sciencespo.fr/mass-violence-war-massacre-resistance/en/document/transitional-justice-new-discipline-human-rights-0 [accessed 5 April 2018].

Bell, Christine. (2009) 'Transitional Justice, Interdisciplinarity and the State of the "Field" or "Non-field"'. *International Journal of Transitional Justice* 3(1): 5–27.

Branch, Adam. (2014) 'Beyond the TJ industry: transitional justice and changing international order'. *Pambazuka News* 703, 21 November, www.pambazuka.org/printpdf/90919 [accessed 5 April 2018].

Brown, Kris and Fionnuala Ní Aoláin. (2015) 'Through the Looking Glass: Transitional Justice Futures through the Lens of Nationalism, Feminism and Transformative Change'. *International Journal of Transitional Justice* 9(1): 127–149.

de Greiff, Pablo and Roger Duthie. (eds). (2009) *Transitional Justice and Development: Making Connections*. New York: Social Science Research Council.

Evans, Matthew. (2016) 'Structural violence, socioeconomic rights and transformative justice'. *Journal of Human Rights* 15(1): 1–20.

Evans, Matthew. (2018a) *Transformative Justice: Remedying Human Rights Violations Beyond Transition*. Abingdon: Routledge.

Evans, Matthew. (2018b) 'A future without forgiveness: beyond reconciliation in transitional justice'. *International Politics* 55(5): 678–692.

Gibson, Nigel C. (2011) *Fanonian Practices in South Africa: From Steve Biko to Abahlali baseMjondolo*. New York: Palgrave Macmillan.

Gready, Paul. (2011) *The Era of Transitional Justice: The Aftermath of the Truth and Reconciliation Commission in South Africa and Beyond*. Abingdon: Routledge.

Gready, Paul and Simon Robins. (2014) 'From Transitional to Transformative Justice: A New Agenda for Practice'. *International Journal of Transitional Justice* 8(3): 339–361.

International Journal of Transitional Justice. (2008) Special issue 'Transitional Justice and Development'. *International Journal of Transitional Justice* 2(3): 253–434.

International Journal of Transitional Justice. (2014) 'Editorial Note'. *International Journal of Transitional Justice* 8(1): 1–5.

International Journal of Transitional Justice. (2015) Special issue 'Transitional Justice – Does it have a Future?'. *International Journal of Transitional Justice* 9(1): 1–192.

Madlingozi, Tshepo. (2007) 'Good victim, bad victim: Apartheid's beneficiaries, victims, and the struggle for social justice'. In Wessel le Roux and Karin van Marle (eds), *Law, Memory and the Legacy of Apartheid: Ten Years After AZAPO v President of South Africa*, 107–126. Pretoria: Pretoria University Law Press.

Madlingozi, Tshepo. (2010) 'On Transitional Justice Entrepreneurs and the Production of Victims'. *Journal of Human Rights Practice* 2(2): 208–228.

Mamdani, Mahmood. (2002) 'Amnesty or Impunity? A Preliminary Critique of the Report of the Truth and Reconciliation Commission of South Africa (TRC)'. *Diacritics* 32(3/4): 32–59.

McAuliffe, Pádraig. (2017) *Transformative Transitional Justice and the Malleability of Post-conflict States*. Cheltenham: Edward Elgar.

Mutua, Makau. (2015) 'What Is the Future of Transitional Justice?'. *International Journal of Transitional Justice* 9(1): 1–9.

Palmer, Nicola, Phil Clark and Danielle Granville (eds). (2012) *Critical Perspectives in Transitional Justice*. Cambridge: Intersentia.

Posel, Deborah. (1999) 'The TRC Report: what kind of history? What kind of truth? A preliminary exploration'. Paper presented at the workshop 'The TRC: Commissioning the Past', Wits History Workshop, University of the Witwatersrand, Johannesburg, South Africa, 11–14 June, http://wiredspace.wits.ac.za/bitstream/handle/10539/8046/HWS-341.pdf [accessed 5 April 2018].

Posel, Deborah. (2008) 'History as Confession: The Case of the South African Truth and Reconciliation Commission'. *Public Culture* 20(1): 119–141.

Renner, Judith. (2014) 'The Local Roots of the Global Politics of Reconciliation: The Articulation of "Reconciliation" as an Empty Universal in the South African Transition to Democracy'. *Millennium: Journal of International Studies* 42(2): 263–285.

Robins, Simon. (2013) *Families of the Missing: A Test for Contemporary Approaches to Transitional Justice*. Abingdon: Routledge.

Waldorf, Lars. (2012) 'Anticipating the past: transitional justice and socio economic wrongs'. *Social and Legal Studies* 21(2): 171–186.

2 Tackling structural violence through the transformative justice framework

Dáire McGill

Introduction

Internal armed conflicts and human rights violations around the world are commonly linked to the existence of structural violence in rural areas (Robins, 2013: 65–69; Pasipanodya, 2008: 380–383; Nagy, 2013: 88–89; Miller, 2008: 282–284). However, transitional justice mechanisms generally deal with land questions, if at all, in terms of property restitution, heavily dependent on political and financial constraints, and ignoring the wider structural problems of land rights and distribution patterns (Pasipanodya, 2008: 390–391; Huggins, 2009: 361; Fitzpatrick and Fishman, 2014; Moyo, 2015: 71–72). These policies neither reconcile competing property claims, nor recognise the distinct economic, social and cultural meanings attached to land, nor question the political economy underpinning existing ownership structures in rural societies (Atuahene, 2010; Huggins, 2009; Fitzpatrick and Fishman, 2014).

Colombia has been in armed conflict for half a century, with 220,000 direct fatalities up until 2012, 80% of those estimated to be civilians. This direct violence exists alongside high levels of structural violence, reflected in lived experiences of inequality and marginalisation (ILSA, 2012: 6; Uribe Kaffure, 2013: 247). Land ownership is highly concentrated and inequitable, especially in regions where the state is weakly or unevenly institutionalised, permitting capture by local elites that dominate economic, political and social life (Ibáñez and Munoz, 2010). While previous conflicts ended with intra-elite political agreements, the Havana Peace Dialogues between the Colombian state and the Fuerzas Armadas Revolucionarias de Colombia – Ejército del Pueblo (FARC) at least rhetorically accepted the need to address structural violence, through recognition that resolving inequities in access to land and services in rural areas is central to the construction of peace (Acuerdo Final, 2016).

This chapter begins by introducing the conceptual category of structural violence, increasingly prevalent in mainstream academic and policy debates, and argues that it is the key problem confronting transitional countries. It will then analyse the successes and failures of transitional justice processes in addressing this central concern. The main argument presented is that reducing structural violence requires transitional processes and mechanisms to embrace the more ambitious transformative justice framework. This framework is operationalised via a matrix that captures the characteristics that any initiative to reduce structural violence must contain, applicable to its diagnostic, process and outcome dimensions. This matrix is then applied to two different public policy initiatives in Colombia, offering a critical look at the boundaries of conflict-related transitional justice in rural areas, with the land restitution programme illustrating the impact of a well-resourced programme as well as its inherent limitations. This paradigmatic transitional justice approach will be set alongside Peasant Reserve Zones, an alternative rural initiative which at least conceptually offers a more transformative response to structural violence.

Structural violence

Johan Galtung famously defined violence as the causal mechanism that explains the avoidable difference between human beings' potential and actual somatic realisations, increasing the distance between them and impeding decrease (Galtung, 1969: 168–169). He distinguishes between personal or direct violence, which involves a clear subject-action-object relation, while violence that occurs without this relation is structural or indirect (Galtung, 1969: 170–171). This work deliberately disrupts Galtung's word-pairs to emphasise that structural violence can have direct, not merely indirect, impacts, while personal violence can be perpetrated by and targeted at collectives. It also fits with Galtung's own later usage of the terms, when he incorporates Direct, Structural and Cultural Violence into a Violence Triangle, with cultural violence conceptualised primarily as a legitimising agent for direct and structural violence (Galtung, 1990). Structural violence occurs when unequal power relationships in societal structures lead to unequal life chances, harming individuals and collectives by preventing them from meeting their basic needs (Vorobej, 2008: 88; McAuliffe, 2015: 93). The phenomenon does not preclude human agency or presume societal stasis, but demonstrates how the institutionalisation of past choices and circumstances affects present societal conditions, and is instantiated anew through time, with harm potentially caused by actions not considered legally, or even morally, wrong (Thomason, 2015; 75; Evans, 2013: 3; Galtung, 1969: 171). Nor does focusing on structural violence deny the severe impact of direct violence on individuals and communities; while they may differ in their nature, perpetrator and intention, both types of violence are serious social problems with significant effects on their victims (Vorobej, 2008: 92–94). Indeed, paying more attention to structural violence can illuminate the origins and true extent of direct violence by showing how it is hidden and normalised within unequal power relations and social structures (Hume, 2009: 6–10). States in the Americas, for example, were constructed on the base of colonial exploitation, displacement and alienation for the majority of the population, a legacy which continued when power passed into the hands of now-independent national elites. Structural violence and severe inequalities continue to characterise the region, as do very high levels of interpersonal, criminal and political violence (Briceno-Leon et al., 2008; Hume, 2009; WHO, 2014: 8). Making visible structural violence requires analytical study of the societal relations and institutions that sustain and render it invisible through social normalisation (Farmer, 1996; Vorobej, 2008: 93; Thomason, 2015: 76).

Structural violence can be conceptually divided into the three major pillars on which it rests: social marginalisation, political exclusion and economic exploitation (Gready, 2011: 15). Normalised patterns of behaviour and relations often mean that inequities do not have to be enforced by recourse to direct violence, but are internalised by individuals and societies, and reinforced through the use of symbolism, ideology, tradition and propaganda (Hume, 2009: 36–38). Modiri (2015) points to the continued social and cultural dominance of whites in South Africa: physically in the number of senior officials and judges; but also symbolically and psychologically in society, with aspirational blacks wanting to have a 'whiter' lifestyle. Patterns of racialised social relations and structures underpin structural violence in South African society, and are in turn reflected within the prevailing political system. Latin American elites have traditionally espoused a 'civilising' or 'modernising' rhetoric that denigrates indigenous cultural identity, and excludes indigenous populations from political and economic power within society (Laplante, 2007: 154; Baquero Melo, 2015: 36). Deeply ingrained and internalised patterns of dominance reinforce the status quo by making change unthinkable and severely castigating challenges (Hume, 2009: 6–7). Political exclusion can be seen in the inability of some members of society to influence political systems given the prevailing power relationships. While a lack of formal political participation is often associated with open denial of civil and political rights under authoritarian regimes, meaningful political participation can also be scarce in countries that hold regular elections given the multiple barriers to participation. The economic component of structural violence is closely related to the existence of widespread poverty, exploitation and inequalities across society (Farmer, 1996). Access to financial resources is a central question here, but it also manifests itself indirectly in the systematic exclusion of certain groups from services and opportunities that are provided to others – reflected in health and education inequities (Hecht and Michalowski, 2012: 5; WHO, 2015).

This tripartite division, while useful in illustrating the extent of structural violence, is merely heuristic, as in practice the political, social and economic spheres are closely interwoven, interdependent and in many ways mutually reinforcing (Muvingi, 2009: 165; Cramer, 2003: 406–409; Harwell and Le Billon, 2009). Structural violence shapes everyday patterns of behaviour by differentially affecting the life chances of groups and individuals (Farmer, 1996; Evans, 2016: 2–3; Galtung, 1969; Mani, 2008). Socioeconomic inequalities based on unequal access to land and other resources were arguably at the heart of apartheid as a project of ongoing economic colonisation (Evans, 2016: 10; Truth and Reconciliation Commission of South Africa Report, 2003: 140, in Miller, 2008: 277), and land ownership patterns have also been historically important in cases such as Rwanda (Miller, 2008: 280–284; Cramer, 2003: 406–408), and Zimbabwe (Muvingi, 2009: 173–176). The social justice claims cited by non-state armed actors in Nepal and Colombia as motivation to adopt violence exemplify the impact of socioeconomic inequalities in driving or fuelling conflicts, even when myriad other social and political factors are in play. Sources of legitimate grievance are likely to fuel conflagrations of violence (Pasipanodya, 2008; Arbour, 2007: 8; Sandoval, 2011: 10; Robins, 2013: 12), fed by an understanding that atrocities are not usually deviations from otherwise peaceful histories, but intimately linked to the background conditions of structural violence that constrain the life chances of some individuals, maintain them in iniquitous relations and increase their susceptibility to human rights violations (Farmer, 1996; Mani, 2008: 254; Miller, 2008; Hume, 2009: 33; Landman and Larizza, 2009; Robins, 2013: 163; Thomason, 2015: 73–78; McAuliffe, 2015: 93). A focus on structural violence provides an analytical framework to look beyond decontextualised acts of violence and the harms they cause and instead make visible the structures underpinning such harms, particularly as the inherent violence of iniquitous social and political structures does not halt during times of civil war and repression (Gready and Robins, 2014: 347; Sharp, 2013a: 157; Evans, 2016: 9; Farmer, 1996: 263; Kent, 2012: 112). The following section will explore the potential of transitional justice to reduce structural violence, before suggesting that a deeper commitment to transformative justice is required to achieve this aim.

Transitional justice

Transitional justice has entered the academic and policy mainstream in recent decades, as a means to deal with violent or authoritarian pasts through processes to prosecute wrongdoers, reveal truth, redress harm, facilitate reconciliation and prevent the recurrence of violence and rights violations (Teitel, 2003; UN Secretary-General, 2004: 4; Olsen et al., 2010: 11; Sharp, 2013a; Obel Hansen, 2014). Transitional justice cohered at an early stage (late 1980s and early 1990s) around a set of four measures: prosecutions, truth-telling, reparation, and reform of abusive state institutions (Arthur, 2009: 325; Patel, 2009: 268–271), with the former subsequently broadened to criminal justice (de Greiff, 2009: 33–41), or justice (Sandoval, 2011: 3–10). The most recent trend is the relabelling of institutional reform as guarantees of non-recurrence (GNR), reflected in the appointment of a United Nations (UN) Special Rapporteur on the promotion of truth, justice, reparation and guarantees of non-recurrence in 2012. Previously conceptualised as one of the five components of reparations programmes, the revised stand-alone GNR dimension encompasses many measures previously labelled institutional reform, while incorporating actions targeted at civil society, individuals or the prevailing culture (UN, 2014: 6; UN Special Rapporteur, 2015a). It appears that transitional goals and processes are increasingly subject to debate, necessitating exploration of each transitional justice component, how each contributes to reducing structural violence, and the factors that prevent them from truly solving the problem.

Justice

According to Olsen et al.'s empirical study tracking the adoption of transitional justice mechanisms, 82% are related to the 'justice process' – understood here to incorporate criminal prosecutions (trials) and decisions not to prosecute (amnesties) (Olsen et al., 2010: 39).[1] The Sierra Leone Special Court's $250 million operating budget, in comparison to the $4.4 million made available for reparations (Ainley, 2015), is one example of the continued dominance of legalistic approaches to transitional justice. The central role given to judicial proceedings is unsurprising given transitional justice's origins in international criminal law and international human rights law, and the duty of states to investigate individuals most responsible for the most serious international crimes. At heart, transitional justice is modelled on corrective criminal justice systems (Arbour, 2007: 2; Waldorf, 2012: 10), with some authors distinguishing the two solely by the scale of challenges faced rather than on any qualitative difference (Posner and Vermeule, 2004; Dyzenhaus, 2012). A pure human rights view holds that 'punishment is the absolute duty of society to honor and redeem the suffering of the individual victim' (Neier, quoted in Arthur, 2009: 358), achieved by recognising victims' suffering and ensuring their future position as valued members of society. Punishment of human rights violators challenges impunity, signals a change in societies' normative values, forestalls vigilante justice, strengthens democratic rule of law, and promotes civic trust (de Greiff, 2009: 56–57; McAuliffe, 2010; Lambourne, 2009: 37–40; Lambourne, 2014: 24–27). Judicial proceedings are linked to deterrence and non-recurrence by virtue of removing perpetrators of abuses from positions of power, and discouraging future abuse based on the credible threat of prosecution (Patel, 2009: 269; Lambourne, 2009: 44; Lambourne, 2014: 32; Sandoval, 2011: 4–5). In transitions from conflict, prosecution is also argued to aid reconciliation by individualising guilt in specific perpetrators, lessening the perception that all ex-combatants are guilty of human rights violations (Patel, 2009: 269). Theoretically this remains true even when amnesties are used, provided they are applied only after the truth of human rights violations has been established and admitted.

The potential for the justice process to reduce structural violence is predicated on broadening efforts away from a narrow focus on perpetrators, or even directors, of physical violence. Increasingly the case is being made to include economic, social and cultural rights (ESCR) violations and economic crimes within the remit of transitional justice (Schmid, 2011; Hecht and Michalowski, 2012; Haldemann and Kouassi, 2014). Latin American studies suggest that prosecutions for corruption can delegitimise autocratic regimes more than those based on human rights violations (Cavallaro and Albuja, 2008; Carranza, 2008). Colombian legislation allows for the prosecution of all individuals implicated in rural displacement, from those who violently seize land to buyers cognisant of the violent and illegal manner in which it was acquired. Prosecuting beneficiaries and enablers (for example local land registrars) of land grabbing would constitute a powerful

1 While their methodology contains some flaws, such as the exclusion of institutional reform and memory projects from the remit, or the potential overcounting of prosecutions by equating a single criminal trial with a reparation programme involving multiple persons, this is a startlingly high figure.

message in rebuilding normative expectations of justice in the country, while truth revealed during trials can form the basis for awarding judicial reparations, and assets seized from convicted parties used to finance victim compensation and broader reparation measures (Hecht and Michalowski, 2012: 2–3; Mani, 2008: 258).

Nevertheless, the very fact that arguments for the contribution of the justice process are made on the instrumental grounds of assisting the development of other mechanisms makes it difficult to sustain a view that they have much relevance in addressing structural violence. Holding accountable the perpetrators of violations through legal proceedings is important in transitions, but insufficient to meet the larger goal of addressing systemic and institutional issues (Thomason, 2015: 76; Muvingi, 2009: 179–180). Focus on discrete events fails to elucidate the structures underpinning rights violations, or uncover the roles of enablers, beneficiaries and bystanders (Miller, 2008: 280–284; Mani, 2005: 520–521; Thomason, 2015: 75), while the causal relationship between prosecution and either deterrence or non-recurrence remains empirically unproven (Ainley, 2015; Robins, 2013: 156). Moreover, prosecutions based on corruption have been selectively pursued, reproduce the flaw of holding up a particular scapegoat when individuals were normally part of a larger system of exploitation, and are circumscribed to blatant acts of illegal enrichment without questioning prevailing economic orthodoxies (Hecht and Michalowski, 2012: 2–4). Judicial enforcement of ESCR has been unsuccessful in reducing structural violence for marginalised groups, with most processes favouring middle- and upper-class sectors of society (Landau, 2012). South Africa's constitutional right to housing did not translate into effective access to housing for those in desperate need (Landau, 2012: 408–410; Haldemann and Kouassi, 2014: 515). Transitional justice's legalistic assumption of a commonly agreed legal baseline, in short, fails to appreciate the social reality of transitional states (Miller, 2008: 276). This applies even to 'tradition inspired' (Nagy, 2013: 85) hybrid justice models, in which 'indigenous' aspects are modified in their encounter with external norms and models (Lambourne, 2014: 20–21; Gready and Robins, 2014: 349). It is apparent that judicial processes cannot be the sole focus of transitions, especially in contexts like Colombia where they fail to engage with the complex and opaque nature of historically rooted direct and structural violence. Instead, an increase in social rights for marginalised groups should rely on political action, supported rather than replaced by human rights law (Gearty, 2011, in Haldemann and Kouassi, 2014: 511).

Truth

The secretive nature of authoritarian regimes in 1980s Europe and South America, political constraints on prosecution and less developed international jurisprudence at this time meant the truth process was often prioritised. Truth commissions – defined as 'a newly established, temporary body officially sanctioned by the state or an international governmental organization to investigate past human rights abuses' (Olsen et al., 2010: 34) – became a nearly ubiquitous transitional justice tool (Collins, 2010: 9; Gready, 2011; Sharp, 2013a: 155). They originate in transitional moments; have official status, a short life-span, and victim-centred approach; focus on past violations of human rights; and investigate patterns of abuses and specific violations rather than a single event (Gready, 2011: 3). An official narrative of repression or conflict is seen to contribute to the pursuit of justice for victims and society at large, by acknowledging suffering and rehabilitating the reputation of marginalised individuals in their community. It also contributes to norm-fulfilment by ensuring perpetrators' actions and ideologies are socially repudiated even if they escape judicial sentences. Such concerns expand transitional justice beyond trials and retributive justice to questions of restorative justice that emphasise peace, reconciliation, and the restoration of societal, community and interpersonal relations by restoring agency to victims, and linking individual actions into wider community dynamics (Kent, 2012; Bell and O'Rourke, 2007: 40–41; Sharp, 2013a: 155; Clamp, 2014).

The restorative element is often believed to come from public participation, with testifying theorised as emotionally cathartic and a symbol of new regimes' willingness to hear the previously voiceless (Daly, 2002: 85; McAuliffe, 2010). Bell and O'Rourke argue that truth commissions' flexible processes, responsiveness to survivor needs, and focus on rebuilding relationships rather than on crime and punishment facilitate the involvement of women in transitional justice processes (Bell and O'Rourke, 2007: 40). It is theorised that truth commissions could deliver a more profound sense of justice by investigating ESCR violations and identifying the root causes of human rights violations (Arbour, 2007: 14; Pasipanodya, 2008: 392–394; Hecht and Michalowski, 2012: 1). Truth commissions in Guatemala and Peru provided empirical evidence of the causal connection between, and correlation in victims of, structural and direct violence (Laplante, 2008: 335–337). East Timor's Commission for Reception, Truth and Reconciliation explicitly investigated violations of economic and social rights, including the abuse of education, price fixing, famine and displacement (Pasipanodya, 2008: 393). These orientations allow the revelation of truth to 'set political agendas for future social justice reforms aimed at true conflict prevention' (Laplante, 2008: 334).

The fundamental question is whether truth commissions can move from analysis to action, requiring enforcement of their recommendations which are currently ignored or subverted by powerful actors (Evans, 2016: 5). The Nepalese peace agreement prioritised socioeconomic violations, yet the truth commission was constrained from the outset by a lack of consultation, insufficient guarantees of independence, a restrictive mandate, the lack of obligation to publish a report, and lack of attention to the rights of victims and witnesses (Pasipanodya, 2008: 392–394). The Guatemalan commission may have examined the roots of conflict, but the findings have not done anything to remedy structural violence against the Maya or to integrate them into the national narrative (Laplante, 2008: 335–337; Gready and Robins, 2014: 346–347; Thomason, 2015: 77). These cases are symptomatic of deeper conceptual flaws, such as the colonisation of commissions by quantitative methodologies and narrow conceptions of human rights that only partially critique power, and the focus on what has changed (civil and political abuses), not what has continued (economic and social concerns) in the transitional period (Gready, 2011: 13). In general truth commissions have failed 'to investigate fully the socioeconomic background to the conflicts in question, to elucidate the structural violence of the past or to fully grapple with the economic aspects of transition' (Miller, 2008: 276), meaning they are experienced as an alien mechanism, rather than a true means of justice (Mani, 2005: 520–521; Muvingi, 2009: 165; Thomason, 2015: 79). So while the truth commission may be an emblematic feature of transitional justice, it cannot be expected to achieve all of its normative expectations. Truth commissions would be more transformative if they analysed ESCR violations, distributive injustices and structural inequalities, and included concrete recommendations to redress these in their final reports (Laplante, 2008: 333; Mani, 2008: 256; Pasipanodya, 2008: 392–394; Harwell and Le Billon, 2009). The major role for truth commissions will be procedural rather than substantive: reports can influence public policy and social mobilisation, and participation in truth commissions could constitute a starting point for citizen empowerment. This requires processes to be deeply participatory, including activities that build the capacity and confidence of the previously marginalised to participate, and remove structural barriers to this involvement (Gready, 2011: 13–14; Freire, 1996). The importance of these procedural requirements in initiatives to reduce structural violence will be set out in greater detail below.

Reparations

Reparation describes a battery of measures aimed at ameliorating and repairing the damages suffered by victims of human rights violations: restitution, compensation, rehabilitation, satisfaction and guarantees of non-repetition. The UN Basic Principles and Guidelines on the Right to a Remedy and Reparation for Victims of Gross Violations of International Human Rights Law and Serious Violations of International Humanitarian Law call for 'adequate, effective and prompt reparation for harm suffered' along with access to equal and effective justice and to relevant information (UN, 2005: 6). Reparations are theorised to provide corrective and distributive justice, define guilt and victimhood, and identify a power shift and redefinition of citizenship in a remade society (Mani, 2005; Arbour, 2007: 17; Miller, 2008: 284; Muvingi, 2009: 180; Gready and Robins, 2014: 346–347). By satisfying victims' urgent basic needs and reaffirming their dignity, reparations can establish the conditions to participate more fully in social and political life (Pasipanodya, 2008: 389; Waldorf, 2012; Robins, 2013; Kent, 2012). Societal demands for reparations can often be the starting point of a more confident and empowered citizenry, with social and political mobilisation more significant and transformative in the long term than the actual reparation payments (Gready, 2015). While reparations have often been a neglected element of transitional justice (Mani, 2005: 524; Thomason, 2015: 72; Ainley, 2015), recent reports by the UN Special Rapporteur (2014) assign greater importance to this dimension.

The Colombian comprehensive reparations programme, based on Law 1448 of 2011 (Victims' Law), aims to directly benefit all conflict-related victims of human rights violations since 1985, restore property lost since 1991, and indirectly benefit wider society through symbolic reparations, truth and guarantees of non-recurrence (Acción Social, 2011: 5–8). The land restitution programme seeks profound transformation in rural societies, including the return of millions of hectares of land (Correa, 2015; Baquero Melo, 2015: 43–44). Certain features make it more responsive to questions of structural violence than many previous reparations attempts: its application in the most deeply affected regions, rather than timidly being rolled out in easier situations; the prioritisation of female-headed households; the reversal of the burden of proof so that current occupiers must prove lawful possession; and parallel implementation of associated rural development policies to create viable livelihood opportunities for returnees. Land restitution is the flagship state initiative towards rural development, transitional justice and victims' rights, with the comprehensive approach to reparation aimed at unleashing its transformative potential (Gready and Robins, 2014; Sandoval, 2011, 2015; de Greiff, 2009).

However, the Colombian reparations programme continues to suffer from a number of commonly occurring failings, particularly difficulties in establishing scope, identifying victims and defining compensation (UN, 2005: 7–8; Sandoval, 2011: 6–7). Land restitution remains limited to individuals who lost land since 1991 for reasons directly attributable to the armed conflict. This excludes important categories *inter alia* those dispossessed pre-1991, the historically landless, and those who suffer socially and economically based structural violence rather than direct violence. Furthermore, individualised compensation for particular groups of victims undermines a focus on inequitable and violent social relations, the political economy of transition and the need for future socioeconomic justice, and fails to redistribute wealth or power on a scale that would dramatically reduce structural violence in transitional states (Miller, 2008: 278–285; Muvingi, 2009: 180; Lambourne, 2009: 41–42; Lambourne, 2014: 28–29; Evans, 2016: 7). Proposals to include vulnerability alongside victimhood as a criterion may facilitate reparations schemes that are affordable and perceived as fair by victims and the broader community (Robins, 2013: 165), with 'land equalisation', for example, ensuring that a wealthy 'victim' is not privileged over an historically marginalised 'non-victim' (Atuahene, 2010). Fundamentally, a transformative paradigm that reduces structural violence needs to move away from individual reparations and towards responses that address systemic exploitation and marginalisation. To this end, the processes of reparation programmes are highly significant, with public participation essential as a tool for empowered citizenship (Gready, 2015; Gready and Robins, 2014: 358). This means participation throughout the process in defining, designing, implementing and monitoring reparations, with this deep engagement building capacity that allows wider participation of marginalised individuals, groups and communities in social and political structures. Civil society will play a role in initiating local processes and leveraging power to advocate for resources from the central state (Muvingi, 2009: 180; Robins, 2013: 210), demonstrating the importance of bottom-up initiatives that can subsequently be scaled-up and transferred to other sectors and localities by building constructive alliances with other interested stakeholders (Gready and Robins, 2014: 360–361; Eriksson, 2009: 141–148).

Institutional reform/guarantees of non-recurrence

Guarantees of non-recurrence recognise that the construction of peace requires changing the societal relations and structures that committed or permitted armed conflict, repression and human rights violations (Sandoval, 2011: 9–10; Lambourne, 2014: 22). Policing reform in Northern Ireland – based on the normative objectives of human rights adherence, competent external oversight, and policing with the community – has increased trust in a vital state institution, contributed to the peace process, and aided societal reconciliation (Bayley, 2008). The peace agreement in Nepal committed the state to creating a State Restructuring Recommendation Commission responsible for planning and implementing comprehensive institutional reform (Pasipanodya, 2008: 385). Legal standards on non-recurrence have grown significantly, and economic and social conditions have increasingly entered into the framing of GNR initiatives, opening the possibility of addressing structural violence in a more transformative approach to transitional justice (Gready et al., 2010; Gready and Robins, 2014; Evans, 2013; UN Special Rapporteur, 2015a: 5–9). Meanwhile, the movement from institutional reform to GNR has led to the incorporation of actions targeted at civil society, individuals or the prevailing culture (UN Special Rapporteur, 2014: 6; UN Special Rapporteur, 2015b).

Institutional reform is considered vital, yet a difficult and often unsuccessful aspect of transitional contexts with powerful actors resisting its challenge to the status quo (Waldorf, 2015; Woollard, 2015). GNR is generally understudied and underutilised (Sandoval, 2015), used often as a rhetorical flourish rather than engaged with seriously (UN Special Rapporteur, 2015a). I argue that the change in terminology, while throwing into relief certain conceptual and practical connections, is unhelpful, and that GNR, like reconciliation, is better seen as a function of transitional justice processes (UN Special Rapporteur, 2015a: 7). Institutional reform is a vital enabling condition to achieve GNR, other transitional goals, and reduction in structural violence and inequalities (Gready, 2011: 7). To succeed, transitional justice reforms must more closely link with other fields, such as security sector reform, which the transitional justice community has long seen as outside its remit and falling to peacebuilding (Sharp, 2013b: 30–31). However, the goal of reforming state institutions implicated in violent conflict and rights violations are shared by both paradigms, and tying Demobilisation, Disarmament and Reintegration (DDR) programmes into transitional justice measures could be mutually beneficial, as they both focus on reintegrating conflict participants back into civil existence (Patel, 2009; Sharp, 2013b). Since 2003, the Colombian Agency for Reintegration (ACR) has assisted the economic reintegration of 60,000 FARC and paramilitary ex-combatants, and recent moves towards a people-centred approach have led to improved results (Thorsell, 2013; BBC, 2016).

Institutional reform is potentially the most transformative transitional justice process, which will be maximised by conceptualising it wider than the prevention of direct violence to encompass the aim of reducing structural violence. Measures in transitional societies must address social, political and economic exclusions and improve overall living conditions if they are to maintain credibility and avoid becoming a series of relatively inconsequential events (Mani, 2008: 254; de Greiff, 2009: 30; Haldemann and Kouassi, 2014: 514). Transformative justice is a better framework to analyse structural violence and responses to it in transitional societies, particularly in a case like Colombia where the socioeconomic aspects related with armed conflict are increasingly widely acknowledged. The following section will explore the development of this new framework and how it differs from transitional justice in its perspective towards structural violence.

Transformative justice

The limitations of the processes set out above derive partly from conceptual limitations of transitional justice, represented by a bias towards legalistic and individualistic responses to dealing with violations of civil and political rights rather than structural approaches or a focus on ESCR (Gready, 2005: 5; Miller, 2008; Gready and Robins, 2014; Franzki and Olarte, 2014). Nevertheless, this is being challenged in practice and theory, with the field increasingly prepared to embrace holistic strategies that combine retributive, restorative and redistributive justice (Arbour, 2007; McAuliffe, 2015: 93–98; Mani, 2002). As former UN High Commissioner for Human Rights Louise Arbour makes clear:

> Transitional justice must have the ambition to assist the transformation of oppressed societies into free ones by *addressing the injustices of the past through measures that will procure an equitable future*. It must reach to – but also beyond – the crimes and abuses committed during the conflict that led to the transition, and it *must address the human rights violations that pre-dated the conflict* and caused or contributed to it.
>
> (Arbour, 2007: 3 (emphasis added))

Transformation has always held an ambiguous position within transitional justice, which traditionally emphasises technocratic and elite-driven sequences of reform (Arthur, 2009: 337–339). However, the expanded GNR remit and aim of constructing more democratic and inclusive societies necessitates deeper transformation on the economic, social and political levels (Arbour, 2007; Lambourne, 2009; Patel, 2009; UN Secretary-General, 2011; Sharp, 2012). However, what does a call for transformation rather than transition mean? How do they differ? While transition can be seen as a bounded change in state to a known destination, and so capable of being managed, transformation is a deeper and more uncertain process. McAuliffe (2011: 35) characterises transition as a finite politically defined epiphenomenal opportunity to re-evaluate or re-establish state norms. Transformation is fundamental change in a society's culture, structures and relationships, even as it undergoes this political transition (Daly, 2002; Evans, 2013: 8). The reconceptualisation of institutional reform as a means to an end illustrates the difference in scope and ambition of transformative justice from the existing transitional blueprint – to ensure non-recurrence of atrocities and armed conflict, radical societal transformation is needed to ensure the once-prevalent becomes unthinkable (Daly, 2002: 181).

Given these differences in foci it is legitimate to question what overlap there is between the two frameworks. Evans argues that transformative justice is not part of transitional justice, and that standard mechanisms can be expected to have very little impact on the structural social and economic issues which are currently peripheral to transitional justice (Evans, 2016: 6–8). Nevertheless, transitional justice is a dynamic field of practice containing mechanisms that can be re-crafted to have deeper societal impacts (Arbour, 2007: 26; Balasco, 2013; Sharp, 2013a; Laplante, 2007: 145; Pasipanodya, 2008: 390; Sandoval, 2015; Gready, 2015). This search for synergies will be facilitated by viewing policies and programmes through the prism of transformative justice (Evans, 2016: 8–10). Transformative justice builds on the contribution of restorative and reparative justice, approaches that place the community at the locus of processes to deal with the past and move forward. Mani treats the three as parallel and complementary notions oriented towards facilitating societal and individual reconciliation to rebuild inclusive political communities (Mani, 2005: 521–525). This is similar to Daly's transformative justice aims of reconciliation and deterrence, respectively defined as people learning to live together, and continuing to do so in the future (Daly, 2002: 84). Restorative justice encompasses a normative shift in which crime is seen primarily as an injury to the community to which both victim and offender belong, and only secondarily as a violation of state law (Eriksson, 2009: 11). Perpetrators are responsible to their direct victim and those affected, and the community may be involved in the process of rectifying the injury and restoring relationships.[2]

The concepts of reparative and restorative justice illuminate a continuum of transitional justice to which transformative justice also belongs; although I argue that reparative and restorative justice are not altogether satisfactory concepts if the intention is to reduce structural violence. To begin with, the terms repair or restore suggest the re-establishment of a previously good state or condition (Clamp and Doak, 2012: 351). However, this is an impossible objective in many transitional contexts because 'What could replace lost health and serenity; the loss of a loved one or of a whole extended family; a whole generation of friends; the destruction of home and culture and community and peace?' (Roht-Arriaza, 2004: 158). There may also be an implication that restoration will be easy or natural, whereas the act of transformation is intrinsically understood to involve significant effort. More substantively, restorative and reparative justice fail to fully engage structural violence and the root causes of conflict. Reparative approaches often continue to work on accountability for specific incidents of individual harm, thus continuing to neglect structural questions (Miller, 2008: 275; Clamp, 2014: 34–35). While reconstructing community relationships is important, reckoning with the past is not limited to correcting unfair transactions, but in putting relationships on a more equitable future footing (Webber, 2012). Local communities where

2 Such approaches are subject to their own criticism, *inter alia* representing a lesser type of justice or not being human rights compliant.

restorative justice processes are implemented often suffer structural disadvantage or violence vis-à-vis wider society, and should not be further stigmatised through association with violent crime, stressing the importance of building an inclusive economic and social, not merely political, community. Mani's call, however, is not accompanied by any mention of institutional reform, redistribution or GNR that would affect the structure of the reconstituted community (Mani, 2005: 524–525), and is not applicable to societies that have never been inclusive. On the contrary, historically unjust social, economic and political orders require transformation, not strengthening or timid reform (Muvingi, 2009: 178; Thomason, 2015: 71). It is also doubtful that reconciliation can be anything more than a tangential outcome of transitional justice (Evans, 2015), dependent on myriad other factors, and with the potential to uphold impunity and prevailing power relations and social structures. Restorative justice proponents themselves call for a more transformative approach that works simultaneously on behaviours, relations, structures and systemic injustices (Robins, 2013: 11; Clamp, 2014: 16). Numerous theoretical linkages and continuities are evident between the concepts, with ambitiously conceived community-based restorative justice able to create space for transformative justice to flourish (Clamp, 2014: 43–44; Eriksson, 2009: 188).

The meaning of transformative justice is still rather nebulous, with no commonly agreed definition or components. Daly's aims of deterrence and reconciliation are almost impossible to operationalise and measure, and have been critiqued as setting the framework up to fail (Evans, 2016: 6). Non-recurrence of violations could be caused by societal reconciliation or by lack of opportunity (for example, a military force blocking armed confrontation), while living together could signify tolerance (or even resignation) rather than reconciliation. The transformative aspects of her approach arise, rather, from the appreciation of local context (Daly, 2002: 77–78), and recognition that transformative institutions must exemplify the values they seek to promote rather than simply reflect the existing balance of power within society (Daly, 2002: 95–100). Lambourne elaborates six principles of transformative justice that establish the conditions, processes, relationships and structures to ensure justice in the past, the present and the future (Lambourne, 2009: 45–47; Lambourne, 2014: 32–34). Lambourne's model is nevertheless undertheorised, leading to conflation, rather than analytical coherence, with related disciplines (Waldorf, 2012: 9–10). The commonality with Daly – and other transformative justice theorists – comes from the need for inclusive processes consistent with local worldviews and cultural understandings of justice. A narrower concept of transformative justice sees it acting to change pre-conflict structures in ways that are more inclusive and equal (Gready et al., 2010: 1). This has the advantage of concentrating on structural questions without unmanageably expanding the field beyond transitional contexts, hence avoiding the conflation of transformative justice with a more general social justice (Evans, 2013: 18; Evans, 2016: 8–9). The emphasis on locally participatory processes recurs, indicating a major definitional building block for transformative justice (see also Robins, 2013; Gready and Robins, 2014; and others). While Waldorf suggests that the transformative justice definition used by Gready et al. is analytically distinct from transitional justice, he asks what this would look like in practice and how it differs from rights-based, conflict-sensitive development (Waldorf, 2012: 10). This remains a pertinent question, indicating the existence of gaps and demonstrating the importance of drawing on theory and practice in other fields. Transformative justice has been better at diagnosing problems – in transitional states and in transitional justice – than offering solutions to these problems (Evans, 2013, 2016; Gready et al., 2010; McAuliffe, 2015).

This work contributes to the search for solutions to structural violence in transitional contexts. This is done by operationalising transformative justice as a three-dimensional model, arguing that a transformative justice model must consider three distinct dimensions: as a diagnostic tool, a process requirement, and a set of outcomes (McGill, 2017). The first requires comprehensive analysis of transitional societies to consider the historical roots and political economy of the current situation in order to successfully diagnose the problem to be resolved. It is important to question critically how a process, programme or mechanism came about, the key debates and mobilisations that shaped it, how – and by whom – decisions were taken, and how aims and beneficiaries were defined. The second emphasises the empowering nature of participatory processes that allow those suffering oppression to construct their own world (Freire, 1996). Operationally, these include building the capacity of local community members or victims to participate, and removing cultural, financial or social barriers to meaningful involvement, thus equipping individuals and communities with the skills and confidence necessary for future mobilisation and participation in society. The empowering nature resides not merely in participation within the transitional processes, but in the construction of wider civic competence and engagement. Processes that do not fulfil this participatory function are not transformative, as they do not change the basis of social relationships or challenge the decision-making monopoly of dominant groups (Lundy and McGovern, 2008; Robins, 2013). The outcome requirements recognise that transitional policies and processes should target more fundamental social changes than ending armed conflict or authoritarianism. This encompasses a variety of contextually specific objectives such as creating a more equitable land-ownership structure or more widespread access to services. Adopting a transformative perspective in all three dimensions will be crucial to reduce structural violence in transitional societies. The final section will investigate the interactions of land with direct and structural violence in Colombia, utilising the model to outline the potential contribution of two public policy initiatives to reducing structural violence in rural areas.

Land and transition in Colombia

Many internal armed conflicts and human rights violations around the world have been rural-based, and often linked to the existence of structural violence (Robins, 2013: 65–69; Pasipanodya, 2008: 380–383; Nagy, 2013: 88–89; Miller, 2008: 282–284). However, transitional justice mechanisms often pay insufficient attention to important questions like land rights and distribution patterns (Fitzpatrick and Fishman, 2014; Moyo, 2015: 71–72; Pasipanodya, 2008: 390–391). Land questions, if addressed, are usually conceptualised as restitution to a pre-existing status quo, heavily influenced by theories of economic efficiency, limited by financial constraints, and ignoring wider structural problems (Huggins, 2009: 361). Land restitution processes are often embarked upon in societies with historically unjust land access patterns and multiple cycles of dispossession and occupation, therefore facing competing claims to land in what is often perceived to be a zero-sum game (Huggins, 2009; Fitzpatrick and Fishman, 2014). One of the most complicated and controversial questions to confront in any land-related process of restitution or redistribution is to which point the clock should be turned back (Atuahene, 2010; Huggins, 2009: 350–352). State policy in post-apartheid South Africa, for example, did not prioritise land redistribution or equalisation (Atuahene, 2010), instead adopting a 'willing seller-willing buyer' approach (Moyo, 2015: 81–82) that did not meet governmental and popular expectations. Failing to acknowledge the diversity of meanings attached to land and how claims to it were justified meant that restitution was not institutionalised as a shared social field, hence hampering implementation (Walker, 2012). Programmes such as South Africa's are socially regressive because they do not transform conditions for marginalised communities, instead prompting a transfer of resources upwards that can reward beneficiaries of the previously unjust system.

Armed conflict in Colombia is estimated to have led directly to the deaths of 220,000 people since 1958, 80% of these civilians, while millions more have been wounded, threatened and displaced (Grupo de Memoria Histórica, 2013). This was preceded by an estimated 200,000 deaths during 'La Violencia' between 1948 and 1958, and a series of other armed conflicts since independence. Understanding the symbiotic relationship between direct and structural violence in Colombia, especially in the countryside, is vital. Entrenched social, political and economic relations and changes in land usage patterns that cause concentration and dispossession are intimately linked to the recurring cycles of armed conflict that have historically begun in rural areas. Guerrilla activity arose in areas that had experienced repeated offensives by state armed forces, initial mass membership was primarily made up of disaffected peasants, and the discursive foundation is one of exploitation and agrarian reform (Otis, 2014: 3; cf. Sendero Luminoso in Peru – Laplante, 2008: 336). The objective of state military offensives had been to destroy peasant communities who had fled La Violencia and were now demanding land reform. Land ownership in Colombia has historically been highly concentrated and this remains the case (PNUD, 2011; Grupo de Memoria Histórica, 2013: 192; Minagricultura, 2014), especially in regions where the state is weakly or unevenly institutionalised, and local elites dominate economic, political and social life (Ibáñez and Munoz, 2010). Ownership and control of land has always been an important economic and social marker, and a constant source of conflict, sometimes violently manifested (ILSA, 2012: 6; Uribe Kaffure, 2013: 247; Minagricultura, 2014: 35–36; Baquero Melo, 2015: 39, 47).

Nevertheless, the situation is more complex than structural violence in rural areas causing armed conflict. The direct violence of the armed conflict has had a massive effect in rural areas with an estimated 5–6 million people displaced from their land (Victims Unit, 2013: 25–27; Grupo de Memoria Histórica, 2013). The high rates of displacement in recent years have increased the number of landless peasants living in the countryside and are closely correlated with the statistical increase in land inequalities as captured by Gini coefficients for land (PNUD, 2011; Minagricultura, 2014: 36). A number of studies suggest that regions experiencing higher numbers of armed conflict incidents, and especially those with a greater paramilitary presence, have seen land concentration and ownership patterns become increasingly unequal (Ibáñez, n.d.; Uribe Kaffure, 2013). In addition, many displaced people have resettled in cities, and this dramatic, unplanned urban growth has put severe pressure on public services, infrastructure and the local ecology, raising important questions around urban property and land rights. Recently internally displaced people often live in unsafe and unhealthy conditions, find it hard to integrate into urban economies, and remain marginalised politically, socially and culturally (Grupo de Memoria Histórica, 2013: 295–299; Ibáñez, n.d.). These cases are powerful examples of how structural violence begets further structural violence, with the inequality in land arrangements, combined with increased exposure to direct violence, precipitating displacement to urban slums where new structural violence occurs. Structural violence severely curtails the life chances of individuals and groups in society, and sustained focus on the phenomenon is necessary to build a more just and peaceful society.

A positive aspect of the Havana Peace Dialogues was recognition of structural violence underpinning armed conflict. The High Commissioner for Peace differentiated between ending armed conflict and building peace, drawing on distinctions of negative and positive peace and indicating the intention to address socioeconomic concerns in the post-accord period (Jaramillo Caro, 2015). The need for fundamental transformation in rural relations and creation of viable economic opportunities in the countryside was accepted by the Colombian government and FARC, with a Comprehensive Agricultural Development Policy point one on the agenda of negotiations and the first agreed upon (FARC-EP, 2014; High Commissioner for Peace, 2014). This policy, which seemingly survived initial public rejection of the peace accord, identifies access to land and land use as the central aspects to confront in order to stimulate social and economic development in zones that have suffered most from conflict and poverty. While it is tempting to regard the Comprehensive Agricultural Development Policy as a fresh start, it has not sprung from a political vacuum, nor will it completely replace all existing agrarian policies. Ensuring it reduces structural violence in Colombia is therefore dependent on assessing existing public policy initiatives, with the most influential being the land restitution programme and Peasant Reserve Zones. The following paragraphs give details of these before analysing to what extent they are compatible with the transformative justice approach elaborated above.

Law 1448 of 2011 (the 'Victims' Law'), is the basis for Colombia's flagship transitional justice initiative, with its ambitious scope aiming to provide comprehensive reparations and guarantees of non-recurrence to all victims of direct violence in the armed conflict since 1985. The central component is the Land

Restitution Programme (LRP), designed to restore millions of hectares of land to people displaced since 1991, issue valid property deeds for this, and improve rural infrastructure and livelihood opportunities (Acción Social, 2011; Correa, 2015; Baquero Melo, 2015: 43–44). The Victims' Law recognises the centrality of economic resources in the armed conflict and the scale of dispossession, and that these must be addressed both inside and outside the official peace process. The declared aim is to stimulate sustained rural development to make the reparations programme transformative (Acción Social, 2011). However, the LRP is highly bureaucratic and legalistic which translates into long implementation timeframes, and it does not address the structural causes of past displacement or impoverishment. The focus on restitution rather than transformation means that deeper problems such as pre-1991 displacement, historic landlessness, and the inadequacy of plots to support livelihoods are not addressed. Moreover, peasant leaders and land rights activists continue to be killed, assaulted and threatened, seemingly to dissuade displaced persons from seeking restitution (Haugaard et al., 2013: 3; Minagricultura, 2014: 41).

Peasant Reserve Zones (ZRC – Zonas de Reserva Campesina) constitute an alternative model. Endowed with legal status by Law 160 of 1994, ZRC were conceived as a strategy to organise rural property, eliminate land concentration, extend peasant landholding, promote rural development, encourage community participation in local development plans, protect the environment, and safeguard peasants' economic, social and cultural rights (Congreso de Colombia, 1994; Incoder, 2011). In accordance with these aims, the land within ZRC is subject to restrictions on the size of individual holdings and the agricultural techniques that can be employed (González Posso, 2011: 2; García Reyes, 2013: 1–2). Zones are created in a collaborative process between local authorities and peasant organisations, and the state is required to safeguard peasant participation in regional planning and decision-making bodies, for example in elaborating the initial sustainable development plan and other foundational documents (Congreso de Colombia, 1994; ILSA, 2012). Six ZRC are formally recognised, while many more are in various stages of legal constitution, some of them operating *de facto*. A National Association of Peasant Reserve Zones (ANZORC) was created in 2011 to facilitate the coordination of common policy positions and transmit them to the government, to the peace negotiations, and to wider society (ANZORC, 2011; ILSA, 2012; García Reyes, 2013).

The remainder of this section will analyse which of these approaches is more transformative of currently unequal rural societies, understood as both empowering local communities and improving peasant farmers' lived realities. For a policy or programme to address structural violence it must begin with an analysis that considers the historical roots and socioeconomic determinants of the existing situation. To put it another way, it must do more than examine the direct violence of conflict, but rather consider the structural violence that underpins, reinforces and surrounds it. Practically speaking, this means that beneficiaries should not be determined solely on the basis of their exposure to direct violence, but to the deeper forces of structural violence. The land restitution programme is specifically geared towards returning land to those displaced by violence or the threat of violence (Acción Social, 2011: Article 75; García Reyes et al., 2015). Furthermore, it is based on a law that was unveiled soon after the inauguration of President Santos, indicating that it was largely drafted by his team rather than through a consultative process. ZRC, on the other hand, are a response to landlessness and unproductive land, containing processes to distribute such land among those requiring access to land and prepared to cultivate it (ILSA, 2012; ANZORC, 2011). They are also a means to collectively manage land and the necessary agricultural inputs to increase production, with the ability to operate to some extent as rural trade unions and collective marketing and production bodies.

In terms of process requirements, the transformative justice framework suggests that ZRC are more suited to reducing structural violence, with significant citizen participation in defining the boundaries and scope of the peasant reserve and elaborating local sustainable development plans (Congreso de Colombia, 1994; García Reyes, 2013: 2). Such participation is empowering, because it grants agency to those previously lacking it, allows diverse views and grievances to be expressed, and challenges established decision-making hierarchies. Vitally, political coalitions have grown both across different regions and among various stakeholder groups in rural society, such as victims' groups, peasant organisations, and indigenous communities. ANZORC was created to bring together 30 different organisations, and 3,800 people attended its third national encounter in 2013 (García Reyes, 2013: 1–4). In contrast, the role of land restitution beneficiaries is that of claimants who register themselves on the victims register, indicate the location of their land and explain the facts of usurpation or dispossession (García-Godos and Wiig, 2014: 22–24). Claimants then pass through an administrative phase of verifying these data and any relevant information, followed by a judicial phase, at which beneficiaries may appear, although primarily to restate their testimony. Claimants are obliged to accept judicial rulings in full, with no recourse to appeal if they disagree (García-Godos and Wiig, 2014: 24). This lack of involvement in designing programme goals and procedures, and of meaningful participation in the implementation stages could be compensated by increased mobilisation of peasants in campaigns to expand and quicken the reparation programme, an important transformative justice aim (Gready, 2015). However, a recent study highlights the low level of participation among the dispossessed in organisations related to the land restitution process (Gutiérrez, García Reyes and Argoty, 2014: 93). According to the model utilised in this chapter, encouraging increased social mobilisation and citizen empowerment to demand further change is a key outcome requirement, so the LRP appears to be deficient on this particular aspect as well. However, in general, it is in the realm of outcomes that the LRP may prove to have more transformative effects than ZRC, primarily because it is the best-resourced mechanism in the country and was symbolically important for the Santos administration. Given the ongoing implementation of restitution and renewed prominence of ZRC as rural actors, empirical investigation could productively be targeted at assessing their substantive impacts on peasants' everyday existence.

Conclusions

Transitional justice processes have generally failed to reduce structural violence in societies where they have been implemented, due to the flaws of specific mechanisms as well as to wider conceptual weaknesses. This is most clearly reflected by the bias towards legalistic and individualistic responses to dealing with violations of civil and political rights rather than considering the historical and economic underpinnings of authoritarianism and armed conflict or focusing on ESCR and inequalities. It is clear that strategies to improve the existence of people at the bottom of highly inequitable hierarchies need to strive towards a more transformative approach that operates on multiple dimensions. As a guide to future theorising and action, this chapter has suggested operationalising transformative justice in a model that can assess initiatives' different dimensions. Diagnoses must consider the social, economic, cultural and political aspects that create structural violence in society; processes should be participatory, with acquisition of confidence and capacity leading to more empowered and engaged citizens; and outcomes should have a positive tangible impact in the life opportunities of those who suffer structural violence.

This matrix was then applied to two public policy initiatives in rural Colombia to illustrate the different impact that a transitional and a transformative mechanism can have across these three dimensions. While the land restitution programme is an important and ambitious undertaking, it is inaccurate to classify it as transformative, notwithstanding the terminology it employs (Acción Social, 2011). The Victims' Law was elaborated quickly with minimal consultation with peasant organisations, and the relationship between peasants and the LRP is mediated by their status as individual claimants. Its transformative aspect resides in state support for economically viable projects for returnees and the commitment to provide rural infrastructure, social services and agricultural inputs (García-Godos and Wiig, 2014: 22). An emphasis on, and extension of, those aspects would help break the zero-sum equations that often arise in conflicts over land by reconceptualising restitution as one among many remedies for structural violence and inequalities in rural areas (Fitzpatrick and Fishman, 2014: 286–287; Haugaard et al., 2013: 22–23). Doing so would allow transitional justice to make a 'modest contribution to achieving the broader aim of reforming land tenure systems in a more just direction' (Huggins, 2009: 353), and fit ANZORC's proposal to institutionalise rural development, equitable redistribution of land and technical assistance for agriculture, articulated in its National Programme as well as in each zone's Sustainable Development Plan (García Reyes, 2013: 6–7). Integration of this wider focus into Colombian rural policies would represent a success for the transformative justice approach, and go some way to reducing structural violence in the country.

References

Acción Social (2011) *Ley de Víctimas y Restitución de Tierras (Ley 1448)*. Bogotá: Acción Social.
Acuerdo Final. (2016) *Acuerdo Final para la Terminación del Conflicto y la Construcción de una Paz Estable y Duradera*, www.altocomisionadoparalapaz.gov.co/p

rocesos-y-conversaciones/Paginas/Texto-completo-del-Acuerdo-Final-para-la-Terminacion-del-conflicto.aspx [accessed 30 August 2018].

Ainley, Kirsten (2015) 'Evaluating Transitional Justice'. Presentation given at the Oxford Transitional Justice Research Seminar Series, University of Oxford, Oxford, UK, 11 May.

ANZORC (2011) *Cartilla Pedagógica de las Zonas de Reserva Campesina en Colombia*, https://issuu.com/anzorc/docs/cartillazonasdereservacampesina [accessed 29 April 2016].

Arbour, Louise (2007) 'Economic and social justice for societies in transition'. *New York University Journal of International Law and Politics* 40(1): 1–27.

Arthur, Paige (2009) 'How "Transitions" Reshaped Human Rights: A Conceptual History of Transitional Justice'. *Human Rights Quarterly* 31(2): 321–367.

Atuahene, Bernadette (2010) 'Property and Transitional Justice'. *UCLA Law Review Discourse* 58: 65–93.

Balasco, Lauren Marie (2013) 'The Transitions of Transitional Justice: Mapping the Waves From Promise to Practice'. *Journal of Human Rights* 12(2): 198–216.

Baquero Melo, Jairo (2015) 'Regional Challenges to Land Restitution and Peace in Colombia: The Case of the Lower Atrato'. *Journal of Peacebuilding and Development* 10(2): 36–51.

Bayley, David H. (2008) 'Post-conflict Police Reform: Is Northern Ireland a Model?'. *Policing* 2(2): 233–240.

BBC (2016) 'Turning guerrilla fighters into entrepreneurs', www.bbc.co.uk/news/business-35873206 [accessed 30 April 2018].

Bell, Christine and Catherine O'Rourke (2007) 'Does feminism need a theory of transitional justice? An introductory essay'. *International Journal of Transitional Justice* 1(1): 23–44.

Briceno-Leon, Roberto, Andrés Villaveces and Alberto Concha-Eastman (2008) 'Understanding the uneven distribution of the incidence of homicide in Latin America'. *International Journal of Epidemiology* 37(4): 751–757.

Carranza, Ruben (2008) 'Plunder and Pain: Should Transitional Justice Engage with Corruption and Economic Crimes?'. *International Journal of Transitional Justice* 2(3): 310–330.

Cavallaro, James L. and Sebastián Albuja (2008) 'The lost agenda: economic crimes and truth commissions in Latin America and beyond'. In Kieran McEvoy and Lorna McGregor (eds), *Transitional Justice from Below: Grassroots Activism and the Struggle for Change*, 121–142. Oxford: Wiley.

Clamp, Kerry (2014) *Restorative Justice in Transition*. Abingdon: Routledge.

Clamp, Kerry and Jonathan Doak (2012) 'More than words: restorative justice concepts in transitional justice settings'. *International Criminal Law Review* 12(3): 339–360.

Collins, Cath (2010) *Post-transitional Justice: Human Rights Trials in Chile and El Salvador*. University Park, PA: Pennsylvania State University Press.

Congreso de Colombia (1994) *Ley 160 de 1994*. Bogotá: Government of Colombia.

Correa, Christian (2015) *From Principles to Practice: Challenges of Implementing Reparations for Massive Violations in Colombia*. New York: International Center for Transitional Justice.

Cramer, Chris (2003) 'Does inequality cause conflict?'. *Journal of International Development* 15(4): 397–412.

Daly, Erin. (2002) 'Transformative Justice: Charting a Path to Reconciliation'. *International Legal Perspectives* 12(1/2): 73–183.

de Greiff, Pablo (2009) 'Articulating the Links between Transitional Justice and Development: Justice and Social Integration'. In Pablo de Greiff and Roger Duthie (eds),

Transitional Justice and Development: Making Connections, 28–75. New York: Social Science Research Council.

Dyzenhaus, David (2012) 'Leviathan as a Theory of Transitional Justice'. In Melissa S. Williams, Rosemary Nagy and Jon Elster (eds), *Transitional Justice*, 180–217. New York: New York University Press.

Eriksson, Anna (2009) *Justice in Transition: Community Restorative Justice in Northern Ireland*. Portland, OR: Willan Publishing.

Evans, Matthew (2013) 'Land, socio-economic rights and transformative justice'. Paper presented at the conference 'Land Divided: Land and South African Society in 2013, in Comparative Perspective', Cape Town, South Africa, 24–27 March.

Evans, Matthew (2015) 'Against reconciliation?'. Paper presented at the conference 'Critical Legal Conference 2015: Law, Space and the Political', University of Wrocław, Wrocław, Poland, 3–5 September.

Evans, Matthew (2016) 'Structural Violence, Socioeconomic Rights and Transformative Justice'. *Journal of Human Rights* 15(1): 1–20.

Farmer, Paul. (1996) 'On Suffering and Structural Violence: A View from Below'. *Daedalus* 125(1): 261–283.

Fitzpatrick, Daniel and Akiva Fishman (2014) 'Land Policy and Transitional Justice after Armed Conflicts'. In Dustin N. Sharp (ed.), *Justice and Economic Violence in Transition*, 263–287. New York: Springer.

Franzki, Hannah and Maria Carolina Olarte (2014) 'Understanding the political economy of transitional justice: a critical theory perspective'. In Susanne Buckley-Zistel, Teresa Koloma Beck, Christian Braun and Friederike Mieth (eds), *Transitional Justice Theories*, 201–221. Abingdon: Routledge.

Freire, Paolo (1996) *Pedagogy of the Oppressed*. Harmondsworth: Penguin.

Galtung, Johan (1969) 'Violence, Peace, and Peace Research'. *Journal of Peace Research* 6 (3): 167–191.

Galtung, Johan (1990) 'Cultural Violence'. *Journal of Peace Research* 27(3): 291–305.

García-Godos, Jemima and Henrik Wiig (2014) *The Colombian Land Restitution Programme: Process, Results and Challenges, with Special Emphasis on Women*, NIBR-report 2014:14, October. Oslo: Norwegian Institute for Urban and Regional Research.

García Reyes, Paula (2013) *III Encuentro Nacional de Zonas de Reserva Campesina*, report. Bogotá: Observatorio de Restitución y Regulación de Derechos de Propiedad Rural [Observatory of Restitution and Regulation of Agrarian Property Rights].

García Reyes, Paula, Laura Ochoa Guzmán, Belén Pardo Herrero and Judith Zableh Orozco (2015) *Informe Sobre el Estado Actual e Impactos del Proceso de Restitución de Tierras en Montes de María*, first half-year report. Bogotá: Observatorio de Restitución y Regulación de Derechos de Propiedad Rural [Observatory of Restitution and Regulation of Agrarian Property Rights].

Godoy, Angelina S. (2005) '"La Muchacha Respondona": Reflections on the Razor's Edge between Crime and Human Rights'. *Human Rights Quarterly* 27(2): 597–624.

González Posso, Camilo (2011) 'Zonas de reserva y comunidades campesinas'. Paper presented at the seminar 'Zonas de Reserva Campesina', Instituto Colombiano de Desarrollo Rural (INCODER), Acción Social and Project to Protect the Land and Assets of the Displaced Population (PPTPPD), Bogotá, Colombia, 3 November.

Government of Colombia and Fuerzas Armadas Revolucionarias de Colombia-Ejército del Pueblo (FARC-EP) (2014) *Informe Conjunto entre el Gobierno de Colombia y las Fuerzas Armadas Revolucionarias de Colombia-Ejército del Pueblo (FARC-EP): Points 1 and 2 of Agenda*. Havana: Government of Colombia and FARC-EP.

Gready, Paul. (2005) 'Reconceptualising transitional justice: embedded and distanced justice'. *Conflict, Security & Development* 5(1): 3–21.

Gready, Paul (2011) *The Era of Transitional Justice: The Aftermath of the Truth and Reconciliation Commission in South Africa and Beyond*. Abingdon: Routledge.

Gready, Paul (2015) 'From Transitional to Transformative Justice'. Presentation at the conference 'The more things change, the more they stay the same? Socio-economic rights in times of transition', Transitional Justice Institute, Ulster Hall, Belfast, 30 April.

Gready, Paul, Jelke Boesten, Gordon Crawford and Polly Wilding (2010) 'Transformative Justice – A Concept Note', https://wun.ac.uk/files/transformative_justice_-_concept_note_web_version.pdf [accessed 30 April 2018].

Gready, Paul and Simon Robins (2014) 'From Transitional to Transformative Justice: A New Agenda for Practice'. *International Journal of Transitional Justice* 8(3): 339–361.

Grupo de Memoria Histórica (2013) *¡Basta ya! Colombia: Memorias de Guerra y Dignidad*. Bogotá: Imprenta Nacional.

Gutiérrez, Francisco, Paola García Reyes and Camilo Argoty (2014) *La Restitución y sus Problemas, Según sus Potenciales Beneficiarios*, first half-year report. Bogotá: Observatorio de Restitución y Regulación de Derechos de Propiedad Rural [Observatory of Restitution and Regulation of Agrarian Property Rights].

Haldemann, Frank and Rachelle Kouassi (2014) 'Transitional Justice without Economic, Social, and Cultural Rights?'. In Eibe Riedel, Gilles Giacca and Christophe Golay (eds), *Economic, Social, and Cultural Rights in International Law: Contemporary Issues and Challenges*, 498–516. Oxford: Oxford University Press.

Harwell, Emily E. and Philippe Le Billon (2009) 'Natural Connections: Linking Transitional Justice and Development Through a Focus on Natural Resources'. In Pablo de Greiff and Roger Duthie (eds), *Transitional Justice and Development: Making Connections*, 282–331. New York: Social Science Research Council.

Haugaard, Lisa, Zoraida Castillo, Winifred Tate and Annalise Romoser (2013) *Far from the Promised Land: Land Restitution on Colombia's Caribbean Coast*. Baltimore, MD and New York: Lutheran World Relief and the Latin America Working Group Education Fund.

Hecht, Lisa and Sabine Michalowski (2012) *The Economic and Social Dimensions of Transitional Justice*. Colchester: Essex Transitional Justice Network.

High Commissioner for Peace (2014) *Learn about the Peace Process in Colombia*. Bogotá: Office of the High Commissioner for Peace.

Huggins, Chris (2009) 'Linking broad constellations of ideas: transitional justice, land tenure reform, and development'. In Pablo de Greiff and Roger Duthie (eds), *Transitional Justice and Development: Making Connections*, 332–374. New York: Social Science Research Council.

Hume, Mo (2009) *The Politics of Violence: Gender, Conflict and Community in El Salvador*. Bulletin of Latin American Research Book Series. Chichester: Wiley-Blackwell.

Ibáñez, Ana María (n.d.) 'La concentración de la propiedad rural en Colombia: evolución 2000 a 2009, desplazamiento forzoso e impactos sobre desarrollo económico'. Presentation at Centro de Investigaciones para el Desarrollo, Universidad Nacional de Colombia, Bogotá.

Ibáñez, Ana María and Juan Carlos Muñoz. (2010) 'The Persistence of Land Concentration in Colombia: What Happened Between 2000 and 2010?'. In Morten Bergsmo, César Rodríguez-Garavito, Pablo Kalmanovitz and Maria Paula Saffo (eds), *Distributive Justice in Transitions*, 279–310. Oslo: Torkel Opsahl Academic EPublisher.

Incoder (2011) *Presentación General Zonas de Reserva Campesina Constituidas*. Bogotá: INCODER.

Instituto Latinoamericano para una Sociedad y un Derecho Alternativos (ILSA) (2012) *Zonas de Reserva Campesina: Elementos Introductorios y de Debate*. Bogotá: Instituto Latinoamericano para una Sociedad y un Derecho alternativos.

Jaramillo Caro, Sergio (2015) 'Peacemaking and Peacebuilding in Colombia'. Seminar at Blavatnik School of Government, University of Oxford, Oxford, UK, 13 May.

Kent, Lia (2012) *The Dynamics of Transitional Justice: International Models and Local Realities in East Timor*. Abingdon: Routledge.

Lambourne, Wendy (2009) 'Transitional Justice and Peacebuilding after Mass Violence'. *International Journal of Transitional Justice* 3(1): 28–48.

Lambourne, Wendy (2014) 'Transformative justice, reconciliation and peacebuilding'. In Susanne Buckley-Zistel, Teresa Koloma Beck, Christian Braun and Friederike Mieth (eds), *Transitional Justice Theories*, 19–39. Abingdon: Routledge.

Landau, David. (2012) 'The Reality of Social Rights Enforcement'. *Harvard International Law Journal* 53: 402–459.

Landman, Todd and Marco Larizza (2009) 'Inequality and Human Rights: Who Controls What, When, and How'. *International Studies Quarterly* 53(3): 715–736.

Laplante, Lisa J. (2007) 'On the indivisibility of rights: truth commissions, reparations, and the right to development'. *Yale Human Rights and Development Law Journal* 10(1): 141–177.

Laplante, Lisa J. (2008) 'Transitional justice and peace building: diagnosing and addressing the socioeconomic roots of violence through a human rights framework'. *International Journal of Transitional Justice* 2(3): 331–355.

Lundy, Patricia and Mark McGovern (2008) 'Whose justice? Rethinking transitional justice from the bottom up'. *Journal of Law and Society* 35(2): 265–292.

Mani, Rama (2002) *Beyond Retribution: Seeking Justice in the Shadows of War*. Cambridge: Polity Press.

Mani, Rama (2005) 'Rebuilding an inclusive political community after war'. *Security Dialogue* 36(4): 511–526.

Mani, Rama (2008) 'Dilemmas of expanding transitional justice, or forging the nexus between transitional justice and development'. *International Journal of Transitional Justice* 2(3): 253–265.

McAuliffe, Pádraig (2010) 'Transitional Justice and the Rule of Law: The Perfect Couple or Awkward Bedfellows?'. *Hague Journal on the Rule of Law* 2(2): 127–154.

McAuliffe, Pádraig (2011) 'Transitional Justice's Expanding Empire: Reasserting the Value of the Paradigmatic Transition'. *Journal of Conflictology* 2(2): 32–44.

McAuliffe, Pádraig (2015) 'Structural Causes of Conflict and the Superficiality of Transition'. In Claudio Corradetti, Nir Eisikovits and Jack V. Rotondi (eds), *Theorizing Transitional Justice*, 93–105. Farnham: Ashgate.

McGill, Dáire (2017) 'Different Violence, Different Justice? Taking Structural Violence Seriously in Post-conflict and Transitional Justice Processes'. *State Crime Journal* 6(1): 79–101.

Miller, Zinaida (2008) 'Effects of invisibility: in search of the "economic" in transitional justice'. *International Journal of Transitional Justice* 2(3): 266–291.

Minagricultura (2014) *La Restitución de Tierras en Colombia: del Sueño a la Realidad*. Bogotá: Ministry of Agriculture and Rural Development.

Modiri, Joel M. (2015) 'Race, law and the incomplete transition in the afterlife of apartheid'. Paper presented at the conference 'Critical Legal Conference 2015: Law, Space and the Political', University of Wrocław, Wrocław, Poland, 3–5 September.

Moyo, Khanyisela (2015) 'Mimicry, transitional justice and the land question in racially divided former settler colonies'. *International Journal of Transitional Justice* 9(1): 70–89.

Muvingi, Ismael (2009) 'Sitting on Powder Kegs: Socioeconomic Rights in Transitional Societies'. *International Journal of Transitional Justice* 3(2): 163–182.

Nagy, Rosemary (2013) 'Centralizing legal pluralism? Traditional justice in transitional settings'. In Chandra Lekha Sriram, Jemima García-Godos, Johanna Herman and Olga Martin-Ortega (eds), *Transitional Justice and Peacebuilding on the Ground: Victims and Ex-combatants*, 81–99. Abingdon: Routledge.

Obel Hansen, Thomas (2014) 'The Vertical and Horizontal Expansion of Transitional Justice: Explanations and Implications for a Contested Field'. In Susanne Buckley-Zistel, Teresa Koloma Beck, Christian Braun and Friederike Mieth (eds), *Transitional Justice Theories*, 105–124. Abingdon: Routledge.

Olsen, Tricia D., Leigh A. Payne and Andrew G. Reiter (2010) *Transitional Justice in Balance: Comparing Processes, Weighing Efficacy*. Washington, DC: United States Institute of Peace Press.

Otis, John (2014) *The FARC and Colombia's Illegal Drug Trade*. Washington, DC: Wilson Center.

Pasipanodya, Tafadzwa (2008) 'A Deeper Justice: Economic and Social Justice as Transitional Justice in Nepal'. *International Journal of Transitional Justice* 2(3): 378–397.

Patel, Ana Cutter (2009) 'Transitional Justice, DDR, and Security Sector Reform'. In Ana Cutter Patel, Pablo de Greiff and Lars Waldorf (eds), *Disarming the Past: Transitional Justice and Ex-combatants*, 262–283. New York: Social Science Research Council.

PNUD (2011) *Informe Nacional de Desarrollo Humano – Colombia Rural: Razones para la Esperanza*. Bogotá: Programa de las Naciones Unidas para el Desarrollo.

Posner, Eric A. and Adrian Vermeule (2004) 'Transitional justice as ordinary justice'. *Harvard Law Review* 117: 761–825.

Robins, Simon (2013) *Families of the Missing*. Abingdon: Routledge.

Roht-Arriaza, Naomi (2004) 'Reparations Decisions and Dilemmas'. *Hastings International and Comparative Law Review* 27: 157–219.

Sandoval, Clara (2011) *Transitional Justice: Key Concepts, Processes and Challenges*, briefing paper ICDR-BP-07/11, Institute for Democracy and Conflict Resolution, University of Essex. Colchester: Institute for Democracy and Conflict Resolution.

Sandoval, Clara (2015) 'The relevance of socio-economic issues to transitional justice'. Paper presented at the conference 'The more things change, the more they stay the same? Socio-economic rights in times of transition', Transitional Justice Institute, Ulster Hall, Belfast, UK, 30 April.

Schmid, Evelyn (2011) 'War crimes related to violations of economic, social and cultural rights'. *Zeitschrift für ausländisches öffentliches Recht und Völkerrecht/Heidelberg Journal of International Law* 71(3): 523–540.

Sharp, Dustin N. (2012) 'Addressing economic violence in times of transition: toward a positive-peace paradigm for transitional justice'. *Fordham International Law Journal* 35(3): 780–814.

Sharp, Dustin N. (2013a) 'Interrogating the peripheries: the preoccupations of fourth generation transitional justice'. *Harvard Human Rights Journal* 26: 149–178.

Sharp, Dustin N. (2013b) 'Bridging the gap: the United Nations Peacebuilding Commission and the challenges of integrating DDR and transitional justice'. In Chandra Lekha Sriram, Jemima García-Godos, Johanna Herman and Olga Martin-Ortega (eds), *Transitional Justice and Peacebuilding on the Ground: Victims and Ex-combatants*, 23–40. Abingdon: Routledge.

Teitel, Ruti G. (2003) 'Transitional justice genealogy'. *Harvard Human Rights Journal* 16: 69–94.

Thomason, Krista (2015) 'Transitional Justice as Structural Justice'. In Claudio Corradetti, Nir Eisikovits and Jack V. Rotondi (eds), *Theorizing Transitional Justice*, 71–80. Farnham: Ashgate.

Thorsell, Stefan (2013) 'Towards people-centred economic reintegration? An analysis of the economic reintegration strategy of demobilised combatants in Colombia'. *Colombia Internacional* 77: 177–215.

UN (2005) *UN Basic Principles and Guidelines on the Right to a Remedy and Reparation for Victims of Gross Violations of International Human Rights Law and Serious Violations of International Humanitarian Law*, www.un.org/Docs/asp/ws.asp?m=A/RES/60/147 [accessed 30 April 2018].

UN Special Rapporteur on the promotion of truth, justice, reparation and guarantees of non-recurrence (2014) *Report A/69/518 on Reparations*, www.un.org/ga/search/viewm_doc.asp?symbol=A/69/518 [accessed 30 April 2018].

UN Special Rapporteur on the promotion of truth, justice, reparation and guarantees of non-recurrence (2015a) *Report A/HRC/30/42 on Institutional Reform*, www.un.org/Docs/journal/asp/ws.asp?m=A/HRC/30/42 [accessed 30 April 2018].

UN Special Rapporteur on the promotion of truth, justice, reparation and guarantees of non-recurrence (2015b) *Report A/70/438 on Vetting*, www.un.org/en/ga/search/view_doc.asp?symbol=A/70/438 [accessed 30 April 2018].

UN Secretary-General (2004) *The Rule of Law and Transitional Justice in Conflict and Post-conflict Societies*, Report S/2004/616, www.un.org/Docs/journal/asp/ws.asp?m=S/2004/616 [accessed 30 April 2018].

UN Secretary-General (2011) *The Rule of Law and Transitional Justice in Conflict and Post-conflict Societies*, Report S/2011/634, www.un.org/en/ga/search/view_doc.asp?symbol=S/2011/634 [accessed 30 April 2018].

Uribe Kaffure, Sonia (2013) 'Transformaciones de tenencia y uso de la tierra en zonas del ámbito rural colombiano afectadas por el conflicto armado. Aproximación desde un estudio de caso'. *Estudios Socio-Jurídicos* 16(1): 245–287.

Victims Unit (2013) *Desplazamiento y Crisis Humanitaria 2012–2013*. Bogotá: Unidad Victimas.

Vorobej, Mark (2008) 'Structural Violence'. *Peace Research* 40(2): 84–98.

Waldorf, Lars (2012) 'Anticipating the past: transitional justice and socio-economic wrongs'. *Social and Legal Studies* 21(2): 171–186.

Waldorf, Lars (2015) 'Less is More: Limiting Transitional Justice's Reach'. Presentation at the conference 'The more things change, the more they stay the same? Socio-economic rights in times of transition', Transitional Justice Institute, Ulster Hall, Belfast, 30 April.

Walker, Cheryl (2012) 'Finite Land: Challenges Institutionalising Land Restitution in South Africa, 1995–2000'. *Journal of Southern African Studies* 38(4): 809–826.

Webber, Jeremy (2012) 'Forms of Transitional Justice'. In Melissa S. Williams, Rosemary Nagy and Jon Elster (eds), *Transitional Justice*, 98–128. New York: New York University Press.

Woollard, Catherine (2015) 'Socio-economic rights and contemporary conflict: implications for policy and practice'. Presentation at the conference 'The more things change, the more they stay the same? Socio-economic rights in times of transition', Transitional Justice Institute, Ulster Hall, Belfast, 30 April.

World Health Organization (2014) *Global Status Report on Violence Prevention 2014*. Geneva: World Health Organization.

World Health Organization (2015) *Health Equity Monitor: Reproductive, Maternal, Newborn and Child Health Interventions, Combined*, http://apps.who.int/gho/data/view.wrapper.HE-VIZ07?menu=hide [accessed 13 May 2016].

3 Addressing historical wrongs in post-transition South Africa

What role for transformative justice?

Matthew Evans

Introduction

The concept of transformative justice has emerged in recent years as a response to perceived shortcomings in the standard toolkit of transitional justice, particularly in relation to addressing structural violence and violations of socioeconomic rights.[1] This chapter asks what role the concept of transformative justice might have in addressing the continuing effects of historical wrongs on South Africa in the post-transition period. There are three areas where the concept may add value to analysis and practice. These are, first, as a means by which measures seeking to address historical wrongs may be analysed and evaluated. Second, as an explicit framework for action shaping policymaking and practice. Third, as a means by which practices and policies may be understood in relationship to one another and in relation to addressing historically rooted structural violence and socioeconomic rights issues (Evans, 2013b). Here each of these possible uses is explored and evaluated with reference to the South African context. Risks and difficulties associated with adopting the transformative justice framework in one way or another are also discussed. The chapter concludes that transformative justice can most readily add value to the analysis of existing and proposed actions (policy and practice) in relation to their contribution to addressing socioeconomic rights violations and other historical wrongs. It is also concluded that the transformative justice framework could play a role in implicitly or explicitly shaping practice. However, it is suggested that there are more significant obstacles to this than there are to the adoption of transformative justice as an analytical lens.

This chapter is not in large part concerned with defining transformative justice. This has been attempted by scholars elsewhere (including in this volume), with some key areas of overlap between most definitions (see, for example, Gready et al., 2010; Lambourne, 2009; Lambourne, 2011; Daly, 2002). It is worthwhile, however, briefly outlining what is and is not considered to be transformative justice for the purposes of this chapter. Here transformative justice is taken to be separate to transitional justice and to general ideas of social justice. Like transitional justice, transformative justice is concerned with addressing historical wrongs

1 See, for example, Gready et al. (2010); Gready and Robins (2014); Evans (2013a, 2016).

in post-conflict and post-authoritarian contexts. However, unlike transitional justice, transformative justice takes a particular focus on socioeconomic rights issues, structural violence and longer-term change, and upon the participation of affected communities, rather than a concentration on elite bargains (Daly, 2002; Gready et al., 2010; Gready and Robins, 2014).[2] Paul Gready and Simon Robins sum up the definition of transformative justice as 'transformative change that emphasizes local agency and resources, the prioritization of process rather than preconceived outcomes and the challenging of unequal and intersecting power relationships and structures of exclusion at both the local and the global level' (Gready and Robins, 2014: 340). This means that in a context, such as South Africa, which could be termed 'post-transition' in that transitional justice mechanisms, such as truth commissions, trials, amnesties and reparations programmes, have largely run their course (successfully or otherwise), transformative justice remains a live concern (see, for example, Gready et al., 2010; Collins, 2010; Waldorf, 2012). Furthermore, this necessitates concern with processes other than the legal and quasi-legal instruments transitional justice (and 'post-transitional justice') typically focuses on (Evans, 2016). Bearing this definition in mind, the analytical utility of the transformative justice framework is discussed next, followed by exploration of its potential role in practice and a discussion of associated risks and difficulties.

Applying transformative justice to analysis

There are several possible analytical roles for the concept of transformative justice. Transformative justice brings together a number of ideas which might otherwise be treated as separate. In particular, transformative justice provides a framework by which (at least some) contemporary struggles for social change in post-transition contexts such as South Africa may be understood in a wider context and as connected to historical wrongs (such as apartheid, conflict and societal division) (Evans, 2013b, 2016; see also Harris et al., 2014).[3] In this sense it is possible to evaluate and distinguish social justice and development issues according to whether they are also transformative justice issues. This affects how contemporary conditions and struggles are understood and responded to from an intellectual and practical point of view. For instance, the profound inequalities in access to land and housing in South Africa are in large part the result of the ongoing influence of apartheid (see, for example, Gibson, 2011). Neither the advent of democracy, nor

2 Paul Farmer, for instance, argues that 'Structural violence is violence exerted systematically – that is, indirectly – by everyone who belongs to a certain social order … In short, the concept of structural violence is intended to inform the study of the social machinery of oppression' (Farmer, 2004: 307). See also Galtung (1969), Gupta (2013) and Farmer (1996) for further elaboration of the commonalities and distinction between structural violence and direct, interpersonal violence. On the question of who might qualify as elites, see McAuliffe (Chapter 5, this volume).

3 Some of the same principles can also be applied to measures seeking to address the effects of historical wrongs rooted in the deeper past, such as colonialism and slavery (see Evans and Wilkins, 2017; also Wilkins, Chapter 8, this volume).

transitional justice mechanisms such as the Truth and Reconciliation Commission directly addressed these. Activism and advocacy around these issues has, however, continued.

With regard to housing, post-apartheid policy has been criticised for failing to provide enough, or adequate, housing (see, for example, Govender, Barnes and Pieper, 2011: 335–342; Goebel, 2007: 291–293; Bond and Tait, 1997). Post-apartheid housing policy has followed a market-oriented approach for the most part (Bond and Tait, 1997: 19–20), based on 'the idea of providing subsidies to poor families to allow them to buy homes produced by the private sector' (Gilbert, 2004: 17). This approach has been supported by the World Bank and other international development institutions and was pioneered in Chile from the late 1970s (Gilbert, 2004: 14). In South Africa the housing subsidy scheme is available to assist 'virtually every family earning less than 3,500 rand' (Gilbert, 2004: 27). However, the size, quality and location (on urban peripheries) of subsidised housing have been criticised.[4] Health and environmental concerns have also been raised as well as criticisms of the bureaucracy and administrative processes associated with accessing the housing subsidy (Goebel, 2007: 291–296; Gilbert, 2004: 28–32). Indeed, '[t]o get onto a housing list may still require becoming a client of a local warlord or neo-traditional powerbroker' (Robins, 2008: 167).

It has been suggested that in attempting to address 'an estimated annual increase in the "housing deficit of 200,000 families"' the African National Congress government's housing subsidy delivery 'effectively chose quantity over quality' (Gilbert, 2004: 24). The government's arguable achievements in terms of the quantity of housing provision and the shortcomings in relation to housing quality are in part shaped by the government's approach to land reform. The current approach to land reform is largely market oriented and focuses more on restitution than on wider redistribution. Consequently, the overarching structures shaping unequal land access, distribution and ownership are largely unchanged (see Evans, 2016). In order to provide housing on well-located land it would be necessary to challenge the existing approach to land reform. The pressures to maintain this approach and the barriers to faster or wider-reaching redistribution of land do not hinder house building on urban peripheries as much as on well-located land. It may be easier to provide a large number of houses in these locations. However, this can reinforce existing ghettoisation and result in houses being built without sufficient access to services, infrastructure and economic opportunities (Bond and Tait, 1997: 27; Goebel, 2007: 292).[5] The provision of housing away from well-located land is in turn a factor contributing to the large number of recipients of housing subsidies who subsequently rent out or sell their houses (frequently at low

4 There is some support for government claims to have made significant progress (especially with regard to the number of houses built). Allison Goebel, for instance, notes that, despite criticism of the policy, 'the low-cost housing and service delivery programs have dramatically increased access to urban services by the poor' and that the United Nations has recognised South Africa's achievements in housing provision (Goebel, 2007: 291–293; see also, Gilbert, 2004: 18–19).

5 See also personal interview with Luthando Ndabambi, Cape Town, 12 August 2010.

prices), often in favour of living in informal settlements closer to economic opportunities (Goebel, 2007: 292; Robins, 2008: 92). Steven Robins further points out that many subsidy recipients also move back to informal settlements 'because the houses are too small and they cannot afford to extend using formal building materials, and/or they cannot afford to pay rates and service fees' (Robins, 2008: 92). The housing subsidy programme provides subsidy recipients 'with a physical structure but not the means to survive under conditions of extreme poverty' (Robins, 2008: 92).

Moreover, given the scale of the housing deficit – even as compared to the large number of subsidised houses built – the quantity and rate of delivery of housing provided through the subsidy scheme has also been criticised as insufficient (Bond and Tait, 1997: 27; Robins, 2008: 167).[6] In Cape Town, for instance, over a decade into democracy, there was 'still a shortage of 250,000 houses' (Robins, 2008: 167; on other parts of South Africa, see also Community Law Centre and Socio-Economic Rights Institute, 2013). This housing deficit, ghettoisation, and their effects, can be seen as a direct legacy of apartheid policies as implementation of Coloured Labour Preference Area and homelands policies have led to an ongoing 'massive shortage of housing for black Africans' in Cape Town (Robins, 2008: 167), as well as parallel problems in other parts of South Africa (see, for example, Community Law Centre and Socio-Economic Rights Institute, 2013). The overarching conditions of injustice surrounding realisation of the right to housing remain untransformed (Huchzermeyer, 2003; Bond and Tait, 1997).

Considering socioeconomic rights issues such as this in terms of the structural violence inflicted by apartheid allows questions to be raised with regard to the justness of the post-apartheid settlement and the justness or otherwise of policies aimed at addressing these issues (see Evans, 2013b: 101–102; Evans, 2016). For instance, in the case of land and housing rights in post-apartheid South Africa it may be concluded that the market-oriented policies put in place to address inequalities rooted in apartheid do not adequately challenge the apartheid-defined status quo. This leads to the further conclusion that some civil society actors promote transformative justice – that is to say, contribute to addressing ongoing effects of apartheid – more than others (Evans, 2013b: 191–192; see also Evans, 2018a). Those which challenge or contest the established, untransformative paradigm contribute towards transformative justice to a greater extent than those actors which accept or work wholly within the established paradigm (see Evans, 2018a).

Furthermore, this conception and application of transformative justice facilitates analysis which transcends the implied dichotomy of pre- and post-transition eras. Whilst perhaps not inevitable, the pinning down of the completion of transition to a date (in South Africa, in 1994 with the first democratic elections, or 1996 when the new constitution was finalised, for instance) can lead to neglect of the importance of pre-transition conditions to contemporary circumstances. From a transformative justice point of view these dates can be seen as largely artificial. It is the

6 See also personal interview with Martin Legassick, Cape Town, 4 August 2010.

case that formal apartheid has come to an end and that transitional justice mechanisms have largely run their course. However, these mechanisms did not address all of the injustices of apartheid. Indeed, there is good reason for thinking that transitional justice mechanisms are not intended to, are not well suited to, and perhaps should not attempt to address structural violence or socioeconomic rights issues (Mani, 2008; Waldorf, 2012). Whilst the case has been made for addressing some socioeconomic rights issues through expanding the established focus of transitional justice mechanisms (for example, Mani, 2008; Pasipanodya, 2008; Skaar, 2011; Sankey, 2014; Schmid and Nolan, 2014), these mechanisms cannot do everything. The expansion of transitional justice to attempt to address socioeconomic rights issues has been criticised, particularly in light of shortcomings in successfully carrying out its established narrower mandate (see Waldorf, 2012).

Indeed, a 2014 editorial in the *International Journal of Transitional Justice*, for instance, noted that 'the implementation of every significant transitional justice initiative has fallen short in meeting the expectations of victims and their advocates' (*International Journal of Transitional Justice*, 2014: 1). Analysis from a transformative justice perspective refocuses attention upon the areas which have not been (or cannot be) addressed by transitional justice mechanisms. Moreover, it is also necessary, from this point of view, to look beyond the transitional lens of these mechanisms and of the notion of *transitional* justice. In doing so further clarity may be provided on what concrete forms transformative justice might take as distinct from the established concrete institutional forms of transitional justice.[7]

The refocusing of analytical attention on to areas which are neglected by transitional justice (whether by accident or design) and on to the links between contemporary development and social justice issues and historical wrongs can also lead to increased analytical attention to the needs and the participation of affected communities (see, for example, Robins, 2011, 2013a). Frequently, socioeconomic rights issues and structural violence have a wider impact than that of violations of civil and political rights and direct personal violence (Waldorf, 2012: 175). In post-transition South Africa much of the population continues to be affected by structural violence rooted in the pre-transition period (such as poverty, economic and social inequalities, and the effects of a highly racialised class system), including many who did not experience (or are too young to have experienced) direct violence by the apartheid regime (see, for example, Robins, 2008; Gibson, 2011). Socioeconomic rights are also often prioritised by those who (civil and political rights-oriented) transitional justice mechanisms are intended to benefit (Waldorf, 2012: 175; Robins, 2011, 2013a). The recognition of this and the intellectual attention this entails in terms of understanding and validating the concerns and experiences of those affected by structural violence is an important role for transformative justice analysis. The need for a different response in policy and practice to that of typical transitional justice mechanisms is implied. This goes some way

7 See, for example, the rest of this book, particularly the chapters by McGill, Lai and Bonora, and Bollaert (2, 4 and 6).

towards defining a distinct area in which transformative justice analysis contributes intellectually, illuminating areas of concern to those affected by conflict and authoritarianism (and potential responses to these) which might be obscured or de-emphasised in alternative analyses.

With regard to the possible value added by transformative justice analysis to discussions around post-transition South Africa it is worthwhile considering the particular influence transformative justice analysis may have upon understanding the role of civil society. A broad definition of civil society is used here, including, for instance, both contentious and non-contentious action taken by informal social movements and more formal organisations such as trade unions and nongovernmental organisations (NGOs).[8] Civil society action is, of course, a broad field. It is possible, however, to apply a transformative justice analytical lens to those elements of civil society which engage in political and social action around human rights issues and socioeconomic grievances. Not all of these are of clear relevance to transformative justice, though an analysis from this point of view allows for action to be assessed with regard to whether it contributes to the addressing of historical wrongs (such as apartheid – and colonial – land dispossession) (see, for example, Harris et al., 2014). This has two aspects. One is to assess whether a given area of civil society action is concerned with a transformative justice issue. The other is to assess whether (or to what extent) the action taken contributes towards promoting transformative justice and why or why not.

At least some of the social movements and wider civil society mobilisation which came to prominence from the end of the first post-apartheid government can meaningfully be considered in terms of transformative justice (see Ballard et al., 2005). In at least some cases, civil society opposition to the post-apartheid government is not simply a question of ideological differences or of criticism of promises left unfulfilled. There is a deeper question about why it is important for certain political issues to be addressed, why civil society actors are concerned with them and what kinds of responses might resolve those issues. As already noted, with regards to activism around land and housing rights, for instance, it may be argued that current inequalities in access to land and housing continue to be shaped by apartheid. It is then possible to evaluate responses to these (see, for example, Evans, 2013b: 171–185).

As argued elsewhere (see Evans, 2013b, 2018a), actors such as the social movements which participate in the Poor People's Alliance and the (to some degree overlapping) groups which participate in the Housing Assembly display a higher degree of transformative potential in their responses to land and housing inequalities than those actors closely associated with Shack/Slum Dwellers International (SDI).[9] SDI's orientation towards working with government as a priority

8 For more detailed interrogation (and problematising) of civil society as a concept, see *inter alia* Robins (2008): 7; Sen (2010).

9 See also Poor People's Alliance (n.d.), as well as personal interview with Mncedisi Twalo, Cape Town, 4 July 2012; personal interview with Lorraine Heunis and Eleanor Hoedemaker, Cape Town, 7 August 2012; personal interview with Michael Blake,

which takes precedence over grass-roots militancy can act as a limiting factor in terms of transformative justice (see Evans, 2018a; also Podlashuc, 2011).[10] Engagement in more contentious tactics and overt criticism of the state does not necessarily produce more transformative results (though it can). However, it is the case that the provision of a platform for the participation of affected communities in shaping priorities and approaches (potentially including contentious tactics) – contributes to transformative processes (see Evans, 2013b, 2018a). There are also challenges and limitations in the approaches taken by Poor People's Alliance linked social movements such as the Western Cape Anti-Eviction Campaign and the shack dwellers' movement Abahlali baseMjondolo, and by the Housing Assembly (which links together community-based and social movement organisations in Cape Town with an NGO – the International Labour Research and Information Group – and the local structures of the South African Municipal Workers' Union).[11] It is, nevertheless, the case that these actors are not constrained to working within the largely untransformative paradigm of the status quo in the same way as SDI (which concentrates on a particular methodology and set of priorities).[12] Furthermore, these actors put forward analysis which is overtly critical of the same structural conditions with which transformative justice is concerned and offer greater potential for politically responsible participation of diverse actors than SDI does (such as through the relationships between the grass-roots community-based elements of the Housing Assembly and the professionalised NGO and trade union elements).[13]

Transformative justice on the ground

In practice there are two broad areas in which the concept of transformative justice may play a role: in overtly shaping how policy and practice is framed or by implicitly shaping practice regardless of its explicit framing. This section of the chapter first discusses the latter possibility then moves on to a discussion of the former.

Regarding the question of whether practice or policies contribute to transformative justice it does not necessarily matter whether these are couched in the terminology of transformative justice. What matters more is the substance of the idea of transformative justice. In this sense a role for transformative justice in practice can be discerned. This links to the application of transformative justice as

Cape Town, 6 July 2012; personal interview with Michael Blake, Johannesburg, 10 April 2015.

10 See also personal interview with Sandra van Rensburg, Johannesburg, 13 March 2015.

11 See, for example, Pointer (2004); Mdlalose (2014); also personal interview with Soraya Hendricks, Cape Town, 11 July 2012; personal interview with Michael Blake, Johannesburg, 10 April 2015. Evans (2018a) explores this in greater detail.

12 See Podlashuc (2011), and personal interview with Sandra van Rensburg, Johannesburg, 13 March 2015.

13 See Evans (2018a). See also, Podlashuc (2011) and personal interview with Michael Blake, Johannesburg, 10 April 2015.

an analytical framework. It is possible to link contemporary struggles for the realisation of socioeconomic rights to the addressing of structural violence rooted in historic injustices. Indeed, these links are reflected in the practice of some actors (such as those linked to the Poor People's Alliance and Housing Assembly) and there can be value added by this. Rhetorically, and in terms of the response invited by duty-bearers, this is important. For instance, the understanding that landlessness and housing inequalities in contemporary South Africa are symptomatic of the ongoing effects of apartheid suggests certain approaches to advocacy and policymaking and precludes – or at least questions – others (see Evans, 2018a). For example, the current policy paradigm regarding land reform (particularly redistribution), and its effects on the realisation of the right to housing (amongst other rights), may be challenged on the grounds that it is insufficiently transformative of apartheid conditions and is therefore insufficiently just (see, for example, Evans, 2016). For instance, market-oriented 'willing buyer, willing seller' processes have been very slow in facilitating redistribution of land and can be said to have failed to transform historically unjust conditions.[14] Actors which work from this understanding can be said to be more likely to contribute to transformative justice in practice (see Evans, 2013b: 185, 189–193). Furthermore, acceptance of (or at least engagement with) this approach by key duty-bearers (such as the state) creates an opening for transformative justice-oriented policies to be pursued.

In addition to this, actors which facilitate the participation of those affected by structural violence contribute in this way to the practice of transformative justice. This is necessary to avoid the pitfalls of elite-oriented transitional justice (Daly, 2002; Waldorf, 2012). Moreover, participation can be beneficial both in terms of placing the concerns of affected communities on broader political agendas and by empowering individuals and communities through the process of participation (Tissington, 2012; Robins, 2013a; Gaventa and Barrett, 2010). Regardless of how action challenging an untransformative policy paradigm is overtly described it contributes to the same idea as transformative justice. As mentioned above, at least some civil society actors in South Africa take this approach.[15] Furthermore, actors taking this kind of approach have had some success in eliciting political and legal outcomes and in facilitating positive processes.[16] Consequently, there is a case to be made that the idea of transformative justice (as it is called here) can play a role in implicitly shaping practice.

With regard to the role of transformative justice in explicitly shaping policy and practice more speculation is necessary. In South Africa there are not (as yet at least) civil society actors overtly framing their practice in terms of transformative justice, likewise government policies have not been explicitly put forward in these terms. This does not, however, preclude the possibility of practice being overtly

14 See, for example, James (2007); Greenberg (2004); Walker (2008); de Satgé (2013).

15 See Evans (2013b) and Evans (2018a) for discussion of social movement organisations, NGOs and trade unions in a South African land and housing rights activist network in this regard.

16 See, for example, Tissington (2012); McKinley (2012).

framed in terms of transformative justice. There could be benefits to the adoption of such a framing. Policies or practices which explicitly adopt transformative justice framing can more easily be evaluated according to the aims and expectations of transformative justice. In practice this could be useful for holding states or other actors to account regarding their rhetorical commitments.[17]

In South Africa the language of 'transformation' has some political currency (see, for example, South African Press Association, 2014; Congress of South African Trade Unions, 2013). Transformation has been defined in a variety of ways. For instance, Thiven Reddy argues that there is a 'minimal consensus' over considering transformation as addressing 'the material "backlog", the material and psychological poverty suffered by the majority of citizens which disadvantages them in exercising the rights enshrined in the new constitution and accessing the resources available in society' (Reddy, 2004: 39). Others put forward understandings of transformation which focus upon poverty, economic inequality and patterns of discrimination relating to race, gender and sexuality, for instance (see, for example, Albertyn, 2007; Liebenberg and Goldblatt, 2007; Gumede, 2012). Much discussion of transformation has considered the extent to which the South African constitution, particularly its socioeconomic rights provisions, is – or can be interpreted to be – transformative (see, for example, Albertyn, 2007; Liebenberg and Goldblatt, 2007; De Vos, 2010). Recent mobilisations around universities, however, have drawn attention to transformation (and the at times overlapping concept of decolonisation) as applied to access to education, curricula content and demographic makeup of staff and student bodies amongst a number of other issues (see, for example, Qukula, 2015; Subramany, 2015; Ntuli, 2015).

At times the notion of transformation suffers from a lack of clarity (see, for example, De Vos, 2010). Nevertheless, there is potential for the practice of transformative justice to be linked to or integrated with existing notions of transformation.[18] Indeed, there might be value added to the discourse around transformation through the adoption of transformative justice as an approach to transformation. If the purpose and scope of transformative justice is clearly defined this could contribute to clarifying what transformation could or should be and what policies and practices contribute towards its realisation.

Particularly given the opening presented by the political currency of transformation in South Africa, it is not inconceivable that the framework of transformative justice could be adopted by, for instance, actors within or seeking to influence the government. Though, as discussed in the next section, there are some difficulties attached to this.

17 See Uvin (2004: 167–201), for a discussion of how rhetorical (and deeper) commitments to human rights framing can be used to hold development actors to account. See also Keck and Sikkink (1998: 16–25), for a discussion of 'accountability politics' – holding powerful actors to account according to their stated commitments.

18 Some commentators have, for instance, linked recent mobilisation of student activism to the addressing of structural violence (see, for example, Godsell, 2015).

Risks and difficulties

So far this chapter has largely discussed the possible value added by a transformative justice approach. Here some of the risks and difficulties attached to adopting such an approach are explored. First, there is the risk of vagueness or imprecision. The second difficulty is in relation to the overt adoption of transformative justice by practitioners as a framework for action and/or policymaking.

The risk of vagueness can affect both analytical and practical application of transformative justice. In essence this is the danger that transformative justice becomes an indistinct idea, that it fails to clarify anything intellectually or that it fails to offer any practical insights. This is a real danger, not helped by the current lack of a large unified or coherent literature theorising and defining transformative justice.[19] The following questions are invited: if transformative justice is simply doing transitional justice better why not call it that? If transformative justice is synonymous with social justice what purpose does the term serve? This chapter argues that for the term to retain meaning it is essential transformative justice is defined and applied as distinct from transitional justice and social justice, even if a degree of overlap is necessary (Evans, 2013b, 95–102; Evans, 2016; Skaar, 2011, Gready et al., 2010). Otherwise transformative justice may on the one hand become a superfluous buzzword or may on the other hand confuse matters through being applied inconsistently to multiple (unrelated) phenomena.[20] The idea of reconciliation, for instance, frequently suffers from this. If the dangers observable in the deployment of reconciliation as an 'empty universal' are to be avoided in efforts to pursue transformative justice then it is necessary to consider and clarify what transformative justice is in practice and how this relates to – or departs from – existing notions and practices, such as those associated with transitional justice (see, for example, Renner, 2014; see also Evans, 2018b).

Consideration of the arguments recently made by Evelyne Schmid and Aoife Nolan, with regard to the extent to which transitional justice can address socio-economic rights, may also be useful here (Schmid and Nolan, 2014). Schmid and Nolan identify that 'the current debate on the economic and social dimensions of transitional justice frequently suffers from terminological and conceptual confusion' (Schmid and Nolan, 2014: 362). There is some risk of the transformative justice concept contributing to this confusion if applied inconsistently to numerous phenomena. Schmid and Nolan claim an authoritative interpretation of economic and social rights (ESR) (Schmid and Nolan, 2014: 365–367). Unfortunately, however, little is provided in terms of an argument supporting this position. Alternative understandings are merely posited as incorrect.[21] Schmid and

19 On this see, for example, McAuliffe (2017). See also Evans (2018a).

20 These questions come to the forefront in reflection upon the range and content of papers presented at the Worldwide Universities Network's (WUN) Transformative Justice Network conferences in 2011 and 2013, for instance.

21 For instance, at various points alternative positions are described as 'improper use and misunderstanding of ESR language and concepts', 'misuse and misunderstanding of ESR standards', 'misapplications', 'inaccurate', 'problematic', and as 'an irritant to ESR

Nolan claim to provide 'clarification' to commentators whose views are not in line with their own and suggest that the implied failure of these commentators to understand the interaction between socioeconomic rights and transitional justice in their terms stems from the fact that many of these commentators are not lawyers (Schmid and Nolan, 2014: 371). Apparently unconcerned with the social construction of human rights or with the multiple different (including non-legal) interpretations, translations and applications of rights (see, for example, Stammers, 1999; Merry, 2006), Schmid and Nolan assert that transitional justice 'has to engage with *rights as they are – as legal standards* – or, alternatively, use different vocabulary' (Schmid and Nolan, 2014: 378, emphasis added). No convincing justification for this 'legal positivism' (see Stammers, 1999: 991–992) is provided.[22] This chapter (and, implicitly, much of the book as a whole) argues that it is necessary to understand and approach human rights (and transitional justice) from a variety of (inter)disciplinary perspectives beyond the narrowly legal.

Despite repeatedly claiming that a narrow conception of socioeconomic rights is the correct one, Schmid and Nolan allow for multiple and broad interpretations of transitional justice and 'do not take a stance on whether or when legalist approaches to transitional justice are suitable' (Schmid and Nolan, 2014: 380, 364). This apparent openness to multiple and broad definitions of transitional justice coupled with an intolerance of alternative understandings of socioeconomic rights does seem likely to add to the conceptual confusion Schmid and Nolan hope to address through attempting to ensure 'participants in the debate on socioeconomic considerations in transitional justice have a way to assess whether they are talking about the same thing' (Schmid and Nolan, 2014: 377).[23] Moreover, in defining some 'socioeconomic issues' as broader than and separate to 'rights', Schmid and Nolan perform something of an intellectual sleight of hand (Schmid and Nolan, 2014: 363–364). Transitional justice is defined (broadly) in such a way as to easily include socioeconomic rights, making alternative notions such as transformative justice unnecessary (Schmid and Nolan, 2014: 380). Simultaneously, socioeconomic rights are defined (narrowly) in such a way as to exclude consideration of many of the issues which concern critics of mainstream transitional justice practice and advocates of alternatives such as transformative justice. This sidesteps key elements of the debate. For instance, Schmid and Nolan's argument that 'When armed forces burn houses, destroy crops, loot healthcare infrastructure or poison drinking water, these are violations of ESR that are neither structural nor relevant to the positive programmatic obligations imposed by those rights' is persuasive (Schmid and Nolan, 2014: 373; see also Sharp, 2012). However, their

advocates'. Schmid and Nolan's claim that their 'aim is not to denigrate the work' of those they criticise does little to mitigate the fact that at times this appears to be what they do (Schmid and Nolan, 2014: 364–381).

22 Evidence is provided to support the case that socioeconomic rights are legally protected, however (Schmid and Nolan, 2014: 365–367).

23 The apparent conflation of laws and norms may also add to this confusion (see Schmid and Nolan, 2014: 365–367).

emphasis on these sorts of socioeconomic rights issues obscures the question of how structural violence, inequalities and other socioeconomic 'issues' (not defined as rights by Schmid and Nolan) might be addressed in (post-)transitional contexts and whether transitional justice is the appropriate or best means to do so (Schmid and Nolan, 2014: 371–372). Many socioeconomic rights issues in post-transition South Africa – such as those surrounding access to land and housing, or education for that matter – *are* experienced structurally, rather than as a direct result of specific actions (see, for example, Gibson, 2011; Evans, 2016; Godsell, 2015).

Also problematic in Schmid and Nolan's account is the failure to distinguish between broad claims of transitional justice advocates and the lived reality of transitional justice in practice. It may very well be true that there is 'no reason why a consideration of ESR within the context of attempts to redress a legacy of past abuses could not be accommodated within the scope of [a] mainstream definition of transitional justice' (Schmid and Nolan, 2014: 380–381). This says nothing about whether socioeconomic rights are frequently or successfully integrated into transitional justice in practice. Few would argue that socioeconomic rights issues were integral to transitional justice in South Africa (or indeed to the majority of transitional justice interventions).[24]

Schmid and Nolan are critical of the suggestion made by some scholars that transitional justice processes typically focus on truth commissions, trials, amnesties and institutional reform, yet they nevertheless almost exclusively cite examples of these processes as means by which socioeconomic rights have been or might be integrated with transitional justice (see, for example, Schmid and Nolan, 2014: 369–370, 374, 376). Furthermore, discussion of the practical scope and limitations of these tools in addressing socioeconomic rights issues is almost entirely absent.[25]

It is right to question the false dichotomy between socioeconomic rights and civil and political rights (Schmid and Nolan, 2014: 371–377). However, Schmid and Nolan's proposals for incorporating socioeconomic rights into transitional justice in some ways highlight the need for transformative justice to be defined separately. Perhaps transitional justice cannot address the root causes of conflict or the broader socioeconomic issues Schmid and Nolan consider to be outside the remit of rights (Schmid and Nolan, 2014: 371–372; see also Waldorf, 2012). These still ought to be addressed. Transformative justice is one means by which a focus may be maintained on these issues and consideration may be given to tools and processes not typically associated with transitional justice. Transformative justice in this case is not merely doing transitional justice better; it is doing something different – though parallel – to transitional justice.

24 See, for example, Gready (2011); Waldorf (2012); Robins (2013a); Gready and Robins (2014).

25 This is despite being discussed in the very work Schmid and Nolan criticise (see Evans, 2013a; Schmid and Nolan, 2014: 380).

The second difficulty, regarding the overt adoption of transformative justice as a framework for action, is now considered. Whilst from an advocacy point of view there may be benefits associated with explicitly adopting transformative justice as a framework for action, it is not clear that this is likely to happen in South Africa.[26] As it stands, explicit discussion of transformative justice (as opposed to the ideas which it links together) has largely come out of academic discourse (see, for example, Gready, 2014). Moreover, in itself, taking up transformative justice as an overt framework may not be particularly worthwhile for civil society actors. Framing action compatibly with others and according to the appropriate advocacy venue may be more important (Keck and Sikkink, 1998: 18; Tarrow, 2005: 165). The payoff associated with analysis and evaluation of policy and practice according to a transformative justice perspective (however framed) is both more obvious and more immediate than the possible payoff associated with explicitly framing practice in terms of transformative justice.

Recalling the above risk of imprecision, it is worth bearing in mind that changing the words describing action does not in itself change the nature of that action. It may be more use practically to facilitate the translation of the transformative justice concept into whatever vernacular form is meaningful and advantageous locally (see, Merry, 2006; Levitt and Merry, 2009). This may include overt transformative justice framing but need not. The abovementioned South African discourse around social and political transformation might indicate a possible opening for mobilisation explicitly framed as transformative justice in this context. However, it may not – though this does not preclude the pursuit of the ideas of transformative justice under an alternative framing.[27]

Indeed, there is a risk that the pursuit of transformative justice as an overt framework might come at the expense of more effective translation and advocacy 'venue shopping' (Merry, 2006; Keck and Sikkink, 1998: 18). Civil society actors in South Africa engaging with issues which can be said to relate to transformative justice utilise a range of (sometimes overlapping) frames for action: human rights, development, anti-poverty, social justice and emancipatory politics, among others. Any of these framings may be equally or more effective than overt transformative justice framing under the right circumstances. Moreover, it is important for advocacy to take place in terms which are meaningful for and relevant to the affected communities participating. This is both to avoid the problems – such as disempowerment – associated with the top-down imposition of outsiders' understandings and in order to maximise the chances of advocacy success.[28]

26 For discussion of challenges and possibilities associated with transformative justice as an explicit framework, see Gready (2014).

27 It is possible, for instance, that the established (though vaguely defined) discourse around transformation might act as a hindrance to the overt adoption of transformative justice – a similar term with some possible overlap in meaning – as a framework for action in South Africa.

28 See Robins (2011, 2013a, 2013b); Merry (2006); Levitt and Merry (2009); Keck and Sikkink (1998: 18); Jordan and Van Tuijl (2000); Tarrow (2005: 165).

Conclusion

In answering the question this chapter set out to address – whether it is analytically and practically useful to consider the shortcomings of transitional justice processes, and the need to address contemporary socioeconomic injustices, in terms of a struggle for transformative justice – three main conclusions may be drawn. Regarding analytical use, it is concluded that there is a role for and value added by applying the concept of transformative justice. In particular, analysis from a transformative justice perspective can refocus attention upon the areas which are not addressed by transitional justice and can usefully link together some issues relating to contemporary social justice and development with historical wrongs – and analysis of how these might be addressed.

Regarding practice, it is concluded that there is a strong case to be made for the utility of transformative justice in implicitly shaping practice regardless of how that practice is overtly framed. Analysis of contemporary socioeconomic rights issues in relation to whether they are rooted in historical injustice, and in terms of whether measures to address these sufficiently take account of this, allows practical contestation of policy and practice which maintains unjust conditions. Practice emerging from this analytical position can be said to follow the principles of transformative justice regardless of how it is explicitly framed. There is a weaker case, however, regarding the possibility of the overt adoption of transformative justice to frame policy and practice. Indeed, it may not always be beneficial for the pursuit of transformative justice to be explicitly framed as such.

The more significant role for transformative justice, then, is in shaping understanding of, and agendas for, practice in terms of linking together ideas concerning structural violence and socioeconomic rights, and in foregrounding the importance of addressing historical wrongs associated with these, including regarding the participation of those affected in these processes. This is important nonetheless. Shifting the focus of analysis of socioeconomic rights issues in order to take account of historical roots of injustices and opening up attempts to address historical wrongs to greater consideration of structural violence potentially adds value to both the understanding of contexts such as post-transition South Africa and to attempts to address these issues in practice.

References

Aberese Ako, Matilda, Nana Akua Anyidoho and Gordon Crawford. (2013) 'NGOs, Rights-based Approaches and the Potential for Progressive Development in Local Contexts: Constraints and Challenges in Northern Ghana'. *Journal of Human Rights Practice* 5(1): 46–74.

Albertyn, Catherine. (2007) 'Substantive Equality and Transformation in South Africa'. *South African Journal on Human Rights* 23(2): 253–276.

Ballard, Richard, Adam Habib, Imraan Valodia and Elke Zuern. (2005) 'Globalization, Marginalization and Contemporary Social Movements in South Africa'. *African Affairs* 104(417): 615–634.

Bond, Patrick and Angela Tait. (1997) 'The Failure of Housing Policy in Post-Apartheid South Africa'. *Urban Forum* 8(1): 19–41.

Collins, Cath. (2010) *Post-transitional Justice: Human Rights Trials in Chile and El Salvador*. University Park, PA: Pennsylvania State University Press.

Community Law Centre and Socio-Economic Rights Institute. (2013) *Executive Summary – 'Jumping the Queue', Waiting Lists and other Myths: Perceptions and Practice around Housing Demand and Allocation in South Africa*. Johannesburg: Socio-Economic Rights Institute.

Congress of South African Trade Unions. (2013) *Mangaung and the Second Phase of the Transition: Discussion Document for the COSATU CEC 25–27 February 2013*. www.cosatu.org.za/docs/discussion/2013/analysis.pdf [accessed 12 June 2014].

Daly, Erin. (2002) 'Transformative Justice: Charting a Path to Reconciliation'. *International Legal Perspectives* 12(1/2): 73–183.

De Satgé, Rick. (2013) *Synthesis Report – Land Divided: Land and South African Society in 2013, in Comparative Perspective*. Cape Town: Phuhlisani Solutions.

De Vos, Pierre. (2010) 'What do we talk about when we talk about "transformation"?'. *Constitutionally Speaking*, 12 August, http://constitutionallyspeaking.co.za/what-do-we-talk-about-when-we-talk-about-transformation-2/ [accessed 22 September 2015].

Evans, Matthew. (2013a) 'Land, Socio-economic Rights and Transformative Justice'. Paper presented at the conference 'Land Divided: Land and South African Society in 2013, in Comparative Perspective', Cape Town, South Africa, 24–27 March.

Evans, Matthew. (2013b) *Advancing Transformative Justice? A Case Study of a Trade Union, Social Movement and NGO Network in South Africa*. Unpublished PhD thesis, Department of Politics, University of York, October.

Evans, Matthew. (2016) 'Structural violence, socioeconomic rights and transformative justice'. *Journal of Human Rights* 15(1): 1–20.

Evans, Matthew. (2018a) *Transformative Justice: Remedying Human Rights Violations Beyond Transition*. Abingdon: Routledge.

Evans, Matthew. (2018b) 'A future without forgiveness: beyond reconciliation in transitional justice'. *International Politics* 55(5): 678–692.

Evans, Matthew and David Wilkins. (2017) 'Transformative justice, reparations and transatlantic slavery'. *Social and Legal Studies*. DOI: 10.1177/09646639177 46490.

Farmer, Paul. (1996) 'On Suffering and Structural Violence: A View from Below'. *Daedalus* 125(1): 261–283.

Farmer, Paul. (2004) 'An anthropology of structural violence'. *Current Anthropology* 45(3): 305–325.

Galtung, Johan. (1969) 'Violence, peace, and peace research'. *Journal of Peace Research* 6(3): 167–191.

Gaventa, John and Gregory Barrett. (2010) *So What Difference Does it Make? Mapping the Outcomes of Citizen Engagement*, IDS Working Paper 347, Institute of Development Studies, University of Sussex. Brighton: Institute of Development Studies.

Gibson, Nigel C. (2011) *Fanonian Practices in South Africa: From Steve Biko to Abahlali baseMjondolo*. New York: Palgrave Macmillan.

Gilbert, Alan. (2004) 'Helping the poor through housing subsidies: lessons from Chile, Colombia and South Africa'. *Habitat International* 28(1): 13–40.

Godsell, Sarah. (2015) 'On violent protest and solidarity'. *Daily Maverick*, 19 October, www.dailymaverick.co.za/article/2015-10-19-witsfeesmustfall-op-ed-on-violentprotest-and-solidarity/#.WXsZi1GQziw [accessed 6 April 2018].

Goebel, Allison. (2007) 'Sustainable urban development? Low-cost housing challenges in South Africa'. *Habitat International* 31(3/4): 291–293.

Govender, Thashlin, Jo M. Barnes and Clarissa H. Pieper. (2011) 'Housing conditions, sanitation status and associated health risks in selected subsidized low-cost housing settlements in Cape Town, South Africa'. *Habitat International* 35(2): 335–342.

Gready, Paul. (2011) *The Era of Transitional Justice: The Aftermath of the Truth and Reconciliation Commission in South Africa and Beyond*. Abingdon: Routledge.

Gready, Paul. (2014) 'Transformation without transition in Egypt?'. *Transformative Justice in Egypt and Tunisia*, 19 July, www.transformativejustice.co.uk/transformation-without-transition-egypt/ [accessed 6 March 2015].

Gready, Paul, Jelke Boesten, Gordon Crawford and Polly Wilding. (2010) 'Transformative Justice – A Concept Note'. Draft concept note developed by the WUN Transformative Justice Group, October.

Gready, Paul and Simon Robins. (2014) 'From Transitional to Transformative Justice: A New Agenda for Practice'. *International Journal of Transitional Justice* 8(3): 339–361.

Greenberg, Stephen. (2004) *The Landless People's Movement and the Failure of Post-Apartheid Land Reform*. Durban: University of KwaZulu-Natal.

Gumede, Vusi. (2012) 'Transformation: SA needs substantial policy reforms'. *Mail and Guardian*, 23 November, http://mg.co.za/article/2012-11-23-00-development-policy-lost-in-the-economic-mix [accessed 20 January 2016].

Gupta, Akhil. (2013) 'Structural violence and politics'. *Economy and Society* 42(4): 686–692.

Harris, Bronwyn, John Eyles, Loveday Penn-Kekana, Jana Fried, Harry Nyathela, Liz Thomas and Jane Goudge. (2014) 'Bringing Justice to Unacceptable Health Care Services? Street-level Reflections from Urban South Africa'. *International Journal of Transitional Justice* 8(1): 141–161.

Huchzermeyer, Marie. (2003) 'A Legacy of Control? The Capital Subsidy for Housing, and Informal Settlement Intervention in South Africa'. *International Journal of Urban and Regional Research* 27(3): 591–612.

International Journal of Transitional Justice. (2014) 'Editorial Note'. *International Journal of Transitional Justice* 8(1): 1–5.

James, Deborah. (2007) *Gaining Ground? 'Rights' and 'Property' in South African Land Reform*. Abingdon: Routledge.

Jordan, Lisa and Peter Van Tuijl. (2000) 'Political Responsibility in Transnational NGO Advocacy'. *World Development* 28(12): 2051–2065.

Keck, Margaret E. and Kathryn Sikkink. (1998) *Activists Beyond Borders: Advocacy Networks in International Politics*. Ithaca, NY: Cornell University Press.

Lambourne, Wendy. (2009) 'Transitional Justice and Peacebuilding after Mass Violence'. *International Journal of Transitional Justice* 3(1): 28–48.

Lambourne, Wendy. (2011) 'Transformative Justice and Peacebuilding: A Psychological Perspective'. Paper presented at the conference 'Transformative Justice: Global Perspectives', Worldwide Universities Network International Conference, University of Leeds, Leeds, UK, 12 May.

Levitt, Peggy and Sally Merry. (2009) 'Vernacularization on the ground: local uses of global women's rights in Peru, China, India and the United States'. *Global Networks* 9 (4): 441–461.

Liebenberg, Sandra and Beth Goldblatt. (2007) 'The Interrelationship Between Equality and Socio-economic Rights Under South Africa's Transformative Constitution'. *South African Journal on Human Rights* 23(2): 335–361.

Mani, Rama. (2008) 'Dilemmas of Expanding Transitional Justice, or Forging the Nexus between Transitional Justice and Development'. *International Journal of Transitional Justice* 2(3): 253–265.

McAuliffe, Pádraig. (2017) *Transformative Transitional Justice and the Malleability of Post-conflict States.* Cheltenham: Edward Elgar.

McKinley, Dale T. (2012) 'The Crisis of the Left in Contemporary South Africa'. In Marcelle C. Dawson and Luke Sinwell (eds), *Contesting Transformation: Popular Resistance in Twenty-first Century South Africa*, 23–43. London: Pluto Press.

Mdlalose, Bandile. (2014) 'The Rise and Fall of Abahlali baseMjondolo, a South African Social Movement'. *Politikon: South African Journal of Political Studies* 41(3): 345–353.

Merry, Sally Engle. (2006) 'Transnational Human Rights and Local Activism: Mapping the Middle'. *American Anthropologist* 108(1): 38–51.

Ntuli, Philile. (2015) 'Students engage in post-apartheid decolonisation'. *Business Day*, 28 October, www.bdlive.co.za/opinion/2015/10/28/students-engage-in-post-apartheid-decolonisation [accessed 20 January 2016].

Pasipanodya, Tafadzwa. (2008) 'A Deeper Justice: Economic and Social Justice as Transitional Justice in Nepal'. *International Journal of Transitional Justice* 2(3): 378–397.

Podlashuc, Leopold. (2011) *The South African Homeless People's Federation: Interrogating the Myth of Participation*, Working Paper, African Centre for Citizenship and Democracy. Cape Town: University of the Western Cape.

Pointer, Rebecca. (2004) 'Questioning the Representation of South Africa's "New Social Movements": A Case Study of the Mandela Park Anti-eviction Campaign'. *Journal of Asian and African Studies* 39(4): 271–294.

Poor People's Alliance. (n.d.) 'About the Alliance', http://sekwanele.wordpress.com/about/ [accessed 1 September 2010].

Qukula, Qama. (2015) 'The meaning of transformation in SA universities after #RhodesMustFall'. *702*, 4 May, www.702.co.za/articles/2714/the-meaning-of-transformation-in-sa-universities-after-rhodesmustfall [accessed 20 January 2016].

Reddy, Thiven. (2004) *Higher Education and Social Transformation: South Africa Case Study*, Report, Council on Higher Education. Pretoria: Council on Higher Education.

Renner, Judith. (2014) 'The Local Roots of the Global Politics of Reconciliation: The Articulation of "Reconciliation" as an Empty Universal in the South African Transition to Democracy'. *Millennium: Journal of International Studies* 42(2): 263–285.

Robins, Simon. (2011) 'Untransformative justice: the limits of civil society and the rights discourse in post-conflict Nepal'. Paper presented at the conference 'Transformative Justice: Global Perspectives', Worldwide Universities Network International Conference, University of Leeds, Leeds, UK, 12 May.

Robins, Simon. (2013a) *Families of the Missing: A Test for Contemporary Approaches to Transitional Justice.* Abingdon: Routledge.

Robins, Simon. (2013b) 'An Empirical Approach to Post-conflict Legitimacy: Victims' Needs and the Everyday'. *Journal of Intervention and Statebuilding* 7(1): 45–64.

Robins, Steven L. (2008) *From Revolution to Rights in South Africa: Social Movements, NGOs and Popular Politics after Apartheid.* Woodbridge: James Currey.

Sankey, Diana. (2014) 'Towards Recognition of Subsistence Harms: Reassessing Approaches to Socioeconomic Forms of Violence in Transitional Justice'. *International Journal of Transitional Justice* 8(1): 121–140.

Schmid, Evelyne and Aoife Nolan. (2014) '"Do No Harm"? Exploring the Scope of Economic and Social Rights in Transitional Justice'. *International Journal of Transitional Justice* 8(3): 362–382.

Sen, Jai. (2010) 'Interrogating the Civil: Engaging Critically with the Reality and Concept of Civil Society', http://p2pfoundation.net/Engaging_Critically_with_the_Reality_and_Concept_of_Civil_Society [accessed 6 January 2011].

Sharp, Dustin N. (2012) 'Addressing Economic Violence in Times of Transition: toward a Positive-peace Paradigm for Transitional Justice'. *Fordham International Law Journal* 35(3): 780–814.

Skaar, Elin. (2011) 'Transformative aspects of formal TJ initiatives: opportunities and limitations'. Paper presented at the conference 'Transformative Justice: Global Perspectives', Worldwide Universities Network International Conference, University of Leeds, Leeds, UK, 12 May.

South African Press Association. (2014) 'Today marks start of 2nd phase of transformation – Jacob Zuma'. *City Press*, 24 May, www.citypress.co.za/politics/today-marks-start-2nd-phase-transformation-jacob-zuma/ [accessed 12 June 2014].

Stammers, Neil. (1999) 'Social Movements and the Social Construction of Human Rights'. *Human Rights Quarterly* 21(4): 980–1008.

Subramany, Deshnee. (2015) 'South Africa: Fees Must Fall protests prove post-Apartheid "born free generation" is a myth'. *International Business Times*, 28 October, www.ibtimes.co.uk/south-africa-fees-must-fall-protests-prove-post-apartheid-born-free-generation-myth-1526059 [accessed 20 January 2016].

Tarrow, Sidney. (2005) *The New Transnational Activism*. New York: Cambridge University Press.

Tissington, Kate. (2012) '"Tacticians in the Struggle for Change"? Exploring the Dynamics between Legal Organisations and Social Movements Engaged in Rights-based Struggles in South Africa'. In Marcelle C. Dawson and Luke Sinwell (eds), *Contesting Transformation: Popular Resistance in Twenty-first Century South Africa*, 201–221. London: Pluto Press.

Uvin, Peter. (2004) *Human Rights and Development*. Bloomfield, CT: Kumarian Press.

Waldorf, Lars. (2012) 'Anticipating the Past: Transitional Justice and Socio-economic Wrongs'. *Social and Legal Studies* 21(2): 171–186.

Walker, Cherryl. (2008) *Landmarked: Land Claims and Land Restitution in South Africa*. Johannesburg: Jacana.

WUN Transformative Justice Network. (2011) 'Transformative Justice: Global Perspectives', Worldwide Universities Network International Conference, University of Leeds, Leeds, UK, 12–13 May.

WUN Transformative Justice Network. (2013) 'Transformative Gender Justice' workshop. University of Leeds, Leeds, UK, 11–12 September.

4 The transformative potential of post-war justice initiatives in Bosnia and Herzegovina

Daniela Lai and Caterina Bonora

Introduction

In the former Yugoslav region, transitional justice scholars and activists have long been frustrated with the shortcomings of judicial approaches and the instrumental use of post-war justice for political purposes. Nonetheless, and despite the frustration, local activism in this field has never stopped. This chapter shifts the attention from established transitional justice processes to initiatives carried out at the level of civil society, arguing that it is among social actors that we might be able to identify transitional justice efforts that can be characterised as 'transformative'. The question, or objective, driving this chapter is thus to locate the transformative potential of transitional justice initiatives in Bosnia and Herzegovina (BiH). We identify three initiatives that will be discussed in greater detail in this chapter: the Regional Commission (RECOM) initiative, the Women's Court, and the 2014 socioeconomic protests. While very different from one another in some respects, these three cases were selected because they represent the most significant efforts to address post-war justice issues that emerged from the Bosnian (or regional, in the case of RECOM and the Women's Court) civil society.

Before we proceed with the analysis, two clarifications are in order. First, why do we refer to transformative 'potential'? Most simply, these grass-roots or civil initiatives, at least in the Bosnian context, still occur at the margins of official transitional justice processes, which have mostly been limited to the judicial realm. This marginalisation, and the lack of institutional support, still limit what these initiatives are able to achieve. Second, given the focus of the chapter, it seems relevant and appropriate to clarify our understanding of 'civil society'. As scholarly interest in the contribution of social actors to political processes has grown over the years, so has the need for debating what characterises civil society. Often defined as the sphere separated from both the state and the market, civil society in post-conflict countries has been heralded as a necessary partner in peacebuilding processes (especially after the 'local turn' questioned top-down approaches to post-conflict reconstruction; see Lederach, 1997 for an early discussion of this, and Leonardsson and Rudd, 2015 for a recent review), but also the object of critique for being too institutionalised, for responding to the priorities of international organisations and losing touch with the broader society (Belloni, 2007). In our view, civil society cannot be reduced to formally established nongovernmental organisations (NGOs), but includes local and grass-roots activists expressing a variety of views. Civil society is a 'terrain of struggle' (Rajagopal, 2003: 261), which includes progressive, socially aware actors, as well as 'English-language speaking, cosmopolitan local activists who know how to relate to Western donors' (Rajagopal, 2003: 261), but also nationalist, religious, or conservative groups who might be opposed to post-war justice processes. The term 'civil society', in this sense, has a neutral, rather than necessarily positive or emancipatory connotation.

The chapter contributes to the current search for an alternative approach to dealing with the consequences of wartime violence and mass human rights abuses. In particular, it draws on and develops the concept of 'transformative justice', engaging with recent work by Lambourne (2009, 2014), Sharp (2012, 2015), Gready and Robins (2014), but also emphasising the need for expanding the scope of critical reflection beyond the field of transitional justice studies to include the work of scholars such as Nancy Fraser (1990, 2005, 2009). The empirical analysis draws on data collected by the authors during several years of fieldwork in Bosnia (2012–2016). This includes interviews with NGOs and local activist groups, transcripts of RECOM proceedings, and observation carried out at RECOM meetings, at the Women's Court events, and at protests and meetings organised by groups involved in the 2014 protests.

The chapter argues that 'transformative' justice in the case of local initiatives in Bosnia means 1 overcoming ethnicity as an organising principle of post-war justice processes; 2 an attempt to include non-institutional actors, going beyond state-sponsored mechanisms and heavily institutionalised civil society organisations; 3 a critique or even rejection of the liberal transition paradigm. The cases we analyse show these issues were identified, implicitly or explicitly, as a form of rupture with conventional transitional justice approaches, and as a way of overcoming some of its limitations. In fact, the most transformative potential can be found, at different levels, among Bosnian post-war justice initiatives that do not resemble transitional justice mechanisms at all.

The chapter is organised as follows. First, we offer a critique of conventional transitional justice approaches, and emphasise the need for an alternative approach to dealing with post-war justice processes. This is followed by a discussion of transformative justice. We focus on three conceptual issues that have been put forward by the literature on transformative justice (the critique of the 'transition', the role of the political, and participation in deliberative processes), but are further developed here with specific reference to their importance for civil society-led justice initiatives. Lastly, the chapter analyses three such initiatives: RECOM, the Women's Court and the 2014 protests. Here it is argued that while RECOM came to be as a response to top-down, legalistic approaches to transitional justice and dealing with the past, it ended up reproducing some of their limitations. The Women's Court, on the other hand, pushed this critique further, and put great effort into rethinking justice models and organisational processes for transitional justice initiatives. Moreover, while the protests may seem the most unorthodox instance of local mobilisation for post-war justice, they were also the most radically transformative in spirit. This is not only because of the type of claims they raised, which were socioeconomic in nature (and linked to the political economies of the war and transition), but also because of the participatory approach they took to collective deliberation.

Rethinking transformative justice and the role of civil society initiatives

Transitional justice has been part and parcel of the broader post-conflict international intervention in Bosnia and Herzegovina and the former Yugoslavia. As a matter of fact, the history of transitional justice, understood here as the ensemble of judicial and non-judicial measures aimed at redressing gross past injustices, is very much intertwined with the post-war justice-seeking experiences in the region. Some of the typical mechanisms of transitional justice were experimented for the first time here (Dragović-Soso and Gordy, 2011: 193). For instance, the International Criminal Tribunal for the former Yugoslavia (ICTY) was the first international tribunal to be established after the International Military Tribunal in Nuremberg. It was the result of the obdurate activism of a group of international lawyers (Hazan, 2004: 49) and part of a broader international justice movement that in the late 1980s and 1990s aimed to consolidate accountability in transitional contexts (Arthur, 2009: 324; Hagan, 2003).

Hence, both in the former Yugoslavia and internationally, the first transitional justice interventions have been characterised by the top-down establishment of international institutions, generally focused on criminal accountability (McEvoy, 2008: 25; Nagy, 2008: 274). While their contribution to normalising the fight against impunity after mass atrocity and consolidating international principles of accountability is indisputable, their limits in tackling complex justice demands in post-war contexts have soon become apparent.

The ICTY, for instance, has been criticised for not being able to live up to its lofty promises of individualising guilt, providing a comprehensive account of the past violence and aiding reconciliation (Clark, 2009: 464). One oft-mentioned problem is the ICTY's physical and conceptual aloofness from those directly affected by the violence in Bosnia and Herzegovina and the region, which has not been remedied after the setting up of the Outreach Program (Delpla, 2007: 219; Mannergren Selimović, 2010: 58). The latter was intended to bring about a better understanding of the ICTY and its procedures through a series of events targeted at the local citizenry and victims' groups, thereby making the tribunal more accessible to them (Arzt, 2006: 230). However, empirical accounts have exposed the incompatibility of the tribunal's understanding of accountability and victimhood with that of the Bosnian public (Mannergren Selimović, 2010: 54).

In the case of the former Yugoslavia, this alienation of international judicial mechanisms from local constituencies has been further exacerbated by the imposition of transitional justice measures as part of the conditionality for European Union (EU) accession, and the ensuing politicisation of transitional justice issues (Subotić, 2011a). Political elites from the region have paid lip service to the principles of international justice incarnated by the ICTY in order to pursue international alliances, while at the same time perpetuating the same conflict-era nationalist rhetoric at the domestic level (Subotić, 2009). Moreover, said conditionality has contributed to reducing transitional justice to retributive justice only, understood primarily as cooperation with international tribunals (Touquet and Vermeersch, 2016: 64). This has further consolidated the focus on individual criminal responsibility as the principal lens through which to look at the injustices of the past in the region (Subotić, 2011b).

However, the problematic dominance of institutional solutions centred on criminal responsibility is not a unique characteristic of transitional justice in the former Yugoslavia. A new wave of transitional justice scholarship has taken issue with the institutional and mainly retributive transitional justice model in many different contexts (for example, Clark and Palmer, 2012; McEvoy and McGregor, 2008; Shaw and Waldorf, 2010), focusing on two key shortcomings. First, it denounced the already mentioned prevailing focus on individual criminal responsibility, which prevents unearthing the roots of the violence (Subotić, 2011b: 158–159). Namely, retributive transitional justice can only offer a very fragmentary analysis of the past violence, which leaves out social inequalities and structural discriminations that may have been at the roots of the violence, and that may continue unabated even after the 'transition' has ended (Nagy, 2008: 284; Ross, 2003: 174). Second, the literature has criticised the prevalence of institutional interventions in transitional justice (McEvoy, 2008: 26–29). Legal institutions, in particular, due to their alleged neutral and apolitical character, are deemed safe to invest in by international organisations and donors (Oomen, 2008: 893; McEvoy, 2008: 20). However, as discussed above with regards to the ICTY, they are seldom able to contribute to reinforcing domestic legal systems, nor to the broader justice and reconciliation process (Gready, 2005: 8).

In addition to these limitations, scholars have also realised that the conceptual tools we use to study post-war justice processes do not seem equipped to capture local activism on justice issues adequately, especially since the work of many groups has surpassed the 'transitional' focus of transitional justice. Here we join the growing debate on transformative justice, and more broadly the new wave of transitional justice scholarship seeking to push its boundaries, to include issues such as socioeconomic justice, gender, and social change (McAuliffe, 2017). While civil society initiatives may be best placed to promote transformative justice, it does not automatically follow that they will. Therefore, in this chapter we reflect on the meaning of transformative justice by pondering on and identifying what elements make local justice initiatives transformative, especially in relation to three conceptual features of transformative justice, briefly discussed below.

The first point to be addressed concerns the problem of post-war justice conceived as merely 'transitional'. On the one hand, its origins as part of the study of democratisation processes in Latin America and Southern Europe (Kritz, 1995; Teitel, 2003) tied transitional justice to the goal of establishing liberal democracy as a necessary and desirable outcome (see Bunce, 1995; Stark and Bruszt, 1998 and Arthur, 2009 for a critique on this). In countries like Bosnia and

Herzegovina, this meant that transitional justice was effectively linked to other elements of institutional, social, and economic transformation that were often contested or viewed as unwelcome by local communities (Laplante, 2008; Nagy, 2008; this is especially visible in the case of socioeconomic reforms). On the other hand, some of the shortcomings of transitional justice processes can be attributed, at least in part, to the fact that 'interim' solutions to the legacy of violence are not sufficient. Local justice initiatives in the Bosnian context, then, can be considered transformative if committed to a process of social transformation that has no predetermined outcomes (Gready and Robins, 2014), and that empowers local actors as agents guiding and directing post-war justice processes, possibly with the support of international organisations.

Second, while there have been efforts to present transitional justice initiatives as technical or neutral, political choices were inevitably behind the decision to privilege approaches that are often legalistic and individualistic in nature. This problem is not even limited to judicial mechanisms, as other internationally supported programmes have often failed to engage with local communities outside mainstream narratives of conflict, thus 'squeezing out' the political or 'the multitude of conflicts inherent in human life' from these initiatives (Jones, 2012: 133). As the Bosnian case illustrates, civil society initiatives risk reproducing this problem, especially when working within the constraints set by international donors who explicitly steer away from politically controversial issues. However, the acknowledgment and critique of the 'political' in transitional justice is a key element underlying transformative justice thinking. Recovering the political in post-war justice initiatives entails a commitment to deal, through open deliberative processes (Lambourne, 2009; Gready and Robins, 2014), with the issues and conflicts that local communities deem relevant to achieve the sustainable transformation of society. In this sense, post-war justice processes resemble more spaces of public contestation, where notions of justice are negotiated, adapted and reworked, and where established assumptions and priorities are questioned. The Bosnian initiatives discussed in the following section illustrate the importance of contestation and deliberation, and represent different levels of engagement with the 'political' in post-war justice processes.

Third, and following from the previous point, transformative justice represents an attempt to respond to the critique that transitional justice is a top-down endeavour that simplifies complex realities on the ground. By acknowledging the diversity of post-war societies, and the presence of overlapping identities and issues, transformative justice can go beyond the call for simply opening up to civil society organisations, and help us reflect on what are the most appropriate and inclusive modes of deliberation and participation. Drawing on Fraser (1990, 2005), we argue that it is not sufficient to address simple forms of exclusion from political deliberation, as even within an 'open' public sphere there might be power relations and differences in resources that prevent participatory parity (Fraser, 1990). Some civil society initiatives, such as the 2014 protests discussed below, promote transformative models of justice by putting the claims and voices of subaltern groups to the forefront of public debate. Transformative justice should also question how boundaries are being set in ways that leave groups of individuals out (for instance, by restricting the definition of 'victimhood'; McEvoy and McConnachie, 2012), and how the space of deliberation is organised in such a way that makes it impossible for certain issues to be included in the debate (Fraser, 2005 refers to this as 'misframing'). To sum up, an alternative approach to post-war justice can be transformative only insofar as it provides for political justice too.

Reflecting on the critique of the transitional paradigm, on the politics of transitional justice, and on processes of deliberation, prompts us to ask questions that can be used as benchmarks to assess the transformative potential of RECOM, the Women's Court, and the 2014 protests: to what extent are these local initiatives open-ended, unbound by the goals of liberal democratic transition? Do they allow for the emergence of alternative political principles, identities, and conceptions of justice? Do they consider the specific features of the transition in each country? Do these initiatives leave the floor open to local communities? Are local communities the initiators, participants, or recipients of the initiatives? To what extent is the initiative guided by international priorities or 'technical', 'neutral' principles that are not up for discussion? Who is allowed to participate? What issues are discussed, and how are these put on the agenda? How is deliberation conducted? Building on the conceptual framework which emerges from these benchmarking questions, the following section provides an overview and assessment of three important justice initiatives conducted at the level of civil society in Bosnia and Herzegovina.

Bottom-up justice initiatives and transformative justice in BiH

This section analyses local justice initiatives and tries to establish to what extent they respond to the features of transformative justice discussed above. While we believe that local initiatives are best placed to promote transformative justice and sustainable social change in post-conflict societies, this does not necessarily imply that they always do, or that they achieve satisfactory results when attempting to do so. Civil society groups vary widely, and so do the three examples discussed below (see Table 4.1 for an overview of their features and key differences). RECOM was initiated by three regional NGOs with the purpose of creating a regional commission and involving victims more actively in shaping the reconstruction of the past. It then obtained the support of international NGOs like the International Center for Transitional Justice (ICTJ), as well as funds and support from international organisations like the EU, the Council of Europe, and various international embassies and foundations. The Women's Court was similarly initiated by regional women's organisations with the purpose of creating a symbolic court for women survivors of various forms of violence related to the conflicts of the 1990s, but it received much more limited external support. Like RECOM, the Women's Court focused on the victims, but it adopted an explicitly feminist approach, and challenged the neat separation of wartime and peacetime violence. The 2014 protests were sparked by industrial workers' protests, but soon revealed deeper social concerns with an aspect of the war, that is socioeconomic violence (and its continuation during the transition), which was not dealt with by conventional transitional

Table 4.1 RECOM, the Women's Court and the 2014 protests

	RECOM	*Women's Court*	*2014 Protests*
Years of activity	*2006–(ongoing)*	*2010–2015*	*2014–(ongoing)*
Purpose	Provide a space for victims to tell their stories; obtain a broader reconstruction of the wartime facts; obtain official acknowledgement by region's politicians	Provide a space for women to tell their (unknown) stories; support a broader concept of justice; point to structural causes of violence	To fight against social injustice and political/institutional system that prevents change in BiH
Participation	Mostly NGOs (regional) and active individuals	Women's organisations (regional) and women affiliated to or approached by them	Citizens' participation in the protests; grass-roots activists established informal groups (some still active)
Institutional support in BiH	None	None	None
International support	Strong (financial support from EU, foundations/embassies; support by Council of Europe, etc.)	Extremely limited	International interest; support from Austrian Initiative

justice approaches in the former Yugoslavia. The three brief accounts of these initiatives, while not being exhaustive, are meant to critically analyse the transformative potential (and limitations) of each.

The initiative for RECOM

The idea of a regional truth commission for the former Yugoslavia emerged out of the failures to establish national truth commissions in the region, and particularly in Bosnia and Herzegovina. Here, three different attempts, in 1997, 2000 and 2005, produced only a series of draft statutes, which were never implemented. All of these attempts had been initiated by or with the strong support of the US Institute for Peace (USIP) and aimed to compensate for the limits of the retributive justice process, by providing a space for victims and producing a more comprehensive reconstruction of the past (Kritz and Finci, 2001). However, these initiatives had never really found the support of the local civil society organisations, which felt that the process lacked transparency (UNDP, 2009: 56), or of the victims' associations, which held that the government should focus instead on more concrete measures to meet their needs (Dragović-Soso and Gordy, 2011: 203). Hence, RECOM's activists had well in mind the limits of top-down processes, both judicial and non-judicial, when they started pondering on the project of a regional truth commission.[1] RECOM was conceived by three human rights organisations, which already worked on the identification of victims of the Yugoslav wars and had signed a protocol of cooperation in 2004: the Humanitarian Law Center from Belgrade, Documenta from Zagreb, and the Research and Documentation Center from Sarajevo. The regional approach was thought to better reflect the regional nature of the Yugoslav wars, and was also translated into the initiative's goal of establishing an intergovernmental commission with the support of governments from all former Yugoslav states.[2] This last, harder step, despite consuming much of the initiative's energy, has so far not been reached, also due to the changing political equilibria in the region.[3]

By consciously addressing the mentioned shortcomings of top-down transitional justice in the region, the organisers aimed at a strongly inclusive and locally owned process. This initiative had the potential to be one of the most transformative attempts carried out in the former Yugoslavia since the end of the conflicts. The

1 Interview with Refik Hodžić, ICTJ, New York, 18 April 2014.
2 Interview with Nataša Kandić, Humanitarian Law Center, Belgrade, 22 May 2013.
3 While in 2014 the changes suggested by the representatives of the various regional governments have been incorporated in the statute of the prospective commission, there has been no further progress toward the establishment of the regional commission. However, a last effort to revive the initiative has been recently made with the launch of a new signature collection campaign in May 2017. So far, about 50,000 signatures have been collected in the region's capitals (RECOM, 2017); this follows a previous signature campaign carried out in 2011, when around half a million signatures were collected (YIHR Serbia and YIHR Croatia, 2011).

leading RECOM activists wanted the prospective truth commission to be the result of a broad consultation process involving numerous and diverse actors of local civil society.[4] From 2007 to 2011, 127 consultations were therefore carried out throughout the seven former Yugoslav countries, involving NGOs, victims' associations (of all ethnic groups), war veterans' organisations, journalists and artists, to discuss the prospective truth commission and adopt a draft statute. Also thanks to the support of the ICTJ from New York, RECOM managed to secure considerable funds for the consultation and awareness-raising process (RECOM, 2011b). Considering its declared bottom-up, inclusive approach and its awareness of the flaws of previous top-down transitional justice approaches, RECOM clearly displayed some transformative potential. Its advocates presented it as an unprecedented effort of inclusiveness and local ownership: 'If you compare this experience with any experience around the world, you will hardly find any initiative that is so inclusive'.[5] Its democratic organisation, with an Assembly of members and a Coordination Council as representative decision-making bodies, lent credibility to these statements.

However, a closer analysis of the consultation process and of the overall initiative points to a narrow and procedural interpretation of inclusiveness. For instance, in singling out the target groups for the consultations, RECOM's activists referred often to the organised, and often professionalised, civil society to represent the abovementioned societal groups. For example, the victims were actually *victims' associations*, the young people were generally *members of youth organisations.* [6] Yet, the extent to which these organised groups may represent society at large is disputable.[7] In the particular Bosnian case, if, on the one hand, RECOM's failure to convince many victims' associations to participate was considered one of the major flaws of the initiative, on the other, the choice to refer to victims' associations to represent the victims was also often criticised.[8] In fact, victims' associations in BiH are often seen as self-interested groups that feature a strong ethnic connotation and often perpetuate the same nationalistic rhetoric that RECOM tried to defeat,[9] while also having limited reach among victims beyond their membership.

With reference to the Serbian case, Obradović-Wochnik (2013) has shown that the idea that NGOs represent the broader public is taken for granted by international actors and scholars. The latter often interpret the silence of the rest of the citizenry as denial or lack of interest, as personal or structural factors that might hinder individuals from participating are generally ignored. Similarly, RECOM's advocates have not engaged in a deeper reflection on structural inequalities among

4 Interview with Marijana Toma, Humanitarian Law Center, Belgrade, 22 May 2013.
5 Interview with Eduardo Gonzalez Cueva, ICTJ, New York, 13 September 2013.
6 See for instance RECOM (2007: 12), where participants themselves notice the problematic focus on youth *activists* only.
7 For a discussion of the representativeness of NGOs, see Steffeck and Hahn (2010).
8 See, for example, telephone interview with Forum Žena II, 11 November 2014; interview with Refik Hodžić, ICTJ.
9 See, for example, interview with Augustina Rahmanović-Koning, Vive Žene, Tuzla, 9 August 2013; Stanojka Tešić, Forum Žena, Bratunac, 16 August 2013.

the various civil society groups that might influence their capacity to participate, and have espoused a conception of civil society as formed exclusively by active and organised individuals/groups. Their emphasis on specialised knowledge on transitional justice, visible in the numerous presentations that often opened the consultation meetings, created distance between the core organisations and those less professionalised, who felt they were not expert enough to contribute in the same way.[10] The kind of engagement that RECOM asked for was demanding even for professional activists in terms of time and resources.[11] As a consequence, as admitted by RECOM's activists themselves, 'the majority did not have the means nor the possibility to participate more actively'.[12]

The impediments to participation in RECOM were therefore not formal, like in top-down, institutional measures of transitional justice, as here a seat in the debate was formally guaranteed to all those interested. It was the lack of a reflection on the informal impediments, like the knowledge of the transitional justice lingo, the unequal access to resources and knowledge among different groups, and the lack of efforts to empower more peripheral and less professionalised groups, that hindered full participatory parity.

In sum, the RECOM experiment displayed the limits of the liberal public sphere as described by Fraser (1990: 63–65), being only formally inclusive, without the substantial social equality necessary for a truly democratic process. Moreover, this shortcoming also had the effect of maintaining, rather than expanding, the discursive space on transitional justice in the region. In fact, the key concepts of justice, victimhood and harm were again defined following international legal standards and therefore through the lens of individual criminal responsibility (RECOM, 2011a: Art. 1). Some participants actually advocated for a more flexible conceptualisation of justice and a broader idea of victimhood, but eventually the reference to international standards sponsored by the organisers prevailed.[13] In this sense, RECOM did not push, but *set* the boundaries of what could be legitimately discussed as a justice claim (and, by implication, what could not be), thus defining what transitional justice meant (and did not mean).

Hence, while the RECOM initiative explicitly tried to make up for the flaws of top-down transitional justice, in practice it reproduced some of its limits by embracing a formal interpretation of inclusiveness and legalistic interpretations of justice and victimhood. Whereas the reference to international standards was supposed to compromise among the different conceptions of justice and victimhood represented in the consultations, it eventually constrained the debate to those options compatible with international standards. Following this chapter's configuration of transformative justice, the transformative potential of the initiative appears to have been limited to challenging ethnic stereotypes and giving a more

10 For instance, interview with Sakib Ahmetović, Bosniak association of prisoners' camps survivors (BUPL), Bratunac, 15 August 2013.

11 Interview with Alma Masić, YIHRs BiH, Sarajevo, 29 April 2015.

12 Interview with Marijana Toma (Serbian in the original, author's translation).

13 See for instance RECOM (2008: 35).

prominent role to the civil society compared to legal mechanisms of transitional justice. However, RECOM's transformative potential was far from being fulfilled with regard to the initiative's potential to produce a substantially inclusive project, able to reach out to the local communities and not only to professionalised NGOs and to encourage the emergence of ideas of justice alternative to the prevalent liberal model.

The Women's Court for the Balkans

Similarly to RECOM, the Women's Court for the Balkans is a truth-seeking initiative initiated by local civil society organisations from all over the post-Yugoslav space (Ženski Sud, n.d.).[14] While RECOM clearly places itself in the transitional justice framework, the main cultural reference of the Women's Court for the Balkans is the tradition, by now consolidated, of women's courts implemented by feminist activists worldwide since the 1990s.[15] These are symbolic courts with no judicial powers where people widely trusted in the local society, the 'judges', issue recommendations based on a series of testimonies by women 'witnesses'. The Women's Court for the Balkans took place in Sarajevo, Bosnia and Herzegovina, from 4–7 May 2015, but it was just the last phase of long preparations that had lasted more than ten years. The first idea had actually come up in 2000, sponsored by local activist Žarana Papić and by the international coordinator of the global Women's Court movement, Corinne Kumar, but it had been abandoned after Papić had passed away (Women's Court, 2011: 14). After the initiative was relaunched by the Belgrade-based NGO Women in Black in 2006/2007, the formal preparatory process started in 2010. It comprised a series of meetings, seminars and presentations with women from throughout the region, during which it was decided who would testify and approximately about what topics.[16]

In the case of the Women's Court, too, similarly to RECOM, there was a strong awareness of the limits of ordinary justice processes, and the secondary and rather passive role victims play therein. Hence, one of the paramount goals of the initiative was to provide a safe space for women whose stories had not been featured in trials or other transitional justice initiatives, to tell their stories. Judicial mechanisms (and more generally the transitional justice framework) were still

14 Its regional organisational committee (*regionalni organizacioni odbor*) comprised: from Srebrenica, Cure, Mothers of Srebrenica, and Zepa; from Croatia, Centre for Women's Studies, and Centre for Women Victims of the War; from Kosovo, Women's Network; from Macedonia, Council for Gender Equality; from Montenegro, Anima; from Serbia, Women in Black, and Centre for Women's Studies; and from Slovenia, Women's Lobby. Other organisations had been involved with a leading role earlier in the preparation stages, e.g. Forum Žena Bratunac and Žene Ženama (the latter dropped out in 2013) (telephone interview with Valentina Pellizzer, feminist activist, Sarajevo, 3 November 2013).

15 The first women's 'tribunals' were actually created in the 1970s, but a new, more informal kind of women's 'courts' has been implemented more consistently since the 1990s throughout the world (Women's Court, 2011: 21–48).

16 Telephone interview with Forum Žena Bratunac II, 11 November 2014.

considered necessary, but were held insufficient to fulfil the needs of the victims and to reflect the complexity of the conflict and its consequences (Zajović, 2015: 11). In order to complement them, a feminist lens had to be adopted, highlighting the various forms of structural violence that accompanied the 1990s conflicts in the region and the ways the latter specifically affected women (Women's Court, 2011: 14).

A broader and more nuanced interpretation of the wartime violence and its consequences was the first and foremost contribution of the Women's Court toward a transformative justice process. In fact, this was the first consistent effort in the region to propose a reading of the violence that would highlight the economic and social consequences of the conflict besides the interethnic and interpersonal violence that are usually in the spotlight. This was realised by including testimonies on various topics, each corresponding to a section of the court featuring several witnesses: 1 war against the civilian population (*Rat protiv civilno stanovništvo*); 2 woman's body: a battlefield (*Žensko tjelo: bojno polje*); 3 militaristic violence and women's resistance (*Militarističko nasilje i otpor žena*); 4 persecution of those who are different in war and peace (*Progon drugačijih i u ratu i u miru*); 5 (un)declared war: social and economic violence and women's resistance (*(Ne) objavljeni rat: socijalno i ekonomsko nasilje i otpor žena*). The women's testimonies were then placed in a broader historical and social context by 'experts' (academics or activists with expertise on the specific topic).

One of the most transformative elements of the Court was that it let histories of violence that had never found an escape valve before, such as the predicament of women who lost their jobs after the mass layoffs ensuing from the privatisations, become part and parcel of the transitional narrative.[17] Attesting to the flexibility of the concept of (in)justice, some testimonies featured several forms of violence. A woman victim of wartime rape, for instance, underlined how she had also been a victim of domestic violence and, after leaving her husband, of multiple discrimination: as a refugee, a single mother and someone suffering from mental health issues. But what currently made her suffer the most was that her sons could not find a job due to the current economic situation in Bosnia and Herzegovina.[18] This example also shows how the Women's Court was able to bring out the interconnectedness of the various forms of violence and, above all, their continuity from wartime into the present. The ability to break the artificial isolation of wartime violence from the present and reveal its significance for current problems is key for a truly transformative process (see Gready and Robins, 2014: 10). In fact, this means directly taking issue with current political problems, like the corruption of ethno-national elites but also the liberal model sponsored by the international community.[19] Through its work, the Court effectively attempted to

17 See field notes on the Women's Court, 7–10 May 2015, Session 6, n.1, woman from Macedonia.

18 Field notes on Women's Court, Session 2, n. 3, woman from Srebrenica.

19 Explicit critiques to these issues were expressed in the preliminary recommendations of the judges (Women's Court, Judicial Council, 2015).

reconceptualise the very meaning of injustice and justice, by relying on a feminist approach and putting women's voices and actions at the centre of the process, in a much more substantial way compared to previous transitional justice initiatives, including RECOM. It did not shy away from political issues, but put them at the centre of its work.

The Court's transformative potential was also visible in the more radical approach it took to increasing local participation. The Court's feminist approach to justice, in fact, meant not only a reformulation of what 'justice' meant, but also a substantial rethinking of the ways in which women (as the focus of the Court's work) took part in post-war justice processes. This meant involving the broader society, beyond those actively involved in NGO work. Women witnesses, some of whom were not affiliated with any organisations, were 'the leading subjects of the Women's Court' (Women's Court, Judicial Council, 2015). The judges who wrote the preliminary conclusions of the Sarajevo events recognised that these women 'have been invisible', and unable to actively take part in 'truth telling, history making, and demanding and defining justice' thus far (Women's Court, Judicial Council, 2015). As we can see, participation here goes well beyond involvement in transitional justice programmes, and refers instead to a fundamental contribution to shaping the whole process of dealing with past (and present) violence. In this sense, the feminist approach to justice of the Women's Court constituted a critique of the structural inequalities of liberal democracy and its forms of participation. It effectively created a 'subaltern' space of confrontation and deliberation (Fraser, 1990) that foregrounded the agency of women. As noted by O'Reilly (2016: 428), one important aspect of the Court was precisely that it was centred around the role of women witnesses rather than that of experts (who were present, but to provide contextualisation to the testimonies rather than guide the process).

Finally, the Court's reference to an alternative, more transformative, justice framework is also visible from its detachment from the restorative justice model. While, as mentioned above, the witnesses constituted the core of the justice-seeking process, the purpose was not merely to assist them as passive victims in need of therapeutic support, but rather to empower them. Hence, very often the histories of violence were also histories of resistance. The violence had often prompted the women to become politically active, to protest or organise.[20] The rebuttal of the restorative model, which was communicated clearly in the very first press conference ('the Women's Court is not a psycho-therapeutic court, but a political court'),[21] may be better understood in light of the tendency (particularly of international organisations and NGOs) to 'pathologise' the Bosnian population, i.e. to focus on the traumatised individual to explain current political and economic problems, while ignoring structural causes (Hughes and Pupavac, 2005: 879–880).

20 Field notes on Women's Court, in particular testimonies from Sections 3 and 5.

21 Ljupka Kovačević of NGO Anima Kotor during the press conference opening the Women's Court for the Balkans, 5 May 2015.

It should be noted that the Women's Court's potential was limited in some important ways. For instance, activists remarked that there was a somewhat unbalanced focus on the broader network of the Women of Srebrenica to testify about sexual violence in Bosnia at the expense of other experiences.[22] O'Reilly (2016: 431) has also pointed out the lack of diversity in the wartime experiences of violence told at the Court, such as the lack of stories of women soldiers, which reinforces the stereotype of the war as a mainly masculine endeavour. However, Women's Court's activists pointed to the difficult task of selecting only some of the numerous women who wanted to testify, due to the short time available and to the scarcity of funds.[23] In sum, despite some limits, in part related to the limited availability of funds and time, which prevented a comprehensive representation of all aspects of the violence, the Women's Court succeeded in producing an alternative interpretive framework and justice model. Perhaps its most serious limitation remains its capacity to impact at the institutional level, by effectively turning this interpretive framework into political action beyond the protected space of the Court activities. In fact, with its limited resort to external funds and support, the Women's Court could not exert the same pressure on regional political elites as more institutionalised initiatives like RECOM.

The 2014 protests

The February 2014 protests were sparked by the frustration of workers in the eastern Bosnian city of Tuzla, where factories had been closing down throughout the transition period, leaving many unemployed. Faced with delayed salaries and social security payments, the workers succeeded in getting a critical mass of protesters to join them, and to surround the cantonal government building. As the police reacted forcefully to the escalation of tensions (the building was damaged by fire and stones thrown at it), citizens and workers in other parts of Bosnia joined the demonstrations. After workers organised informally in Tuzla, other citizens joined the demonstrations spontaneously in other cities. While some political parties made instrumental claims regarding the demonstrators to gain popularity, what characterised this wave of discontent was precisely its informal and grass-roots nature. The scope of the protests quickly broadened to include calls for the resignation of governments at cantonal, entity and state levels,[24] the revision of privatisation agreements, as well as an end to privileges accorded to political elites (see BH Protest Files, 2014a for a concise summary of the protesters' demands).

22 Interview with feminist activist, Sarajevo, 27 May 2015.

23 For example, interview with Jadranka Miličević, Foundation 'Cure', Sarajevo, 15 December 2015.

24 Bosnia and Herzegovina is divided into two entities: the Federation of Bosnia and Herzegovina, and Republika Srpska, each with their own government, and the Brčko District. The Federation is further divided into ten cantons, which also elect cantonal governments. Both the cantons and the entity of Republika Srpska are composed of municipalities.

Among the cases analysed in this section, the 2014 protests are the least immediately recognisable as a post-war justice initiative, as the crucial concern of the protesters was socioeconomic. How are these events connected to the war and wartime violence?

The protests were in fact linked directly to the war, but in a different way than usually foreseen by the transitional justice literature. Their origins lay in the political economy of the Bosnian conflict, which was mostly based on trafficking, profiteering, and on the seizure of socially owned property. Economic power was, in many cases, a crucial factor fuelling the military effort (Strazzari, 2003; Pugh and Cooper, 2004; Andreas, 2009). As infrastructure was shelled and industry reduced to a fraction of its pre-war capacity, in parts of the country ethnic cleansing overlapped with theft, dismissals from employment, and other measures of social exclusion that constituted a major part of people's experiences of the war. In Prijedor, a city in north-western BiH, the first impression that the non-Serb population got from the war was the loss of employment on an ethnically discriminatory basis. This was often followed by internment in some of the very industries from which workers had been fired, such as the Omarska iron ore mines and the Keraterm ceramics factory, which were turned into prison camps in 1992.[25] This story of the war as one of economic clashes, destruction, and profiteering went rather unnoticed, especially from the point of view of dealing with the legacy of (socioeconomic) violence. In February 2014, still suffering from the consequences of asset stripping, economic decline and failure to compensate workers in any way, Bosnian citizens mobilised for socioeconomic justice.

While not falling within the canon of transitional justice initiatives, the protests exhibited transformative features, probably to a greater extent compared to the other cases analysed here. Referring to the concepts developed in the previous section and to the questions raised, we can say that the transformative potential of the protests resides in their radical claims related to socioeconomic redistribution, and to the modes of participation and democratic deliberation they adopted.

The 2014 protests effectively turned the experiences of socioeconomic violence experienced in Prijedor, Tuzla, and many other Bosnian cities during the conflict, into a public and political issue for the first time since the end of the war. Experiences of unjustified dismissal, followed by the impossibility of regaining employment after the war, led protesters to make work, and the rights related to work, a central claim.[26] The protests' focus on privatisations and on regaining control of the economic production process shows the transformative nature of the demonstrators' demands, as they claim that issues that have, so far, been subject to the neoliberal logic of the market should instead be dealt with through a social justice approach (BH Protest Files, 2014b). These socioeconomic demands expanded quickly into the political realm. The protesters saw the institutional framework established at Dayton as an obstacle to achieving social justice, and as a

25 Based on interview research conducted in Prijedor in the summer of 2015.

26 See interviews with activists, Sarajevo, 5 May 2015 and 21 May 2015, and activist, Zenica, 7 May 2015. See also BH Protest Files (2014c).

way of maintaining unfair privileges reserved for the elites, while common citizens struggle to get by (Kurtović, 2015; see also the claims made by protesters in different cities, for example at BH Protest Files, 2014d). The analysis of these justice claims thus shows two things: on the one hand, the 2014 protests begin as a critique of the liberal transition model established in Bosnia with the support of international organisations. They see economic reforms in the area of privatisation, labour laws, and welfare not as redressing the everyday forms of socioeconomic violence they suffered during the war, but as aggravating the situation. On the other hand, they discuss justice issues as inherently political, and envisage redistributive policies and changes in the political and economic model of the country as the primary way of redressing the dire conditions faced by Bosnian people. This has little to do with individual claims brought forward in courts: structural change is needed.

From the point of view of the modes of participation and deliberation, the 2014 protests were characterised by a rejection of ethnicity as a form of identification, and the adoption of a civic model that valued open discussion and direct democracy. In this sense, February 2014 represented a radical response to the rigid ethno-nationalist frameworks of political participation characterising the Bosnian system. Some of the slogans that appeared during the demonstrations exemplify the importance given to socioeconomic issues, beyond any ethnic dimension: 'we are hungry in three languages' (*gladni smo na tri jezika*), 'freedom is my nation' (*sloboda je moja nacija*), 'death to nationalism' (*smrt nacionalizmu*).[27] As one activist put it, the protests had nothing to do with ethnicity, but 'had everything to do with the positions of an ordinary citizen in this system'.[28] If participants considered themselves citizens (without the need for identifying with an ethnic group), they were also invited to take part in the process of debating and developing the protest claims. City after city, 'plenum' assemblies of citizens were formed, which were defined as 'public gatherings, open to any citizen, through which collective decisions and demands can be made and action taken beyond guarantees of leadership. They are open, direct, and transparent democracy in practice' (Arsenijević, 2014: 47–48). Plenum assemblies did not have leaders or an internal hierarchy. Each citizen had one vote, and decisions were made at general meetings where everyone had the right to speak, and the discussion was conducted by a moderator (who had no role in representing the plenum outside the assembly). While the absence of leaders and structure was criticised for curbing the potential of the protest movement (Weber, 2015; Sicurella, 2016), horizontality was a crucial feature of the movement, where activists were trying to encourage a more meaningful form of democratisation than had been promoted through internationally sponsored 'civil society building' projects or 'local ownership' (Donais, 2009). Indeed, this radical approach to inclusiveness went hand in hand

27 Fieldnotes, Tuzla, 1 May 2015; see also the *Bulletin of Plenum Zenica* (Plenum Zenica, 2016).
28 Interview with activist, Sarajevo, 21 May 2015.

with criticism of the NGO sector, despite the fact that NGO workers were often present at the meetings in personal capacity.[29]

To sum up, the 2014 protests were a transformative moment because they questioned the necessity and desirability of the liberal transition, while promoting alternative forms of identification that went beyond ethnicity (and that were civic, or based on socioeconomic status), and opening up spaces of public deliberation to common citizens. The protesters' concern with widening political participation and reclaiming public spaces mirrored new forms of social activism which emerged in the wake of the Arab uprisings and the Occupy movement (Pickerill and Krinsky, 2012; Kaldor and Selchow, 2015). It also demonstrated the relevance of social and economic rights within contemporary forms of activism (Evans, 2015). As the protest movement faded, though, questions regarding their legacy were raised. Many of the informal, grass-roots groups formed in February 2014 were quite small, or became so once the street protests ended. Some of these groups still exist in different parts of Bosnia, and were assisted with a limited amount of unconditional funding coming from Austria, but social mobilisation in Bosnia has never reached the levels of 2014 again. For their part, international actors have largely failed to understand the nature of the protests and their connection to the legacy of the war, or how they could have supported the transformative change promoted by the activists (Lai, 2016). Instead, they pushed forward a programme of economic reforms that follows the blueprint of previous attempts at liberalising the market and completing the privatisation process.

However, the 2014 protests also facilitated the creation of activist networks across Bosnia. Citizens of both entities (the Federation and Republika Srpska) saw that a civic mobilisation was indeed possible, and that there are possibilities for entertaining progressive debates on the future of the country.[30] Building on these newly formed networks, for instance, the so-called Austrian Initiative supported activists and plenum groups from all over Bosnia by providing funding for their running costs, and for activities that the groups themselves could establish, without any form of conditionality, and without requiring them to formally register as an NGO (Ludwig Boltzmann Institute, 2016). In another case, the long-term commitment of the workers of the DITA company in Tuzla succeeded in keeping the detergent factory open and workers employed (Pepić, 2015). While the structural problems affecting Bosnia have not been solved, the protests showed what a potentially transformative mobilisation for post-war social justice can look like.

Conclusion

Bosnia is definitely a country in need of transformation: many international actors, NGOs, activists and common citizens would agree. However, if we consider the field of transitional justice, the focus of international efforts has been limited to

29 Interview with activist, Sarajevo, 16 September 2015.
30 Interview with activist, Sarajevo, 16 September 2015.

'conventional' transitional justice mechanisms, and especially judicial ones. Trials have contributed to establishing a record of what happened during the war, and acknowledged the suffering of thousands of victims. They have also, according to some scholars, promoted local mobilisation around justice issues, which has contributed to the democratisation of Bosnian society (Nettelfield, 2010). Without contesting the vital importance of war crimes trials, though, attempts at transformative justice have mostly come from local actors, who have been able to look beyond the transitional focus of the ICTY, and sought comprehensive ways of dealing with the legacy of the conflict, in all its facets.

In this chapter, we analysed what transformative justice might look like in the case of Bosnia and Herzegovina. We argued that several attempts were made to overcome the limitations of judicial, top-down approaches to dealing with the past, and that these attempts originated within the civil society. In our understanding, the 'transformative' potential of civil society initiatives is characterised by a critique of the liberal transition paradigm, an engagement with the political nature of transitional justice, and a commitment to more radically open forms of participation and deliberation. The analysis of the case studies shows a great deal of variation between RECOM, the Women's Court and the 2014 protests, with the latter two initiatives presenting more transformative features than the first: it seems that the further away we move from the transitional justice model, the more transformative potential the initiative contains. At the same time, we might find that, in the long run, the more institutionalised RECOM initiative might have a more prominent legacy, at least in shaping future attempts at dealing with past injustices in the former Yugoslav region. RECOM (similarly to the Women's Court) also shows that regional activism may be better equipped to deal with a common legacy of violence, and highlight common trends of criminality and injustice that continue into the transition. Scholars such as Bilić (2012) have indeed pointed out that talking about activism while considering the countries of the former Yugoslavia separately constitutes an artificial endeavour. In fact, even the 2014 protests, which were primarily a Bosnian phenomenon, drew on the experiences of social mobilisation from below of, and exchanges between, activist groups from different parts of the former Yugoslavia.

Overall, the chapter suggests that if transitional justice is to survive criticism of its politics, and especially accusations of Western-centrism, legalism, and ineffectiveness, it needs to engage seriously with these grass-roots initiatives, not close itself. It should recognise that local actors are varied, and they include potential spoilers of peace and justice processes (Arnould, 2016; McAuliffe, 2017), but also progressive and socially aware activist groups that, as in the Bosnian case, have been left without institutional and political power by the war and transition, but which could play a crucial role in promoting transformative change. Our emphasis on local initiatives, though, might lead some to question whether the international community should have a role in post-war justice processes at all. We believe that, in today's globalised world, it is indeed impossible for international actors not to influence these processes. International organisations are present on the ground and have an impact on the daily life of the country, and on its population. Support for certain political, economic and institutional reforms inevitably affects the context within which post-war justice initiatives develop and operate. Moreover, withdrawing financial and organisational commitment from transitional justice programmes in order to promote 'local ownership' is in itself a form of intervention that could well have adverse effects. Rather, the international community might seek alternative ways of supporting local processes of dealing with the past, more akin to the Austrian Initiative implemented after the 2014 protests than to formalised projects with complex forms of conditionality. This is a limited example, but is indicative of the need for transformative thinking on the part of donors and external actors as well.

One issue that emerges from this chapter, and that would be worth pursuing in further research, is thus related to the role of international actors in transformative justice. From a conceptual point of view, is it possible for international organisations and donors to be involved in local processes without compromising their success or potential for sustainable social change? And from a practical point of view, what would this international support entail? Aside from these questions, this chapter clearly suggests that much of the transformative potential of local initiatives still remains unrealised. The challenge for researchers and practitioners with a serious commitment to developing this transformative potential will be in understanding these initiatives, their connections to the broader society, and how they might (or could, in the future) support transformative change in post-conflict societies.

References

Andreas, Peter. (2009) 'Symbiosis Between Peace Operations and Illicit Business in Bosnia'. *International Peacekeeping* 16(1): 33–46.

Arnould, Valerie. (2016) 'Transitional Justice in Peacebuilding: Dynamics of Contestation in the DRC'. *Journal of Intervention and Statebuilding* 10(3): 321–338.

Arsenijević, Damir. (2014) 'Protests and the Plenum: The Struggle for the Commons'. In Damir Arsenijević (ed.), *Unbribable Bosnia and Herzegovina: The Fight for the Commons*, 45–50. Baden-Baden: Southeast European Integration Perspectives, Nomos.

Arthur, Paige. (2009) 'How Transitions Reshaped "Human Rights": A Conceptual History of Transitional Justice'. *Human Rights Quarterly* 31(2): 321–367.

Arzt, Donna A. (2006) 'Views on the ground: the local perception of international criminal tribunals in the former Yugoslavia and Sierra Leone'. *The Annals of the American Academy of Political and Social Sciences* 603(1): 226–239.

Belloni, Roberto. (2007) *State Building and International Intervention in Bosnia*. Abingdon: Routledge.

BH Protest Files. (2014a) 'Visualizing the Plenum Demands', 13 May, https://bhprotestfiles.wordpress.com/2014/05/13/visualizing-the-plenum-demands/ [accessed 20 July 2017].

BH Protest Files. (2014b) 'Declaration of the Sarajevo Citizens' Plenum (#3)', 9 February, https://bhprotestfiles.wordpress.com/2014/02/09/declaration-of-the-sarajevo-citizensplenum-3/ [accessed 12 September 2017].

BH Protest Files. (2014c). 'The Tuzla Declaration of Citizens and Workers of 7 February 2014 (Tuzla #1)', https://bhprotestfiles.wordpress.com/2014/02/07/declaration-of-citizens-and-workers-in-tuzla-1/ [accessed 25 September 2017].

BH Protest Files. (2014d) 'Proclamation of the Plenum of Citizens of the Tuzla Canton', 13 February, https://bhprotestfiles.wordpress.com/2014/02/13/announcement-of-the-plenum-of-citizens-of-the-tuzla-canton/ [accessed 20 July 2017].

Bilić, Bojan. (2012) *Resisting the Evil: [Post-]Yugoslav Anti-war Contention.* Baden-Baden: Nomos.

Bunce, Valerie. (1995) 'Should Transitologists Be Grounded?'. *Slavic Review* 54(1): 111–127.

Cassese, Antonio. (2003) *International Criminal Law.* Oxford: Oxford University Press.

Chandler, David. (2011) 'Post-conflict Statebuilding: Governance without Government'. In Michael Pugh, Neil Cooper, and Mandy Turner (eds), *Whose Peace? Critical Perspectives on the Political Economy of Peacebuilding*, 337–355. Basingstoke: Palgrave Macmillan.

Clark, Janine N. (2009) 'The limits of retributive justice. Findings of an empirical study in Bosnia and Hercegovina'. *Journal of International Criminal Justice* 7(3): 463–487.

Clark, Janine N. (2016) 'Transitional justice as recognition: an analysis of the Women's Court in Sarajevo'. *International Journal of Transitional Justice* 10(1): 67–87.

Clark, Phil and Nicola Palmer. (2012) 'Challenging transitional justice'. In Phil Clark, Nicola Palmer and Danielle Granville (eds), *Critical Perspectives on Transitional Justice*, 1–16. Antwerp: Intersentia.

Delpla, Isabelle. (2007) 'In the midst of injustice: the ICTY from the perspective of some victim associations'. In Elissa Helms, Ger Duijzings and Xavier Bougarel (eds), *The New Bosnian Mosaic*, 211–234. London: Ashgate.

Donais, Timothy. (2009) 'Empowerment or Imposition? Dilemmas of Local Ownership in Post-conflict Peacebuilding Processes'. *Peace & Change* 34(1): 3–26.

Dragović-Soso, Jasna and Eric Gordy. (2011) 'Coming to terms with the past: transitional justice and reconciliation in the post-Yugoslav lands'. In Dejan Djokić and James Ker-Lindsay (eds), *New Perspectives on Yugoslavia. Key Issues and Controversies*, 193–212. Abingdon: Routledge.

Evans, Matthew. (2015) 'Trade Unions as Human Rights Organizations'. *Journal of Human Rights Practice* 7(3): 466–483.

Fraser, Nancy. (1990) 'Rethinking the Public Sphere: A Contribution to the Critique of Actually Existing Democracy'. *Social Text* 25/26: 56–80.

Fraser, Nancy. (2005) 'Reframing Justice in a Globalizing World'. *New Left Review* 36: 69–88.

Fraser, Nancy. (2009) *Scales of Justice. Reimagining Political Space in a Globalizing World.* New York: Columbia University Press.

Gready, Paul. (2005) 'Reconceptualizing transitional justice: embedded and distanced justice'. *Conflict, Security and Development* 5(1): 3–21.

Gready, Paul, and Simon Robins. (2014) 'From transitional to transformative justice: a new agenda for practice'. *International Journal of Transitional Justice* 8(3): 339–361.

Hagan, John. (2003) *Justice in the Balkans. Prosecuting War Crimes in the Hague Tribunal.* Chicago, IL and London: The University of Chicago Press.

Hazan, Pierre. (2004) *Justice in a Time of War – The True Story behind the International Criminal Tribunal for the Former Yugoslavia.* College Station, TX: Texas A&M University Press.

Hughes, Caroline and Vanessa Pupavac. (2005) 'Framing post-conflict societies: international pathologisation and the post-Yugoslav states'. *Third World Quarterly* 26(6): 873–889.

Jones, Briony. (2012) 'Exploring the Politics of Reconciliation through Education Reform: The Case of Brčko District, Bosnia and Herzegovina'. *International Journal of Transitional Justice* 6(1): 126–148.

Kaldor, Mary and Sabine Selchow (eds). (2015) *Subterranean Politics in Europe.* Basingstoke: Palgrave Macmillan.

Kritz, Neil J. (1995) *Transitional Justice: How Emerging Democracies Reckon with Former Regimes.* Washington, DC: United States Institute of Peace.

Kritz, Neil and Finci, Jakob. (2001) 'A truth and reconciliation commission in Bosnia and Herzegovina: an idea whose time has come'. *International Law Forum* 3: 50–58.

Kurtović, Larisa. (2015) '"Who Sows Anger, Reaps Rage": On Protest, Indignation and Redistributive Justice in Bosnia and Herzegovina'. *Southeast Europe and Black Sea Studies* 15(4): 639–659.

Lai, Daniela. (2016) 'Transitional Justice and Its Discontents: Socioeconomic Justice in Bosnia and Herzegovina and the Limits of International Intervention'. *Journal of Intervention and Statebuilding* 10(3): 361–381.

Lambourne, Wendy. (2009) 'Transitional Justice and Peacebuilding after Mass Violence'. *International Journal of Transitional Justice* 3(1): 28–48.

Lambourne, Wendy. (2014) 'Transformative Justice, Reconciliation and Peacebuilding'. In Susanne Buckley-Zistel, Teresa Koloma Beck, Christian Braun and Frederike Mieth (eds), *Transitional Justice Theories*, 19–39. Abingdon: Routledge.

Laplante, Lisa J. (2008) 'Transitional Justice and Peace Building: Diagnosing and Addressing the Socioeconomic Roots of Violence through a Human Rights Framework'. *International Journal of Transitional Justice* 2(3): 331–355.

Lederach, John Paul. (1997) *Building Peace: Sustainable Reconciliation in Divided Societies.* Washington, DC: United States Institute of Peace Press.

Leonardsson, Hanna, and Gustav Rudd. (2015) 'The "local turn" in peacebuilding: a literature review of effective and emancipatory local peacebuilding'. *Third World Quarterly* 36(5): 825–839.

Ludwig Boltzmann Institute. (2016) *Supporting Informal Citizens' Groups and Grass-root Initiatives in Bosnia and Herzegovina 2015, Interim Report – First Implementation Phase (July 2015 – December 2015)*, February. Vienna: Ludwig Bolztmann Institute.

Mannergren Selimović, Johanna. (2010) 'Perpetrators and victims: local responses to the International Criminal Tribunal for the former Yugoslavia'. *Focaal – Journal of Global and Historical Anthropology* 57: 50–61.

McAuliffe, Pádraig. (2017). 'Reflections of the nexus between justice and peacebuilding'. *Journal of Intervention and Statebuilding* (online first): 1–16.

McEvoy, Kieran. (2008) 'Letting go of legalism. Developing a "thicker" version of transitional justice'. In Kieran McEvoy and Lorna McGregor (eds), *Transitional Justice from Below. Grassroots Activism and the Struggle for Change*, 15–45. Oxford: Hart Publishing.

McEvoy, Kieran, and Kirsten McConnachie. (2012) 'Victimology in transitional justice: victimhood, innocence and hierarchy'. *European Journal of Criminology* 9(5): 527–538.

McEvoy, Kieran and Lorna McGregor (eds). (2008) *Transitional Justice from Below: Grassroots Activism and the Struggle for Change.* Oxford: Hart Publishing.

Nagy, Rosemary. (2008) 'Transitional Justice as Global Project: Critical Reflections'. *Third World Quarterly* 29(8): 275–289.

Nettelfield, Lara. (2010) *Courting Democracy: The Hague's Tribunal Impact in a Post-war State.* New York and Cambridge: Cambridge University Press.

Obradović-Wochnik, Jelena. (2013) 'The silent dilemma of transitional justice: silencing and coming to terms with the past in Serbia'. *International Journal of Transitional Justice* 7(2): 328–347.

Oomen, Barbara. (2008) 'Donor driven justice and its discontents: the case of Rwanda'. *Development and Change* 36(5): 887–910.

O'Reilly, Maria. (2016) 'Peace and Justice through a feminist lens: women's justice and the Women's Court for the former Yugoslavia'. *Journal of Intervention and Statebuilding* 10 (3): 419–445.

Pepić, Andjela. (2015) 'Reclaiming the Factory: A Story from Bosnia', *Open Democracy*, www.opendemocracy.net/can-europe-make-it/andjela-pepic/reclaiming-factory-story-from-bosnia [accessed 1 August 2017].

Pickerill, Jenny and John Krinsky. (2012) 'Why Does Occupy Matter?'. *Social Movement Studies* 11(3/4): 279–287.

Plenum Zenica. (2016) *Bulletin* (*Bilten*) No. 1, on file with the authors.

Pugh, Michael and Neil Cooper. (2004) *War Economies in a Regional Context: Challenges of Transformation*. Boulder, CO and London: Lynne Rienner Publishers.

Rajagopal, Balakrishnan. (2003) *International Law from Below: Development, Social Movements and Third World Resistance*. New York: Cambridge University Press.

RECOM. (2007) *Minute of National Consultations with Young People*, Sarajevo, 27 June.

RECOM. (2008) *Minute of National Consultations with the Associations of Victims on the Mechanism for the Establishment for the Facts and Truth-telling on War Crimes in the Former Yugoslavia*, Belgrade, 15 July.

RECOM. (2011a) *The Statute Proposal of the Regional Commission for Establishing the Facts about War Crimes and Other Gross Violations of Human Rights Committed on the Territory of the Former Yugoslavia*. RECOM, http://recom.link/wp-content/uploads/2012/01/Proposed-Statute.pdf [accessed 30 September 2017].

RECOM. (2011b) 'RECOM Budget, 2011', www.zarekom.org/documents/Financial-Report.en.html [accessed 9 February 2015].

RECOM. (2017) 'Prikupljeno 50.361 potpisa podrške da se REKOM osnuje u okviru berlinskog procesa' ['50,361 signatures collected in support of the establishment of RECOM in the framework of the Berlin process'], RECOM, http://recom.link/sr/prikupljeno-50-361-potpis-podrske-da-se-rekom-osnuje-u-okviru-berlinskog-procesa [accessed 30 September 2017].

Ross, Fiona. (2003) 'Using rights to measure wrongs: a case study of method and morals in the case of the South African Truth and Reconciliation Commission'. In Richard Wilson and Jon P. Mitchell (eds), *Human Rights in Global Perspective. Anthropological Studies of Rights, Claims and Entitlements*, 141–163. London: Routledge.

Sharp, Dustin N. (2012) 'Addressing Economic Violence in Times of Transition: Toward a Positive-peace Paradigm for Transitional Justice'. *Fordham International Law Journal* 35(3): 780–814.

Sharp, Dustin N. (2015) 'Emancipating Transitional Justice from the Bonds of the Paradigmatic Transition'. *International Journal of Transitional Justice* 9(1): 150–169.

Shaw, Rosalind and Lars Waldorf (eds). (2010) *Localizing Transitional Justice. Interventions and Priorities after Mass Violence*. Stanford, CA: Stanford University Press.

Sicurella, Federico G. (2016) 'Usurpatori o Portavoci? La Mancata Alleanza tra Intellettuali Pubblici e Movimenti di Protesta in Bosnia-Erzegovina nel 2014'. In Giuseppe Motta (ed.), *A venti anni dagli accordi di Dayton*, 201–217. Rome: Aracne Editrice.

Stark, David and Laszlo Bruszt. (1998) *Postsocialist Pathways: Transforming Politics and Property in East Central Europe*. Cambridge: Cambridge University Press.

Steffeck, Jens and Kristina Hahn (eds). (2010) *Evaluating Transnational NGOs*. London: Palgrave Macmillan.

Strazzari, Francesco. (2003) 'Between Ethnic Collision and Mafia Collusion: The "Balkan Route" to State-making'. In Dietrich Jung (ed.), *Shadow Globalization, Ethnic Conflicts and New Wars*, 140–162. London and New York: Routledge.

Subotić, Jelena. (2009) *Hijacked Justice: Dealing with the Past in the Balkans*. Ithaca, NY: Cornell University Press.

Subotić, Jelena. (2011a) 'Europe is a state of mind: identity and Europeanization in the Balkans'. *International Studies Quarterly* 55(2): 309–330.

Subotić, Jelena. (2011b) 'Expanding the scope of post-conflict justice: individual, state and societal responsibility for mass atrocity'. *Journal of Peace Research* 48(2): 157–169.

Teitel, Ruti G. (2003) 'Transitional Justice Genealogy'. *Harvard Human Rights Journal* 16: 69–94.

Touquet, Heleen and Peter Vermeersch. (2016) 'Changing frames of reconciliation: the politics of peace-building in the former Yugoslavia'. *East European Politics and Societies and Cultures* 30(1): 55–73.

United Nations Development Programme (UNDP). (2009) *Vodić kroz tranzicijsku pravdu u Bosni i Hercegovini* [*A Guide to Transitional Justice in Bosnia and Herzegovina*], prepared by Dragan M. Popović. Sarajevo: UNDP.

Weber, Bodo. (2015) *Bosnia and Herzegovina after the February 2014 Protests: Is there a Potential for Renewed Violent Social Unrest?* Policy Note #2, September. Berlin and Sarajevo: AI-DPC BiH Security Risk Analysis.

Women's Court. (2011) *Ženski Sud feministicki pristup pravdi* [*Women's Court, a Feministic Approach to Justice*]. Belgrade: Art Print Novi Sad/ Women in Black Belgrade and Centre for Women's Studies.

Women's Court, Judicial Council. (2015) 'Preliminary Decisions and Recommendations, Delivered in Sarajevo, 9 May 2015'. Women's Court, www.zenskisud.org/en/pdf/2015/Womens_Court_Preliminary_Decision_Judicial_Council_2015.pdf [accessed 30 July 2017].

YIHR Serbia and YIHR Croatia. (2011) *Report of Youth Initiative for Human Rights in Serbia and Youth Initiative for Human Rights in Croatia on 1,000,000,000 signatures for RECOM campaign*. Documenta, www.documenta.hr/assets/files/REKOM/ENG/11_f_2184_en.pdf [accessed 30 September 2017].

Zajović, Staša (ed.). (2015) *Ženski Sud: o procesu organizovanja* [*Women's Court: On the Process of Organisation*]. Belgrade: Art Print Novi Sad/Women in Black Belgrade and Centre for Women's Studies.

Ženski Sud. (n.d.) 'Ženski Sud. Feministički pristup pravdi' ['Women's Court. A Feminist Approach to Justice'], www.zenskisud.org [accessed 2 October 2017].

5 The problem of elites

Pádraig McAuliffe

Introduction: transformative justice's biggest lacuna

The transformative 'turn' in transitional justice (TJ) that animates many of the contributions to this volume is a welcome development inasmuch as it renders justice its full meaning. However, the transformative turn is generating its own discontents even among those sympathetic to the re-orientation of TJ. This is largely because transformative justice still appears to be defined more by what it is not (liberal, legalist, technicist) than what it is. Sandoval (2017: 168, 177), for example, argues that transformative justice 'remains vague and unclear, as are its desired goals and the ways to achieve them', noting that 'missing from the transformative justice literature is a detailed examination of the capacity and potential for the field to be truly transformative'. Core issues that define the prospects for transformation like the existence or not of basic security, the state's revenue base or its ability to raise revenues and the relationship of localities, tribes, regional power-brokers, etc., with the state have largely gone under-explored. Enlarging the focus of TJ is distinct from transforming social conditions; articulating norms is distinct from establishing them. Recent arguments that 'there has been little analysis to date of what it means to achieve structural change and socio-economic justice in a post-conflict setting' and that TJ 'lacks the tools for identification and implementation of such a broader agenda for change' are more than defensible (Balint, Lasslett and Macdonald, 2017: 4).

This is true of both top-down and bottom-up theories of transformative justice. Because victims increasingly use the language of rights to appeal to the state to respond to their needs, some more top-down theories of transformative justice stress the normative power of the state as duty-bearer re-oriented towards the pursuit of economic justice. These scholars emphasise the state's capacity to define and then secure what can or should be regarded as important through the promulgation of rights, the creation of social capital for the disempowered and the definition of key concepts like justice that have a direct bearing on development programmes or national budgets (Arthur, 2009). Others stress the bottom-up potential of grass-roots conceptualisations of justice to coalesce and catalyse broader national change (Gready and Robins, 2014). There are problems with both top-down and bottom-up visions, however. In the areas of limited statehood within which most transitional justice takes place, the state lacks the administrative reach, resource base or legitimacy to effectively place the state at the centre of economic justice guarantees. States are typically hybrid, mixing rational governance structures with competing economic, traditional or regional power structures that intermingle and interact. In these environments the state has no monopoly on loyalty or the provision of social goods, sharing as it does authority and capacity with other individuals or institutions (Boege, Brown and Clements, 2009: 17). Bottom-up visions of transformative justice commendably emphasise this local agency, but lack the sort of programmatic links (the 'missing middle') that might link up micro-local projects with broader structural change (McAuliffe, 2017a).

It is clear then that a discourse premised around the twin poles of rejecting liberal-legalist models and celebrating the emancipatory potential of localised justice projects cannot identify the political levers or economic tools that might catalyse the desired broader agenda for change. International actors and local nongovernmental organisations (NGOs) or victim groups can only be understood as two (albeit important) parties to ongoing domestic struggles over resources and opportunities, struggles neither has any realistic hope of taming on their own. TJ is never simply an exported expert activity or a pristine reference point for emancipatory activity, but a conflict-ridden process in which numerous different societal actors are inevitably involved. Scholars sympathetic to the need for structural change have begun to move away from the reductive liberal-local binaries that characterise the discourse to examine the political economy of the states in question. This mode of analysis concentrates on how power and wealth are apportioned and disputed in a given society. It explores how domestic actors work as both promoters and resisters of justice projects for reasons largely but not exclusively endogenous to that political culture, and how the frictions between these actors condition all opportunity for change (see for example Arnould, 2016; Jones and Bernath, 2017; McAuliffe, 2017b; Leclercq, 2017). Transformative justice always challenges an existing order that did not permit such progress to develop organically. Systemic, structural violence that disenfranchises distinct sectors of society must be deliberately sustained by a political system that distributes power and resources unequally. The operation and effect of any model of TJ we promote on the spectrum from narrowly juridical accountability to socioeconomic transformation is inevitably 'mediated by domestic responses to it, which can vary from compliance to adaptation, instrumentalization, resistance or non-participation' (Arnould, 2016: 324). If it is to bridge the gap from critique to programmatic relevance, the evolving literature on transformative transitional justice needs to comprehend the main poles of effective political agency.

Of these actors involved in negotiating TJ, it is here argued that the most important, but least well understood, are domestic elites. Strategic options that are theoretically available to TJ implementers may not be 'incentive compatible' insofar as they do not accord with the other compelling interests of critical politically effective groups to adopt (the government, faction leaders and economic elites, for the most part). As discursively framed in the TJ literature, elites emerge as a homogenous coterie of bogeymen pursuing a clearly definable class interest whose position is actively perpetuated by traditionally corrective TJ at the expense of empowering the marginalised (Aguirre and Pietropaoli, 2008: 367). However, though identified as one of the main barriers to transformation, there has been no sustained analysis in the transformative TJ literature of who elites are, what they do, the divisions between them or the incentives they might have to ameliorate the conditions of those in their society.

The homogenising and emphatically pejorative use of the concept of elites is striking as it is distinctly at odds with how other large-scale projects for economic or social transformation see them and interact with them. Peacebuilding operations, for example, are conceived as means of helping domestic elites surmount the difficulties presented by post-conflict transition, while democratisation projects live or die by the active participation of domestic elites (Zürcher, Manning and Evenson, 2013: 4, 6). Post-conflict constitutions 'are typically not the brainchildren of the people at large, but rather of established or newly dominant elites' (Reynolds, 2005: 65). State-building is increasingly understood as the means by which powerful groups and individuals institutionalise their power as a legitimate form of state (Bliesemann de Guevara, 2010: 116). The resilience of that state, and its power in turn to pursue poverty reduction, depends crucially on the inclusiveness of the bargains struck between elites. For the UK Department for International Development's (DFID) work in post-conflict states, for example, elite political settlements supporting the state 'should be a first-order priority – even if these settlements come at the cost of accelerated development' (DFID and UKAID, 2010: 15). State-building agencies likewise accept that any social contract that emerges in fragile states must revolve first around the expectations of society within the state (a matter transformative TJ literature is attentive to), second the state's resources and capacity to provide services (distinctly underexplored), and third elite will to direct these resources and services towards the fulfilment of those expectations (again, underexplored) (Organisation for Economic Co-operation and Development, 2008: 17). We might wish that transitional states become more responsive to inequalities and poverty, but any state that does so can only achieve this by reconciling transformation with at least some elite interests. Even the most sensitive bottom-up and grass-roots forms of participation will have limited effects on political or economic life without conscious engagement and dialogue with elites. It would be a mistake, therefore, to associate the reliance on existing elites with a conscious preference on the part of international interventionary actors. Reliance is better explained by necessity or unavoidability. Sovereignty inevitably makes national governments and the powerful economic and identity group leaders within the state the fundamental interlocutors for any form of intervention beyond the most grass-roots. Peacebuilding, state-building and TJ actors engage with elites because they have to, even though the normative standards through which the international community bestows legitimacy on the state may often conflict with the unspoken norms and informal rules of elite pacts (Salmon and Anderson, 2013: 49). Elite political settlements 'set the constraints for what can and cannot be achieved' in all developing states (Di John and Putzel, 2009: 18). They can do so negatively and positively.

In negative terms, most areas of limited statehood, and particularly those emerging from conflict, are subject to informal but pervasive elite pacts. As Whaites (2008: 7) notes, 'the structures of the state are determined by an underlying political settlement; the forging of a common understanding, usually among elites, that their interests or beliefs are served by a particular way of organising political power'. This political economy means the state is rarely capable of rational means-end planning to address structural injustice, but must instead incorporate sectoral, regional, religious and economic elite interests. Furthermore, these political settlements create or calcify unequal power relations, which in turn produce economic realities that place material constraints on international actors and local reform constituencies.

In the more positive sense, paying attention to elites can also help in crafting transformative approaches to justice by understanding the political economy of elite accumulation and contestation patterns and the potential levers for altering them. It can help identify elite incentives to invest in state functionality, progressive taxation or welfare to alleviate the problems of commitment or insecurity that lead to accumulation or predation. Evans (2016: 14) is correct to argue that social movements, trade unions and NGOs offer valuable insights as to how a transformative agenda might be pursued, but if marginalised groups are to realise their rights to a living wage, water, housing or health, responsive elite institutions matter. Elites are a key determinant of the success of social movements – some elites will have incentive to orchestrate or respond to reform movements or victim networks in society, while others will have incentives to thwart them. However, a literature that only emphasises in a generic and binary sense the impact of dominant classes on dominated classes will miss the internal clashes between reformist dominant groups and non-reformist ones. As Akmeemana and Porter (2015: 126) argue, two particular choices appear to be especially important in determining the scope, depth, and durability of a successful transition for society as a whole. The first is the ability of elites to impose centralised arrangements to collect and distribute rents. The second is the 'ability of central actors and the modalities they use to project authority and distribute resources to places where people live, including them in the settlement by delivering public safety, services, livelihoods and other opportunities' (Akmeemana and Porter, 2015: 126). Colombia's land restitution programme is a state-driven exercise passed via thoroughgoing land restitution legislation by some national elites that prejudiced the interests of many other elites like faction leaders, drug trafficking and large agricultural and mining corporations (Nilsson and Taylor, 2017). TJ scholarship has quite rightly commended the agreement as an example of holistic and transformative response to marginalisation, but has evinced little interest in how this came about. Theories of transformative justice lack a practical politics to explain why domestic elites might elect to make these difficult choices and so have distinct limitations.

Though critics of TJ pride themselves on their greater attention to questions of power and agency, the core argument propounded herein is that existing conceptions of transformative justice lack a sufficient understanding of the obstructive or facilitative roles elites play in the maintenance or reform of economic structures.

Without a strong understanding of those informal, shadow networks of privilege and patronage where real economic and social power lies, outsiders will always 'grope in the dark and their actions will continue to produce perverse and unintended consequences' (Berdal, 2009: 92). This chapter is not intended to be an exhaustive introduction to the study of elites in TJ, but I draw on disciplines like conflict studies, peacebuilding and elite theory that present more rigorous and instructive scholarship on elites to outline the ambiguous and contradictory political implications of (dis)engagement with them. The key question at all points is how to get domestic elites to improve individual welfare for the people as a whole when it is not in their immediate interests to redistribute resources. Elites are not homogenous and their coalitions are not static – effective links between TJ and transformation require a sophisticated approach that both identifies how elite relationships are drawn and re-drawn through alliances and resistances as they engage with international actors, the state and other social forces. To this end, the second section examines why transitional justice as a discipline has unhelpfully homogenised elites. The third section examines what scholars in other disciplines understand by the concept of elites. The fourth section explores elites as barriers to transformation, while the fifth section looks at their transformative role.

Elites in TJ discourse

Because TJ is a self-consciously victim-centred discipline, it should not be surprising that elites have generally been ignored or disdained in the literature. TJ as a field self-identifies as 'part of a larger turn toward embracing victims and the oppressed rather than the traditionally dominant victors and heroes of history' (Rothschild, 2017: 459). However, the roots of the discourse surrounding elites can actually be found in attempts to transcend the victim-perpetrator dichotomy that initially characterised the field. The trial and truth commission models reliant on distinguishing victims from perpetrators that initially dominated TJ could not capture the moral grey zone where these polarised identities became blurred, where people become complicit in violence or engaged in resistance to it as part of the struggle to survive (Drexler, 2013). Fletcher and Weinstein (2002: 626), notably, questioned whether and how individualised guilt might contribute to myths of collective innocence. As scholars began to acknowledge that directly and indirectly committed gross human rights violations can only occur while the majority of the population passively supported it, the concept of bystander complicity ('guilt through apathy') began to emerge (Borer, 2003: 1107). A further sense developed that the victim-perpetrator, guilt-innocence binaries were a convenient focus for 'those who most benefit' from existing structures but could not be fitted into any existing mode of analysis (Evans, 1998: 16–17). Over time, and as concerns about socioeconomic injustice became mainstreamed within TJ, this concern with the relatively inert figure of the bystander morphed into a concern for the more active concept of the beneficiary. An early theorist of this concept as it applied to TJ was Mahmood Mamdani (1996). In arguing that the definition of injustice had to extend beyond bodily integrity abuses that preoccupied the South

African Truth and Reconciliation Commission (TRC), he turned his attention to beneficiaries, those who accumulated wealth while by no means directly involved in apartheid. They are a larger group than direct perpetrators, but a much smaller group than the mass of victims impoverished by apartheid. Mamdani (1996) argued that those who do and do not benefit from conflict or the logic of authoritarian systems should become the focus of TJ. With the increasing focus on structural injustice, Marxist ideas of beneficiaries as 'would-be perpetrators' emerged, and

> claims for historical justice consequently include all those who profited from the past regime ... in this context, initial victory over the perpetrators of oppression 'would be merely a first stage in a longer struggle against the passive beneficiaries of the old regime'.
>
> (Franzki and Olarte, 2014: 209, citing Meister, 2011: 21f)

In a broader discourse premised on principles of equality, it is naturally problematic that some groups concentrate more wealth and power than others. 'Elites' has become the dominant catch-all for conceptualising these beneficiaries in contemporary TJ discourse, invariably seen as unrepresentative of their societies' needs, manufacturing consent through corruption and clientage, the self-interested upholders of the radically inegalitarian status quo. Critics argue that the norms TJ emphasises are articulated *by* the powerful *for* the powerful (Robins, 2012: 4). They worry that TJ's legalist discourse 'can empower elites and outsiders at the expense of victims, particularly the most disempowered' (Gready and Robins, 2014: 343). Elite political behaviour is furthermore associated with the masculinisation of politics and exclusion of women (Brown and Ní Aoláin, 2014: 132). It is argued that inequality stems from the 'entrenched ideology of elites' (Miller, 2008: 268). Theories or projects of justice 'from below', by contrast, are seen as inherently resistant to powerful hegemonic political and economic forces, and so are morally more worthy of our attention – indeed, a subaltern focus is presented as a welcome antidote to a fixation on elites (McEvoy and McGregor, 2008). Critics perceive 'a need, as far as possible, to externalise transitional justice from political elites' (Hansen, 2014: 119).

Even if the intellectual history and moral commitment of TJ to victims fosters a natural suspicion of elites, it still does not explain the tendency to essentialise their identities as uniformly conservative or predatory figures estranged entirely from community, culture, tradition or everyday life. For TJ activists in Bosnia, for example, the elite

> were represented exclusively in a homogenized and negative way, as the main group responsible for the lack of progress in the country and for creating a divided society, unable to reach any consensus and interested only in remaining in power.
>
> (Seixas, 2013: 81)

The failure to explore elites or to disaggregate the 'top' in 'top-down' might be explained by the preference for exploring vast impersonal forces of structural injustice in analysing harmful social structures over actor-centred examinations of 'great' or 'bad' men that insufficiently capture wider relations of exploitation. The role of elites is also difficult to parse – the relationship of elites to each other and their supporters is opaque and often unreliable, while policy decisions are adopted in secret without much visible public discussion. Patterns of elite accommodation, clientage and informal patrimonialism and 'off-budget' practices relating to rents will appear outside the official reform 'radar', but will critically condition the resources available for welfare or redistribution and the motivations that might inform compliance or resistance to transformation.

The shape TJ assumes contains expressive messages about the individuals or communities that matter, and it is natural to wish to redress the power balance in favour of victims without bargaining leverage. It also is natural to esteem power that resides in communities over that of artificially constructed states, and to prefer social movements that reflect immediate place-based concerns over external blueprints. However, the exaltation of social movements of the indigenous, poor and marginalised as a means of 'challenging institutions steered by elites' (Gready and Robins, 2017: 964–965) carries one obvious danger, namely the assumption that genuine social transformation can be envisaged without accounting for elite support or opposition. As the rest of this chapter argues, to ignore elites is to ignore the loci of effective political power that condition all opportunity for meaningful change.

Identifying elites

Elite theory attempts to explain why all societies are characterised by asymmetrical distributions of political and economic power (Zuckerman, 1977: 324), and why organised minorities tend to dominate unorganised majorities (Mosca, 1939: 53). It begins with the deep historical sociology of state formation. In the social state of nature, groups that attempt to establish self-defence and at least some form of community goods organise themselves hierarchically. These and subsequent, more complex forms of organisation require leaders. Though we attribute action to classes, tribes or social movements, what we generally mean is that some members of these groups, namely elites or sub-elites, have taken common action (Etzioni-Halevy, 1993). As Mann (1986: 6) puts it:

> In pursuit of their goals, humans enter into cooperative, collective power relations with one another. But in implementing collective goals, social organisation and division of labour are set up. Organisation and division of function carry an inherent tendency to distributive power, deriving from supervision and coordination.

The authority this process generates gives leaders or groups thereof the wherewithal to speak for groups and represent them to others. With this authority comes both the potential for abuse but also the potential for creating effective social contracts. States essentially represent the imposition of order on a territory by a particular class or group of elites, even if they enjoy some degree of consent (Call, 2008: 61). The further up one goes in the state hierarchy the greater the coercive and/or bureaucratic power over actors at lower levels. However, while much of TJ critique inveighs against the formal, technocratic state-building it is implicated in, all states mix formal governance with informal governance. The latter 'are based on implicit and unwritten understandings' and 'reflect socio-cultural norms and routines, and underlying patterns of interactions among socio-economic classes and ethnic groups' (Brinkerhoff and Goldsmith, 2002: 1). Critiques of TJ as liberal, formalist or technocratic are limited because they ignore the vast extent to which *de facto* informal practices of national or localised elites dominate, subvert or compromise *de jure* governance. Along similar lines, criticism of TJ for the limits of the formal liberal-democratic model it promotes pays insufficient attention to the way power is actually exercised, which bears little relation to this model. In many African states, for example, the public at large is seldom consulted in policy-making as decision-making in public affairs 'is typically restricted to elites with a narrow social base' (Bratton and Van de Walle, 1994: 470). The typical post-conflict or post-authoritarian state is a complex set of relationships between state frameworks, these domestic socio-political forces and ideational notions of authority (existing, of course, within an international political economy) (Jayasuriya, 2003: 383). TJ faces a crisis of relevance if it cannot extend beyond homogenisation of elites to understand these relationships.

Because the identity of elites is murky and difficult to research, they are notoriously hard to define precisely. Some delineation is possible. Dahl (1958: 464), for example, writes of that 'minority of individuals whose preferences regularly prevails in cases of differences on key political issues'. For Etzioni-Halevy (1993: 29) the term 'refers to those who wield power and influence on the basis of their active control of a disproportionate share of society's resources'. In relation to societies outside the West, scholars have developed theories and typologies of elite power that are distinct from the homogenisation we see in most TJ literature. The 'elite' is a composite notion that refers less to a full characterisation of real people than to a specific agency at national and sub-national levels defined by competence (ability) and/or because they enjoy a superior status, be it political, social or economic (Madsen and Christensen, 2016). Some individuals enjoy sufficiently loyal constituencies (tribes, unions, political parties, other corporatist institutions) to legitimate relationships of supremacy and subordination and so can speak for the bulk of their followers (Bhuta, 2010: 806). Others control sufficient resources or wealth to dominate whatever regulatory process exists to ensure the guiding principles of the economy serve them well. The concept mixes state elites and non-state elites, formal and informal, political and economic, rural and urban. In Weberian terms, they might evince or mix charismatic, traditional and rational authorities (Weber, 1947). They may exercise power through elaborate systems of political beliefs, or do so entirely privately. Relationships can be cemented through alliances, business dealings, religious or tribal affiliation, or even marriage. They are united not by common positions (as the fifth section, below, argues, elites are often divided by interest or geography), but by the disproportionate power and influence they wield. Hossain and Moore (2002: 1) speak of 'the most powerful 3–5 per cent of people within any political system', those who 'define what issues are to be taken up as political and policy problems and which are to be ignored or sidelined; how these issues are to be tackled; and what count as legitimate and feasible policy options'. Land-grabbing in Afghanistan, for example, is dominated by an unusually precise figure of '15,831 people as "relatives of high status government officials, members of parliament and other powerful and individual people"' (Saeed and Parmentier, 2017: 25, citing *Daily 8AM* newspaper).

TJ as a discipline used to have an acute understanding of how the attitudes and interests of elites fundamentally conditioned opportunities for justice. All initial debates around impunity revolved around the 'enormous causal power' of elite bargaining in authoritarian transitions in Latin America and Eastern Europe (Arthur, 2009: 346). This remains the case with post-conflict transitions (Aroussi and Vandeginste, 2013). Subsequent treatments of elites in the context of post-conflict accountability were similarly sophisticated, most notably Subotić's argument that the traditional accountability goals of transitional justice are contested between three types of elite, namely true believers, instrumentalists and resisters (Subotić, 2014: 127). Scholars are conscious of how elites can undermine traditional TJ, notwithstanding the discursive hegemony of TJ and its normalisation as peace processes become internationalised:

> Research on the politics of transitional justice suggests that domestic elites may be swayed to engage in transitional justice when faced with strong international pressure or domestic demand, but often they will try to circumscribe or reshape these policies so that they better serve their interests or in order to contain their potential negative political impact.
>
> (Arnould, 2016: 324)

Scholars worry that ownership of truth commissions worldwide has shifted from populations to national elites and the international community. In Ghana, for example, implementation of the truth commission's plan depends largely on which party is in power (Aciru, 2017: 73, 76). The Kenyan government and political elites have attacked the legitimacy of the International Criminal Court (ICC) and refused to nominate commissioners to the national Truth, Justice and Reconciliation Commission (Paffenholz, 2015: 866). The Maoist-led government in Nepal resiled from earlier commitments to implement TJ as the exigencies of domestic politics dictated (Robins, 2012: 12), a process replicated in Afghanistan as the Karzai government and parliamentary elites legislated for blanket amnesty (Saeed and Parmentier, 2017: 21–22). Domestic elites in the Democratic Republic of Congo (DRC), Burundi and East Timor have instrumentally adopted TJ as a means of including and excluding faction leaders from government as a form of conflict management (Ottendörfer, 2013; Arnould, 2016; Leclercq, 2017). Reparation mechanisms 'created by political elites can often silence and marginalise non-elites, and women in particular, who are not part of the political negotiation' (Moffett, 2017: 67), and so often take the form of undelivered promises.

The narrow legalism that the transformative turn rejects is widely believed to be derived from the initially circumscribed opportunities for justice that sprang from elite bargaining in Latin America and Eastern Europe. However, a baby has been thrown out with this bathwater – the acutely fine-grained analyses of the rational calculi of elites so familiar in the early TJ literature have been conspicuous by their absence in the transformative turn, to say nothing of Subotić-esque attempts to establish typologies of elite actors. In the critical TJ literature, once one gets beyond references to homogenised 'elites', less attention is paid to these powerful spoilers who have something to lose from transformation than it is to the multiplicity of bottom-up resistances manifested in localised processes, non-engagement, public dissent, etc. The discourse presumes a hydraulic relationship between the interests of elites driving transitional justice and 'those most affected by the events of the conflict and indeed over the broader needs of the nation' in which the interests of the former are inherently irreconcilable with the latter (Robins, 2012: 16).

One notable aspect of the failure to meaningfully scrutinise the relationship of elites to the political economy of post-conflict states is the insistence that these origins in elite negotiations produced a preference among TJ policy-makers to maintain existing normative and political hierarchies at the national level over the interests of the many (Arthur, 2009: 347; Aguirre and Pietropaoli, 2008: 367). Critics are correct that the liberal intervention package of democratisation, peacebuilding and TJ invariably leaves elite power intact, but this is more a result of the inherited national political economy than choice. While international interventionary actors present conditionality criteria that demand co-operation with defined outcomes, the institutions and norms that emerge are co-opted, compromised, distorted and instrumentalised by local power-brokers to suit their interests. Far from establishing the liberal and democratic peace consistently assailed in the discourse of the transformative turn (or even the shell thereof), international intervention typically culminates in conditions of hybridity in which liberal and illiberal, democratic and traditional elements coexist (Mac Ginty and Sanghera, 2012), but with a distinct tendency towards the latter. In many cases, liberal interventionary processes become

> coopted by domestic elites who use the legitimacy and power resources granted by transitional governance, and the subsequent aid economy, to turn the state into an arena of rent-seeking and distribution that is then employed in the struggle for political power.
>
> (Barma, 2012: 274)

While there is little doubt that many of the most salient inequalities and elite behavioural incentives are produced at the global level, the practices that result from intervention lie at the far end of the spectrum from the liberal governance models propagated by international actors. The problem is not that the liberalism of international actors unduly limits the potential for structural transformation (though it does little to help) – the problem instead is that in areas of limited statehood, interventionary prescriptions over domestic governance of any stripe exercise very little influence over a political economy that is defined by (a) historically non-liberal incentives and (b) the pressing contemporary need for stabilisation. The TJ literature around transformation tends to assume the relationship that matters most for structural change is that between interveners and domestic elites. As the fourth section goes on to argue, it is instead those intra-elite bargains that exercise the most influence over the distribution of resources or opportunity in a state.

How and why elites resist transformation

The social structures of contemporary developing states, the sites for most TJ and those which most animate the transformative turn, cannot be explained by this model of capitalist bargaining and reciprocal demands for revenue and services that explains the historical sociology of state formation in the West (Tilly, 1990). Post-colonial politics were instead characterised by state capture by elites claiming legitimacy on the basis of liberation politics (Bates, 2015: 33–54). Because poorly institutionalised states lacked capacity to implement and enforce central decisions and because broad-based civil society organisations like parties or unions with clear programmes were non-existent or weak, politics was highly personalised among those aforementioned figures that commanded the loyalties of constituencies through ethnopolitical mobilisation or domination of the military hierarchy, or who controlled sufficient inherited wealth or power to exercise decisive influence over politics. Ethnically oriented patronage, clientelism and 'pork' became key connecting tissue of nation-building in pluralistic African, Asian, Caribbean and Pacific states (Brinkerhoff and Goldsmith, 2002: 20). In societies that developed as more relationship-based than rule- or institution-based, these became the foundation for more enduring political settlements, an 'underlying or emerging "social order" based on political compromises between powerful groups that sets the context for institutional and other policies' (Khan, 2010: 4).

Elites are generally committed to the endurance and stability of these settlements because they derive benefits from them. They maintain this stability through formal administration of government, constitutional deliberation, bargaining and adaptation at the top, but also through manipulation of the economy. Most pacts or settlements demonstrate the capacities of 'grasping' (extracting rents and revenues from domestic actors and international aid/trade) and 'reaching' (the redistribution of rents and services to supporters across the national territory) (Craig and Porter, 2014: 6). Historically based forms of 'reaching' that we in the West would describe as neopatrimonialism, patronage and clientelism endure and routinise the political economy of the state in the absence of governmental bureaucratic sway. These complex chains of personal bonds between political patrons and their clients are fundamental to the 'politics of survival' in fragile and under-developed states as they guarantee mutual advantage – resources (jobs, opportunities) flow to dependants while support (votes, political support) flows to patrons (Migdal, 1988). These 'Limited Access Orders' quell tendencies toward violence by awarding privileged elites control of economic opportunities (monopolies, government contracts, tax exemptions, land rights, government employment), creating disincentives to grab more and incentives to maintain the flow of rents through peace (North, 2007). While clientelism and patrimonialism are associated with state failure, they should better be understood as context-sensitive apparatuses for social control and capital accumulation within the historical constraints imposed by post-colonial environments (Di John, 2010: 2, 24). True state failure and conflict follows when they break down.

There are many reasons why conflict erupts in those societies TJ later deploys to, but they generally tend to be those where powerful groups are unable to maintain a stable coalition as exclusionary behaviour violates the expectations of key socio-political groups (for example, Tunisia, DRC, Côte d'Ivoire). In conflicts over access to state power or secessionist struggles, elites fight to (re)gain access to economic or political privileges they are excluded from or to protect those they enjoy. Some African conflicts in the likes of DRC, Chad and the Central African Republic have been described as 'elite recycling' (Tull and Mehler, 2005: 378–79). This narrow range of actors also dominate the terms under which conflict ends. As Aroussi and Vandeginste (2013: 190) note, peace agreements seldom result from societal pressure from below, but instead are initiated by military and/or political figures at national elite level. Though unrepresentative of the population, future stability must be rooted in their expectations – 'elite agency is the locus for examining the chances of recurrence of internal armed conflict' (Call, 2012: 217). In positive terms, power-sharing usually becomes the immediate short-term point of coalescence among conflict elites sufficient to engender acquiescence among their supportive populations, dependent on the distribution of material and psychological resources between those individuals and groups who can undermine the settlement. In more negative terms, there is an acknowledgment by domestic leaders (one shared by the international community) that most instability flows from situations where factionalised, winner-takes-all contestation can re-emerge. As Khan (2010: 4) notes, 'if powerful groups are not getting an acceptable distribution of benefits from an institutional structure they will strive to change it'.

I have elsewhere described the tendency of post-conflict power-sharing towards policy stagnation and economic cartelisation that cripples the short-term prospects for transformation (McAuliffe, 2017c). It is important to remember, however, that these one-off political settlements are supplemented (and sometimes succeeded) by ongoing processes of mediation, contestation and collaboration in areas like security, markets, capital, resources and public appointments that will draw on longer-established ways of doing things (Salmon and Anderson, 2013: 44). Indeed, these constantly modified settlements are increasingly understood as crucial to all longer-term development and peacebuilding. Successful transitions are those where settlements 'are deepened, made more democratically inclusive and gradually institutionalised through security and service delivery out to the edge of the national territory' (Craig and Porter, 2014: 2). However, elite settlements are rarely composed exclusively of statesmen and faction-leaders intent on institutionalising peace, or where these figures exist they can rarely divorce leadership from other claims to patronage or clientelism. Even those who are not involved as government or faction leaders may have benefited from conflict in terms of power and prestige sufficiently to develop a 'political-criminal nexus' between the governing establishment and the criminal underworld so powerful its demands have to be taken into account (Godson, 2003: 260). In states like South Africa and East Timor, new elites, for instance among the black community or resistance leaders, benefit from the inequitable structures of the old system. Peacebuilding does little to affect these dynamics (Cheng, 2013: 73).

While scholars in the transformative turn place much faith in the resistant capability of communities and grass-roots organisations to alter social structures, their repertoires of action are often subtle and non-confrontational forms of self-exclusion or boycott (Fatogoma, 2017: 18–19). By contrast, the most powerful informal elites have much broader repertoires of action. They enjoy power in the classic Weberian sense of the capacity to realise their will even where others oppose it – they have sufficiently loyal and clear constituencies to mobilise public demonstrations, can amass sufficient means of control or coercion to deploy strategic violence to maintain or alter the balance of resources (Boyle, 2009). They can credibly wield the threat of capital flight, while political parties function as tools of their entrenched interests. While the putative majority beneficiaries of transformative justice are diffuse and latent, the minority of elites are easier to organise and more coherent. These sub-state vested interests have great bargaining leverage with state elites or peacebuilders, who may be too weak or too distant to confront them, to say nothing of the grass-roots actors TJ seeks to empower. Elites mobilise to counter economic reform or alternative welfare modalities. The post-conflict political economy calculus that emerges orients elites towards traditionally legitimate forms of patronage generation that undermines institutional governance models (Barma, 2012: 274).

In terms of transformative justice, this is most obviously problematic because most of the resources that would underpin a redistributive or welfarist approach to justice are employed in servicing patronage and clientelist practices. The tendency of elites to coalesce around a politics of stability instead of transformation also has other harmful knock-on effects that can stymie a transformative agenda. The manageable instability of elite settlements fosters short-term horizons as leaders try to maximise immediate returns over longer-term investment in infrastructure or people – it is more important to accommodate elite factions than to stimulate the sort of growth that conduces to structural reform (Di John, 2010: 24). Elites are seldom able to commit to singularly normative goals because maintaining the informal settlement usually means responding to elites and ignoring the needs of the masses (Brinkerhoff and Goldsmith, 2002: 9).

When we speak of transformative justice, we do so in an environment where domestic elites have a monopoly on power and where they have compelling reasons to promote short-term security over long-term development or transformation. Analysis of elites makes clear that their economic interests are born more out of issues of culture in under-institutionalised polities and the need for security than simple greed or familiar models of capitalist accumulation as the critical TJ literature implies. Even so, the pressures on them to adopt pro-poor policies are negligible. There are few obvious points where changing opportunity structures can influence or force formerly mobilised elites to prefer broad-based public goods provision to narrow patronage distribution or rent-seeking. Some do, however, exist.

Developmental and redistributive functions of elites

Elites can fulfil constructive redistributivist or welfarist roles in post-conflict societies. If they did not, then those top-down progressive policies we occasionally see in transitions like progressive taxation, quotas for employment or education, regional investment programmes or anti-discrimination legislation would be impossibilities, as opposed to rarities. Scholars in the transformative turn are blind to the possibilities for this (like the aforementioned land reform in Colombia) if their conceptualisation of elites remains uniformly pejorative and homogenised. Two possibilities in particular are worth considering. The first responds to the homogeneity question – while critical TJ discourse treats elites as an inherently interconnected and interchangeable oligarchy, this obscures divisions between them that are productive of transformative or reformist impulses. The second builds on this and addresses the pejorativeness question to assert the malleability of elite incentives given their reliance on the provision of at least some social goods to maintain their status.

To begin with productive divisions between elites: political scientists, development scholars and peacebuilders have long been aware that different types of elites exist, often with conflicting interests. For example, rural land-holding elites are often the most adamantly opposed to pro-poor policies to keep the price of agricultural labour cheap, while bureaucratic elites in the civil service are often relatively pro-poor in the interests of a more functional state (Hossain and Moore, 2002: 18–19). Transitional states are riven with such conflicts. Robins's examination of elites in Nepal reveals the disparity between elites promoting a high-caste Hindu ideal and newer Maoist elites in government opposed to exclusion on the basis of caste or ethnicity. Conflicts between landlords and the Communist Party of Nepal – Maoist over redistribution of the former's land illustrate how elite interests can clash and open opportunities to co-operate with some elites against others (Robins, 2012: 18). Similarly, the (admittedly unsatisfactory) progress made in relation to redistribution and restitution of land in South Africa reflects the clash of interest between African National Congress (ANC) political elites in post-apartheid governments that monopolised political power after 1994 and the white landowners who owned up to 87% of the land there (Evans, 2016: 10). In El Salvador post-conflict economic elites and military elites clashed over the reputational damage ongoing impunity for the latter had on national recovery in terms of investment (Kirschner and Von Stein, 2009: 294). The inevitability of clashes of interests is significant because, as noted above, the political settlement that is (re-)established after peace is not a one-off, enduring monolith – in the post-conflict period it is iterative as shifts in the economy, degree of statehood, international incentives, etc., affect the organisational cohesion of elites who came together to make peace. Transformation of any sort requires contestation and contention at elite level. Instead of empowering bottom-up groups exclusively, effective TJ might be that which exploits cleavages between reformist and conservative elites or allies with some of them.

In societies not divided vertically by class but horizontally by ethnicity, religion or clan, there is an even less homogenous elite culture. A typical feature is clashes of state elites (themselves divided, as noted above) attempting to extract from society, and local elites that block consolidation of effective authority at the centre (Lake and Fariss, 2014: 569). In many states, political life takes the form of an 'auction of loyalties' where competing provincial elites extract a price for their allegiance from divided state elites (De Waal, 2009: 103). The boundaries between the state and the local are not sharply demarcated but drawn and re-drawn through negotiations over the exercise of political and economic authority. In those typically hybrid states where interpenetration of state and local elites through patronage relationships or clientelism is the norm, a proper understanding of the potential for change requires close analysis of the conflicts between them as they promote projects that grant access to certain resources to some groups over others. One thing greater attention to the hybrid nature of most transitional states makes clear is that combinations of state, traditional and community structures produce the best welfare outcomes. Effective bottom-up TJ again should look to weigh in favour of reformist state elites against conservative rural elites where appropriate, or alternatively support local redistribution over the dispersal of resources to the metropolis.

Where elites are fragmented (and particularly where they have no concentrated revenue source like oil or minerals), ruling elites must work constructively to address the demands of constituencies and potential rivals in order to gain their political and financial support. These create the most propitious conditions for building strong institutions that extract revenue (taxation) from society and distribute benefits widely to broaden the national support base (Berg, 2012: 12). DFID and UKAID (2010: 5), for example, consistently 'highlight the role of contestation and bargaining between the state, elites and citizens in building the public institutions that deliver development'. The homogenised, broad cultural label of 'elites' found in the transformative TJ literature hides important distinctions of power and incentive that we risk not understanding as these distinctions and identities develop in response to the evolving settlement after peace.

These clashes are important because they remind us that any progress towards amelioration of unfair social structures will be less the product of rational design from the top down or successful agitation from the bottom up than the outcome of compromises struck between different elites. Relationships between the elite and public are, after all, to a greater or lesser extent reciprocal. Clientelistic practices deliver access to resources or governmental support to poor individuals or communities, and 'pork' for regions or groups can provide even broader general gains. Elite settlements cannot survive without a threshold degree of public support because otherwise they could not mobilise supporters. As Brinkerhoff and Goldsmith (2002: 2) put it, reciprocal traditions between elites and supporters that endure:

> usually do so because they provide some value to people. They are functional in the jargon of social science – or else they would disappear through disuse. One of the challenges of development is figuring out how to separate the de facto governance institutions that serve, or at least do not contradict, the majority's needs and well-being, from similar-looking institutions that block or even reverse improvements in social welfare.

In areas of limited statehood, these practices may constitute pockets of effective governance even in the midst of wider state failure (Leonard, 2010), and this conditions support for elites outside of those who simply extract natural resources. As such, 'elites can rarely take social constituencies for granted, they must maintain an ability to organise, persuade, command or inspire' (Whaites, 2008: 4). The elite politics of political representation disdained in the TJ literature as irrelevant to the needs of citizens is the tip of an iceberg – often below the waterline we will find 'followers' or 'masses' whose support is underpinned by a collective preoccupation with the economic and social well-being of the group. Public opinion can constrain even the most ostensibly exclusive or impregnable elite power (Etzioni-Halevy, 1993: 32).

The best prospects for transformation (or, at least, poverty alleviation or better provision of social minima) may therefore lie not with challenging elites, for that challenge is sure to fail given their indispensability to stability and social provision. Instead, bearing in mind (a) the transformative TJ focus on the rearticulation of norms and the empowerment of reform constituencies and (b) the importance of good governance for the poorest and most vulnerable, the best prospects for transformation may lie with binding existing elites' practices to a broader and more inclusive national project. Development actors in particular acknowledge that enhancing the incentives of elites to support inclusive long-term development is at the core of any pro-poor politics (DFID and UKAID, 2010: 8). Hossain and Moore (2002: 5), most notably, argue that elites hold the key to developing meaningful anti-poverty strategies not out of any altruistic ethos, but out of self-interest in a more effective state to better project their influence, a bigger economic cake to divide up between their clients or wider welfare provision to expand the client base (Hossain and Moore, 2002: 10). Inasmuch as transformative TJ aspires to truth commissions that diagnose socioeconomic ills, reparations programmes that conduce to broader welfare outcomes or grass-roots empowerment, the best results are likely to emanate from constructive dialogue with elites about solutions to structural inequality and the sorts of framing of economic justice issues that bind elites to a greater commitment to address them. The most powerful arguments are those that not only accord with shared norms about what is morally right, but which tap into notions of elite self-interest and common gains (Hossain and Moore, 2002: 10). Transformative aspirations like better education, housing and fertility control might better be justified in the instrumental language of development and economic growth than in terms of rights or of their intrinsic worth. Though the transformative turn emphasises bottom-up empowerment and resistance, better results may flow from activities that foreground some of the more inclusive elite incentives by foregrounding those 'persuasive narratives that justify policies that might reduce poverty in terms of the achievement of other broadly accepted goals' (Hossain and Moore, 2002: 16).

Conclusion

This chapter has argued that while transformative justice as a rough normative orientation can be commended for its greater responsiveness to the needs of communities than liberal-legalist forms of TJ, its scope is increasingly attracting criticism for being too conceptually opaque. A policy–practice gap is apparent in the divergence between vaguely stated aspirations for structural change and the methods by which it might be implemented. One of the biggest lacunae in the transformative justice literature is the treatment of elites, which are addressed parenthetically, if at all, in a homogenised and pejorative fashion that generates more heat than light. Because of this, it is far from clear that scholars and practitioners have the wherewithal to productively engage with those national- or local-level actors who enjoy direct control over events and whose decisions are the critical factor in shaping the political culture that conditions all possibilities for change. Peacebuilders, development agencies and democracy promoters have long acknowledged that the prospects for any norms, practices or structural changes they and domestic allies promote can only be realised if they understand how existing forms of economic and political organisation (like settlements based on patronage, pork, resource monopolies, clientelism) are shaped by, and reproduce, the interests of elites and their constituencies.

This chapter started with the assumption that it is *not* primarily 'the retributive roots and narrow agenda of its practitioners' that prevents the emergence of a practice that addresses social injustice (Robins, 2012: 21), though undoubtedly these have unduly limited the imaginary of justice. The primary impediment to change is not how justice is framed, but the conditions in which it must be conceptualised. While political institutions might change dramatically after transition, prior political, economic and social elites are likely to endure. While some may disappear, others may even emerge stronger, to say nothing of those who rise to prominence during the events preceding transition. In environments where elites have jealously guarded their privileges and their particular constituencies against attempts to redistribute wealth or opportunity on a wider basis, it is uncommon for them to voluntarily concede such advantages where they have the option not to concede. The political economy of clientelism, neo-patrimonialism and pork are underpinned by pressing security logics and culturally legitimate relations. Transformation requires an explicit and constantly reinforced resolve to challenge constraints imposed by historic and contemporary socio-political circumstances. Because critiques of TJ do not engage with this reality in anything but a superficial fashion, it results in significant interpretative errors when trying to understand why post-conflict conditions take the shape they do, most notably the imputations of primary culpability for socioeconomic stasis to the field itself. If the proposals truth commissions, reparations programmes or grass-roots actors formulate do not reflect at least some interests of at least some of these elites, their changing balances of power and shifting informal alignments, then it will appear superfluous.

Conflict with some elites is inevitable, but not necessarily all – what is essential for transformative TJ is first to identify and second to work with those elites willing to balance construction with extraction, support for their constituencies with other constituencies in common self-interest, who prefer more inclusive settlements to exclusive ones. Reynolds posits a realistic, if sobering, scope for amelioration (if not transformation) of society when he argues that '[i]f elite dominance is to be the reality, perhaps the best that one can hope for is that the relevant elites will decide to prefer long-term stability and state-building to short-term partisan advantage' (Reynolds, 2005: 65). If transformative justice is to become meaningfully prescriptive and develop some means-end forms of analysis, it needs a research agenda that foregrounds how credible commitments elites make to the public, and the gradual expansion or greater inclusivity of the goods they deliver to retain or build public support, occur. Instead, by focusing to a large degree on the liberal legalism of TJ and the liberal prescriptions of democracy, the market and rule of law it is supposedly embedded in, we concentrate on formal political institutions at the expense of the socio-political informal structures of power and practice, most notably elite settlements or 'ways of doing things' that ultimately underwrite them and alter them beyond recognition.

To do these things, we need to develop an infrapolitics of TJ, one where the concealed sites of agency – culture, identity and self-preservation at the top – have a telling effect on more visible institutional or liberalising dynamics (to adapt phraseology in Richmond, 2011: 116). Such an infrapolitics might (a) provide a practical language for policy proposals, (b) generate a more productive analysis of the entrenched hierarchies to be challenged, and (c) help us recognise the limits of change in transitional environments. Instead of asking who TJ should be for (this has been well answered in the transformative justice literature), it would ask what elite actors (local/national, traditional/formal, economic/political) count, and how they interact to produce outcomes. It would shift analysis from the realm of victim-centred values and transformative norms, where we are comfortable, to the arena of compromises and negotiations, where we are not. Indeed, while the bottom-up grass-roots actors transformative TJ theorists wish to empower are disparate, those political, economic and institutional elites who possess concentrated power may be easier targets to both identify and to focus reform efforts on. Though in no way dismissive of grass-roots empowerment, it remains to be seen whether a literature that has fetishised the local, the bottom-up and subaltern resistance can mimic the pragmatic embrace of elites we see increasingly in development and peacebuilding discourses.

References

Aciru, Monica. (2017) 'Rethinking Post-Truth Commissions: Empowering Local Capacities to Shape Post-Truth Commissions Discourse'. *Human Rights & International Legal Discourse* 11(1): 71–82.

Aguirre, Daniel and Irene Pietropaoli. (2008) 'Gender Equality, Development and Transitional Justice: The Case of Nepal'. *International Journal of Transitional Justice* 2(3): 356–377.

Akmeemana, Saku and Doug Porter. (2015) 'Securing a New Ordering of Power in Timor-Leste: The Role of Subnational Spending'. In Sue Ingram, Lia Kent and Andrew McWilliam (eds), *A New Era? Timor-Leste After the UN*, 117–140. Acton: Australian National University Press.

Arnould, Valerie. (2016) 'Transitional Justice in Peacebuilding: Dynamics of Contestation in the DRC'. *Journal of Intervention and Statebuilding* 10(3): 321–338.

Aroussi, Sahla and Stef Vandeginste. (2013) 'When Interests Meet Norms: The Relevance of Human Rights for Power-sharing'. *International Journal of Human Rights* 17(2): 183–203.

Arthur, Paige. (2009) 'How "Transitions" Reshaped Human Rights: A Conceptual History of Transitional Justice'. *Human Rights Quarterly* 31(2): 321–367.

Balint, Jennifer, Kristian Lasslett and Kate Macdonald. (2017) '"Post-conflict" Reconstruction, the Crimes of the Powerful and Transitional Justice'. *State Crime Journal* 6 (1): 4–12.

Barma, Nazneen. (2012) 'Peace-building and the Predatory Political Economy of Insecurity: Evidence from Cambodia, East Timor and Afghanistan'. *Conflict, Security & Development* 12(3): 273–298.

Bates, Robert H. (2015) *When Things Fell Apart*. Cambridge: Cambridge University Press.

Berdal, Mats. (2009) *Building Peace After War*. Abingdon: Routledge.

Berg, Louis-Alexandre. (2012) 'Guns, Laws and Politics: The Political Foundations of Rule of Law and Security Sector Reform'. *Hague Journal on the Rule of Law* 4(1): 4–30.

Bhuta, Nehal. (2010) 'New Modes and Orders: The Difficulties of a *Jus Post Bellum* of Constitutional Transformation'. *University of Toronto Law Journal* 60(3): 799–854.

Bliesemann de Guevara, Berit. (2010) 'Introduction: The Limits of Statebuilding and the Analysis of State-formation'. *Journal of Intervention and Statebuilding* 4(2): 111–128.

Boege, Volker, M. Anne Brown and Kevin Clements. (2009) 'Hybrid Political Orders, Not Fragile States'. *Peace Review* 21(1): 13–21.

Borer, Tristan Anne. (2003) 'A Taxonomy of Victims and Perpetrators: Human Rights and Reconciliation in South Africa'. *Human Rights Quarterly* 25(4): 1088–1116.

Boyle, Michael. (2009) 'Explaining Strategic Violence after Wars'. *Studies in Conflict & Terrorism* 32(3): 209–236.

Bratton, Michael, and Nicolas Van de Walle. (1994) 'Neopatrimonial Regimes and Political Transitions in Africa'. *World Politics* 46(4): 453–489.

Brinkerhoff, Derick and Arthur Goldsmith. (2002) *Clientelism, Patrimonialism and Democratic Governance: An Overview and Framework for Assessment and Programming*. Washington, DC: USAID.

Brown, Kris and Fionnuala Ní Aoláin. (2014) 'Through the Looking Glass: Transitional Justice Futures through the Lens of Nationalism, Feminism and Transformative Change'. *International Journal of Transitional Justice* 9(1): 127–149.

Call, Charles. (2008) 'Building States to Build Peace? A Critical Analysis'. *Journal of Peacebuilding & Development* 4(1): 60–74.

Call, Charles. (2012) *Why Peace Fails: The Causes and Prevention of Civil War Recurrence.* Washington, DC: Georgetown University Press.

Cheng, Christine. (2013) 'Private and Public Interests: Informal Actors, Informal Influence, and Economic Order after War'. In Mats Berdal and Dominik Zaum (eds), *Political Economy of Statebuilding: Power after Peace*, 63–78. Abingdon: Routledge.

Craig, David and Doug Porter. (2014) *Post-conflict Pacts and Inclusive Political Settlements: Institutional Perspectives from Solomon Islands*, ESID Working Paper No. 39. Manchester: Effective States and Inclusive Development Research.

Dahl, Robert. (1958) 'A Critique of the Ruling Elite Model'. *American Political Science Review* 52(2): 463–469.

De Waal, Alex. (2009) 'Mission Without End? Peacekeeping in the African Political Marketplace'. *International Affairs* 85(1): 99–113.

DFID and UKAID. (2010) 'The Politics of Poverty: Elites, Citizens and States', www.oecd.org/derec/unitedkingdom/48688822.pdf [accessed 11 July 2018].

Di John, Jonathan. (2010) *Conceptualizing the Causes and Consequences of Failed States: A Critical Review of the Literature.* London: Crisis States Research Centre.

Di John, Jonathan and James Putzel. (2009) *Political Settlements Issues Paper.* Birmingham: Governance and Social Development Research.

Drexler, Elizabeth. (2013) 'Fatal Knowledges: The Social and Political Legacies of Collaboration and Betrayal in Timor-Leste'. *International Journal of Transitional Justice* 7(1): 74–94.

Etzioni-Halevy, Eva. (1993) *The Elite Connection: Problems and Potential of Western Democracy.* Cambridge: Polity Press.

Evans, Matthew. (2016) 'Structural Violence, Socioeconomic Rights and Transformative Justice'. *Journal of Human Rights* 15(1): 1–20.

Evans, Tony. (1998) 'Introduction: Power, Hegemony and the Universalization of Human Rights'. In Tony Evans (ed.), *Human Rights Fifty Years On: A Reappraisal*, 2–24. Manchester: Manchester University Press.

Fatogoma, Adou DjaneDit. (2017) 'Resistance to Transitional Justice in the Context of Political Violence in Côte d'Ivoire'. In Briony Jones and Julie Bernath (eds), *Resistance and Transitional Justice*, 17–34. Abingdon: Routledge.

Fletcher, Laurel and Harvey Weinstein. (2002) 'Violence and Social Repair: Rethinking the Contribution of Justice to Reconciliation'. *Human Rights Quarterly* 24(3): 573–639.

Franzki, Hannah and Maria Carolina Olarte. (2014) 'Understanding the Political Economy of Transitional Justice: A Critical Theory Perspective'. In Susanne Buckley-Zistel, Teresa Koloma Beck, Christian Braun and Friederike Mieth (eds), *Transitional Justice Theories*, 201–221. Abingdon: Routledge.

Godson, Roy. (2003) 'Transnational Crime, Corruption, and Security'. In Michael E. Brown (ed.), *Grave New World: Security Challenges in the 21st Century*, 259–278. Washington, DC: Georgetown University Press.

Gready, Paul and Simon Robins. (2014) 'From Transitional to Transformative Justice: A New Agenda for Practice'. *International Journal of Transitional Justice* 8(3): 339–361.

Gready, Paul and Simon Robins. (2017) 'Rethinking Civil Society and Transitional Justice: Lessons from Social Movements and "New" Civil Society'. *International Journal of Human Rights* 21(7): 956–975.

Hansen, Thomas. (2014) 'The Vertical and Horizontal Expansion of Transitional'. In Susanne Buckley-Zistel, Teresa Koloma Beck, Christian Braun and Friederike Mieth (eds), *Transitional Justice Theories*, 105–124. Abingdon: Routledge.

Hossain, Naomi and Mick Moore. (2002) *Arguing for the Poor: Elites and Poverty in Developing Countries.* Brighton: Institute of Development Studies.

Jayasuriya, Kanishka. 2003. 'Beyond Institutional Fetishism: From the Developmental to the Regulatory State'. *New Political Economy* 10(3): 381–387.

Jones, Briony and Julie Bernath. (2017) 'Introduction: Resistance and Transitional Justice'. In Briony Jones and Julie Bernath (eds), *Resistance and Transitional Justice*, 1–14. Abingdon: Routledge.

Khan, Mushtaq. (2010) *Political Settlements and the Governance of Growth-enhancing Institutions.* London: School of Oriental and African Studies.

Kirschner, Shanna A. and Jana Von Stein. (2009) 'The Pieces of Peacemaking: Understanding Implementation of Civil War Settlements'. *Civil Wars* 11(3): 279–301.

Lake, David and Christopher Fariss. (2014) 'Why International Trusteeship Fails: The Politics of External Authority in Areas of Limited Statehood'. *Governance* 27(4): 569–587.

Leclercq, Sidney. (2017) 'Injustice through Transitional Justice? Subversion Strategies in Burundi's Peace Process and Postconflict Developments'. *International Journal of Transitional Justice* 11(3): 525–544.

Leonard, David. (2010) '"Pockets" of Effective Agencies in Weak Governance States: Where Are They Likely and Why Does it Matter?'. *Public Administration and Development* 30(2): 91–101.

Mac Ginty, Roger and Gurchathen Sanghera. (2012) 'Hybridity in Peacebuilding and Development: An Introduction'. *Journal of Peacebuilding & Development* 7(2): 3–8.

Madsen, Michael Rask and Mikkel Jarle Christensen. (2016) 'Global Actors: Networks, Elites and Institutions'. In *Oxford Research Encyclopedia of Politics*, http://politics.oxfordre.com/view/10.1093/acrefore/9780190228637.001.0001/acrefore-9780190228637-e-9 [accessed 11 July 2018].

Mamdani, Mahmood. (1996) 'Reconciliation without Justice'. *Southern African Review of Books* 46(1): 3–5.

Mann, Michael. (1986) *The Resources of Social Power I: A History of Power from the Beginning to A.D. 1760.* Cambridge: Cambridge University Press.

McAuliffe, Pádraig. (2017a) 'Localised Justice and Structural Transformation: How New Approaches to Transitional Justice Pull in Different Directions'. *Human Rights & International Legal Discourse* 9(1): 96–107.

McAuliffe, Pádraig. (2017b) *Transformative Transitional Justice and the Malleability of Post-conflict States.* Cheltenham: Edward Elgar.

McAuliffe, Pádraig. (2017c) 'Dividing the Spoils: The Impact of Power Sharing on Possibilities for Socioeconomic Transformation in Postconflict States'. *International Journal of Transitional Justice* 11(2): 197–218.

McEvoy, Kieran and Lorna McGregor. (2008) 'Transitional Justice from Below: An Agenda for Research, Policy and Praxis'. In Kieran McEvoy and Lorna McGregor (eds), *Transitional Justice from Below: Grassroots Activism and the Struggle for Change*, 1–14. Oxford: Hart Publishing.

Meister, Robert. (2011) *After Evil: A Politics of Human Rights.* New York: Columbia University Press.

Migdal, Joel. (1988) *Strong Societies and Weak States: State-Society Relations and State Capabilities in the Third World.* Princeton, NJ: Princeton University Press.

Miller, Zinaida. (2008) 'Effects of Invisibility: In Search of the "Economic" in Transitional Justice'. *International Journal of Transitional Justice* 2(3): 266–291.

Moffett, Luke. (2017) 'Reparations in Transitional Justice: Justice or Political Compromise'. *Human Rights & International Legal Discourse* 11(1): 59–70.

Mosca, Gaetano. (1939) *The Ruling Class.* New York: McGraw-Hill.

Nilsson, Manuela, and Laura Taylor. (2017) 'Applying the Security-Development Nexus on the Ground: Land Restitution in Colombia'. *Conflict, Security & Development* 17(1): 73–89.

North, Douglass. (2007) *Limited Access Orders in the Developing World: A New Approach to the Problems of Development.* Washington, DC: World Bank Publications.

Organisation for Economic Co-operation and Development (OECD). (2008) *From Fragility to Resilience: Concepts and Dilemmas of State Building in Fragile States.* Paris: OECD.

Ottendörfer, Eva. (2013) 'Contesting International Norms of Transitional Justice: The Case of Timor Leste'. *International Journal of Conflict and Violence* 7(1): 24–35.

Paffenholz, Thania. (2015) 'Unpacking the Local Turn in Peacebuilding: A Critical Assessment Towards an Agenda for Future Research'. *Third World Quarterly* 36(5): 857–874.

Reynolds, Andrew. (2005) 'Constitutional Medicine'. *Journal of Democracy* 16(1): 54–68.

Richmond, Oliver. (2011) 'De-romanticising the Local, De-mystifying the International: Hybridity in Timor Leste and the Solomon Islands'. *Pacific Review* 24(1): 115–136.

Robins, Simon. (2012) 'Transitional Justice as an Elite Discourse: Human Rights Practice Where the Global Meets the Local in Post-conflict Nepal'. *Critical Asian Studies* 44(1): 3–30.

Rothschild, Amy. (2017) 'Victims versus Veterans: Agency, Resistance and Legacies of Timor-Leste's Truth Commission'. *International Journal of Transitional Justice* 11(3): 443–462.

Saeed, Huma and Stephan Parmentier. (2017) 'When Rabbits are in Charge of Carrots: Land Grabbing, Transitional Justice and Economic-state Crime in Afghanistan'. *State Crime Journal* 6(1): 13–36.

Salmon, Jago and Catherine Anderson. (2013) 'Elites and Statebuilding'. In David Chandler and Timothy Sisk (eds), *Routledge Handbook of International Statebuilding*, 42–51. Abingdon: Routledge.

Sandoval, Clara. (2017) 'Reflections on the Transformative Potential of Transitional Justice and the Nature of Social Change in Times of Transition'. In Roger Duthie and Paul Seils (eds), *Justice Mosaics: How Context Shapes Transitional Justice in Fractured Societies*, 166–201. New York: International Center for Transitional Justice.

Seixas, Eunice Castro. (2013) 'How Activists See Civil Society and the Political Elite in Bosnia: Relevance to Prospects of Transitional Justice'. In Olivera Simić and Zala Volčič (eds), *Transitional Justice and Civil Society in the Balkans*, 69–86. New York: Springer.

Sriram, Chandra Lekha. (2014) 'Liberal Peacebuilding and Transitional Justice: What Place for Socioeconomic Concerns?'. In Dustin Sharp (ed.), *Justice and Economic Violence in Transition*, 27–49. New York: Springer.

Subotić, Jelena. (2014) 'Bargaining Justice'. In Susanne Buckley-Zistel, Teresa Koloma Beck, Christian Braun and Friederike Mieth (eds), *Transitional Justice Theories*, 127–143. Abingdon: Routledge.

Tilly, Charles. (1990) *Coercion, Capital, and European States, AD 990–1990.* Oxford: Blackwell.

Tull, Denis and Andreas Mehler. (2005) 'The Hidden Costs of Power-sharing: Reproducing Insurgent Violence in Africa'. *African Affairs* 104(416): 375–398.

Weber, Max (1947) *The Theory of Social and Economic Organization* (trans. A.M. Henderson and Talcott Parsons). New York: Oxford University Press.

Whaites, Alan. (2008) *States in Development: Understanding State-building*. London: Department for International Development.
Zuckerman, Alan. (1977) 'The Concept "Political Elite": Lessons from Mosca and Pareto'. *Journal of Politics* 39(2): 324–344.
Zürcher, Christoph, Carrie Manning and Kristie Evenson. (2013) *Costly Democracy: Peacebuilding and Democratization After War*. Stanford, CA: Stanford University Press.

6 Culture

The missing link in transitional justice; an imperative for transformative justice

Cathy Bollaert

Introduction

Transitional justice has been coming under growing critique by transformative justice scholars for its failure to address the social and economic inequalities at the expense of less powerful groups when addressing the legacy of gross violation of human rights for countries in transition (Muvingi, 2009; Gready and Robins, 2014; McAuliffe, 2017). Shifting from the largely legal approach of transitional justice and the emphasis it has historically placed on state and institutional building, transformative justice emphasises local agency and the promotion of social and economic transformation which tend to be prioritised by victims and formerly marginalised groups, which, if left unaddressed, can contribute to the return of violence. Given the emphasis that transformative justice gives to challenging structural inequalities and their associated power relations, this chapter argues that to be holistic in its transformative agenda it also needs to engage with culture and the diversity of worldviews this carries with it. Using South Africa as a case study, the chapter explores the influence that different systems of meaning-making had on the Truth and Reconciliation Commission (TRC) and on transitional justice and peacebuilding more broadly. These differences were made apparent through South Africa's truth recovery process (Tutu, 1999; Krog, 2008, 2015; Shutte, 2009a).

Talking about cultural differences can sometimes be seen as politically incorrect, possibly even racist given the way, historically, it was tied to biology and (ab)used to support colonialism and justify the subjugation of Africans and other forms of racism. In moving away from theories that reinforce racial difference the language of universalism, as expressed in 'universal values' and 'universal rights', which emphasise similarity, is increasingly being used. While this is important for protecting human dignity, implicit in such language is the assumption that all societies share similar systems of (often Western) meaning-making. By failing to uncover and understand the worldviews within which other societies live, finding contextually relevant solutions to peacebuilding is impeded. It also undermines a person's sense of identity and dignity; particularly those from previously marginalised groups.

The identity-culture-worldview nexus

Identity, culture and worldview are complex, dynamic and interconnected concepts. In considering the impact this nexus has on transitional justice it is necessary to define each of these terms. Within the literature there are three broad schools of thought relating to how identity is understood, including primordialism, instrumentalism and constructivism (Arthur, 2011; Malan, 2011; Eriksen, 2001). In this chapter, identity is located within the constructivist paradigm which argues that identity is not something that is chosen or innate but is produced and constructed through the narratives that people use to interpret their lived reality (Lawler, 2008). Nonetheless, identity is the unit of survival that speaks to one's sense of safety and belonging in the world including physically, psychologically, socially and even spiritually (Maslow, 1954; Northrup, 1989). Identities are not fixed but understood to be flexible, emerging and continually shifting as the context in which they are embedded changes (Arthur, 2011; Weedon, 2004; Eriksen, 2001).

Integral to understanding identity is the culture in which it is embedded. Drawing from Geertz's (1973) definition of culture, Ross defines culture as 'a shared system of meaning that helps people make sense of the world in which they live and interpret the actions of others' (Ross, 2009: 3; see also Berger and Luckmann, 1966). It includes shared meanings of how the self and one's reality are interpreted, as well as shared religious and spiritual beliefs, group values, and social rules of conduct (Staub, 1996: 117). It is expressed through a range of rituals, symbols, language, emotions and customs, and is embodied in social institutions such as religious, educational, legal, and security systems (Staub, 1996; Eriksen, 2001; Ross, 2007, 2009; Bryan and Stevenson, 2009).

Distinguishing identity from culture, identity can be understood as one's unit of survival where one's sense of self and belonging is derived. While culture, on the other hand, can be understood to be that which houses the rules and behaviours governing and determining group membership (Ross, 2007, 2009). Further to this, culture is also what is deemed as logical or common-sense within a group. Significantly, a failure to understand the actions and behaviours of the 'other' can lead to stereotyping and the hardening of intergroup boundaries (Avruch and Black, 1993).

Culture is integral to maintaining the coherency and ability of a group or society to function and survive and can contribute to exacerbating conflict (Bryan and McIntosh, 2005; Ross, 2007, 2009; Atran, 2010). This is well illustrated in the intensity of violence that ensued following the printing of cartoons of the Prophet Mohammed by the French magazine, *Charlie Hebdo* (BBC News, 2015a; *The Guardian*, 2015), the furore and threat of violence that followed the painting of (then-president of South Africa) Zuma with his genitals exposed (*Mail and Guardian Online*, 2012; Times Live, 2012), and the hostility and sometimes violent confrontation in Northern Ireland over the meaning and practice of certain symbols and traditions (Bryan, 2000). Integral to such conflicts are a society's or group's sacred values which Atran (2010: xiv) defines as those 'deeper cultural values that are bound up with people's identity which often trump other values, particularly economic ones'. Citing the example of Islamic suicide bombers, he argues sacred values are fundamental to understanding why people are willing to martyr their lives for a cause. While these values are often rooted in religion they can also be related to sustaining traditions and values such as justice and honour. As they speak to the core of one's sense of self and security in the world (identity), efforts to protect them can provide the impetus for instigating violence.

Pointing to a lack of conceptual clarity within the literature between culture and worldview, a third observation relates to how Ross (2009) likens culture to worldview. If culture is all encompassing of our social world, as suggested in this definition of culture, it can be rendered useless. While not replacing culture, differentiating between the two allows one to look more deeply at how people within a particular group interpret the world around them. Distinguishing between culture and worldview, worldview can be understood to be embedded in culture and acts to inform the way a society is organised. Significantly, a society's cultural expressions including its institutes, rules, rituals, customs, symbols and language communicate a worldview held by an individual or group. For example, in the case of apartheid South Africa, beliefs of superiority and privilege based on 'scientific' theories of racism informed and justified its racist institutions. Although deeply intertwined, this suggests that worldview has a deeper reach than culture.

Deeply intertwined with culture, worldview is understood as the ontological and epistemological assumptions through which one's social reality is interpreted (Naugle, 2002; Goffman, 1986; Pepper, 1942; Clark, 1989; Docherty, 2001, Berger and Luckmann, 1966; Koltko-Rivera, 2004). It refers to the way in which the nature of reality is interpreted and to how knowledge is attained and can be known (Guba and Lincoln, 1998). This can be through the structures of authority, tradition, the senses, rationality, science, intuition, divination or revelation (Koltko-Rivera, 2004). As the infrastructure for deeper meaning-making, it contains the scripts and assumptions which inform how one behaves and engages with one's social reality and how the behaviours of others are interpreted. It provides meaning and coherence to the world, without which reality cannot be understood. This has led to the distinction between an objective or scientific worldview and a spiritual or interconnected worldview. These dimensions are where one places one's sense of security and well-being (identity): i.e. in scientific and objective knowledge or in the spiritual realm. Significantly, there is growing recognition of the way in which ontological and epistemological differences are contributing to the breakdown of transitional justice and peacebuilding processes in non-Western societies (Palmer, Jones and Viebach, 2015; Merry, 2006, Sriram, 2007; Kelsall, 2009; Krog, 2008, 2015).

Worldview diversity in South Africa

South Africa is an amalgam of diverse cultures. To understand how the critiques surrounding South Africa's truth commission are shaped by ontological difference, it is helpful to deconstruct idealised conceptions of an objective and interconnected worldview. Recognising there are multiple strands of thought within

Western philosophy I will focus on two dominant views that have shaped South African society: the Western liberal worldview and nationalism. It is likely that, with their European heritage, a scientific or Western worldview will be more dominant among 'white' South Africans, while an interconnected worldview is argued to be more reflective of an indigenous African way of being in the world. Before continuing it should be recognised that an individual's worldview is more complex than these idealised forms connote. When individuals with different ontological assumptions encounter each other these worldviews can overlap, fuse or possibly compete. As a result, hybrid identities can develop in which individuals may appear to hold contradictory worldviews. The chapter applies this analysis to investigate the way in which they shaped the proceedings of the TRC and to interpret some of the criticisms it received.

The Western liberal worldview is rooted in the Enlightenment which was a period in European history (late 1600s to early 1800s) which challenged the authority of the Church, perceived ignorance and superstitious beliefs (Gay, 1971; Tarnas, 1991). This resulted in the separation of the scientific world from the spiritual world. Underpinned by objectivist ontology, the Enlightenment promoted rationalism, secularism, progress, truth that could be scientifically quantified, individualism, freedom and personal autonomy (Tarnas, 1991; Balcomb, 2014; Gay, 1971; Nürnberger, 2007). Its valuing of scientific experimentation, progress, efficiency, improvement and productivity drove many of the inventions of the agricultural and industrial revolutions (Gay, 1971; Nürnberger, 2007). Furthermore, the Enlightenment also promoted what was referred to as the 'ideal society' (Gay, 1971: 56). This was a vision for a secular society that followed the rule of law for political and legal purposes and not on the basis of religion or tribe (Gay, 1971). This speaks to Max Weber's notion of rational-legal authority, in which claims to legitimacy or authority are rooted in rules that are legally or contractually determined (Bendix, 1977). Flowing from this are social values of justice, equality, freedom and order (Dunne, 2006). These values are central to informing the Western liberal approach to peacebuilding which emphasises individual freedom and prioritises the rule of law, human rights, good governance, social and economic development, the building of state institutions, and concern for social justice (Richmond, 2011; Richmond and Mitchell, 2012). Although a Western liberal worldview emphasises the individual, there is also a collective element that sees itself working for the benefit of the collective and its security (Hernández-Truyol, 2004; Dunne, 2006).

The Enlightenment also contributed to the development of nationalism (Eriksen, 1997; Anderson, 1983; Halliday, 2006). With the formation of the secular society Anderson (1983) argues that a new sense of community, which nationalism spoke to, was needed. This, he argues, was supported by capitalism and the introduction of print technology. In addition to this, nationalism was also influenced by Romanticism, which challenged the rapidly growing faith in reason, and the attitude of superiority that accompanied it (Tarnas, 1991; Eriksen, 1997; Gelvin, 2005). In doing so, Romanticism maintained a more spiritual view of the world and is what inspired much of the arts in Europe during the eighteenth and early nineteenth centuries including music, literature and architecture. However, as Tarnas (1991) explains, Romanticism shared the Enlightenment's rejection of institutional hierarchies and forced belief, and its promotion of individualism, quest for human freedom and interest in exploration. Within nationalism, freedom and self-determination were interpreted within the framework of a national identity (Smith, 1983; Halliday, 2006). In turn, this influenced the nationalist ideal for every group to have the right to defend its language, religion and other aspects of its culture (Eriksen, 1997; Halliday, 2006). Influenced by the Enlightenment and Romanticism, nationalism promotes individualism and freedom within an autonomous but unified community (Gelvin, 2005; Smith, 2001, Halliday, 2006). Further to this, it promotes national pride, loyalty to the state or collective, cultural and national unity, and attachment to one's ancestral history (Smith, 2001). Distinguishing between a Western, civic and ethnic nationalism (which represent idealised forms of nationalism), Smith (2001: 39) explains that civic nationalism emphasises the rational individual within a unified collective that is bound by common laws while within ethnic nationalism the collective transcends the individual.

In contrast to a scientific worldview, an interconnected worldview is underpinned by an ontology that sees the physical and spiritual world as unified and interconnected (Turner, 1977; Mbiti, 1969; Bediako, 2004; Balcomb, 2014; Krog, 2008, 2015; Ashforth, 2005; Nürnberger, 2007). It does not separate the spiritual world from the material or physical world in the way that it was separated during the period of the European Enlightenment. To understand the interconnected worldview it is useful to turn to the work of Harold Turner (1977), who develops several related key features.

First, Turner (1977) explains that within the interconnected worldview there is a deep-rooted belief in a spiritual world which consists of spiritual forces or beings greater and more powerful than oneself. Speaking to an identity rooted in 'spiritual insecurity' a greater power outside oneself is needed to maintain a sense of safety and security in such a world (Nürnberger, 2007; Ashforth, 2005). Further to this, Turner (1977) explains that this world consists of both benevolent and malevolent forces. Benevolent forces include one's ancestors, as well as other spirits and divinities. Malevolent forces include evil spirits, demons, and the occult power of witches and wizards. Further to this, witchcraft is widely understood as akin to jealousy and can be used to deter those who are seen to be successful (Ashforth, 2005). This is illustrated in the report of a traditional healer in South Africa who interpreted the bones that appeared outside her house as a sign of jealousy for the way she was healing people (*Daily Sun*, 2015).

Second, in an interconnected worldview Turner (1977) explains that the physical world is seen as a reflection of the spiritual world whereby the physical acts as a vehicle through which spiritual power can be accessed. One is able to share in the power of these forces both whilst alive and after death, and able to form a relationship with the benevolent spirits to gain protection from malevolent forces. These serve to strengthen an individual's and society's resistance to potential malice (Zulu and Wilhelm-Solomon, 2015). It is here that the role of ancestors becomes important, because, while their physical bodies are dead, they are nonetheless perceived in some respects as being alive (the 'living dead'), maintaining their benevolent support of the community in which they formerly lived (Nürnberger, 2007). Consequently, security and well-being in the world are attained through submission to elders and those in authority, and ultimately to ancestors whose role is to protect and maintain stability in everyday life.

Protocols, customs and rituals are closely observed to ensure protection from witchcraft and the malevolent world (Zulu and Wilhelm-Solomon, 2015). For example, Zulu and Wilhelm-Solomon (2015) explain how among African migrants to the city of Johannesburg a person's misfortune is interpreted either as a result of 'metaphysical disorder' (which can include ancestors who are angry with the living for failing to observe necessary cultural rituals) or exposure to malevolent spirits. To ensure protection from misfortune, and to ensure one's sense of safety and well-being in the world, rituals aimed at protection, purification and healing are practised. The relevance of rituals in securing protection is further illustrated in an incident surrounding a rescue mission of South African mineworkers trapped in a container. The families of those who were trapped attributed the failed rescue attempts to failure to conduct a particular ritual, which is said to be carried out at all mines in the region (*Mail and Guardian Online*, 2016). The strength of these beliefs is well evidenced in the Marikana shootings. Following a consultation with a *sangoma* (someone who is 'trained to communicate with and utilise the powers of ancestors in diagnosing a disease or mishap'; see Ashforth, 2005: 53), some of the victims believed they would be protected from the bullets if they used a certain medicine associated with these practices (locally known as *muthi*) which would turn the bullets into water (Bond, 2014; ENCA, 2014).

Within this worldview, the motive of the instigator behind an event becomes the interpretative framework through which issues pertaining to poverty, suffering, ill health, early death and personal difficulties can be understood and resolved (Turner, 1977; Ashforth, 2005). Zulu and Wilhelm-Solomon (2015: 140–145) cite several examples including that of a migrant woman living in poverty who interpreted the miscarriage of her twins as the result of being bewitched or cursed by someone living in the same building as her, and the labourer who attributed the swelling of his feet to someone who had bewitched him following the disappearance and then sudden reappearance of his work boots. This interpretative framework is fundamentally different to a scientific ontology which is concerned with *what* is the causal factor and not *who* caused it (Nürnberger, 2007). As Ashforth (2005) notes, this contributes to the complexity surrounding the issue of personal responsibility. It can also compete with values within individualism which prioritise personal responsibility and accountability (Blankenburgh, 2013).

The philosophy of *ubuntu* is an expression of an interconnected worldview that shaped South Africa's TRC (Truth and Reconciliation Commission, 1999a; Munyaka and Motlhabi, 2009; Krog, 2008; Tutu, 1999; Shutte, 2009b). Although the term *ubuntu* is an isiZulu term, the concept is expressed in a number of languages in South Africa and across Africa (Mbiti, 1969; Munyaka and Motlhabi, 2009; Kenyon, 2015). Reflecting a collectivist sense of identity, it recognises that the well-being of one's society, community and spiritual worlds are inextricably intertwined and cannot be detached (Munyaka and Motlhabi, 2009; Krog, 2008; Tutu, 1999, Mbiti, 1969; Shutte, 2009b). It encapsulates what it means to be human and speaks to a reality or identity that only makes sense in relation to others (Munyaka and Motlhabi, 2009; Murithi, 2009; Shutte, 2009a, 2009b; Tutu, 1999; Krog, 2008; Metz, 2011). Further to this, one's sense of value, dignity and fulfilment in life is found in relationship with others. As a worldview *ubuntu* also serves to inform moral conduct and what is seen to be acceptable forms of behaviour. Strong emphasis is given to placing communal interests above individual interests and on maintaining positive relationships. Respect and compassion for others are considered the most essential values from which other values such as loyalty, hospitality, tolerance, generosity and courtesy stem (Munyaka and Motlhabi, 2009; Shutte, 2009b; Metz, 2011; Masina, 2000). Centred on people and relationships it encourages forgiveness and openness to others (Munyaka and Motlhabi, 2009; Murithi, 2009; Shutte, 2009a).

The concept of *ubuntu* presented above is an idealised depiction of the philosophy. The possibility of individuals functioning within this worldview yet committing crimes and bringing harm to a society should be acknowledged (Shutte, 2009a). Munyaka and Motlhabi (2009) explain that the extent of the violence witnessed in many South African communities laying claim to this worldview is due to the degradation of values within the *ubuntu* worldview. The reasons they cite for this breakdown include: the impact of colonialism and the loss of land that accompanied it; the impact apartheid had on stripping people of their dignity and identity; the influence of Western interpretations of reality on 'black' Africans as they moved into urban areas; and the impact that conflict has on diminishing the value of life (Munyaka and Motlhabi, 2009). Despite this, Ashforth asserts it is essential to understand the gravity of these beliefs; otherwise, he warns, 'the social and political dynamics of vast portions of humanity will remain incomprehensible' (Ashforth, 2005: xiv).

The Truth and Reconciliation Commission: a worldview perspective

The South African Truth and Reconciliation Commission, while heralded for its contribution to the society's peaceful transition, has received extensive criticism for the way it interpreted its mandate (Asmal, 2000; Boraine, 2000; Borer, 2004; Gibson, 2004; Mamdani, 2000). However, receiving little attention in the literature is the extent to which these interpretations relate to worldview and how one interprets one's reality. Drawing from the idealised delineation of worldviews described above, the aim of this section is to explore the significance of worldview in South Africa's TRC. In doing so, three core aspects of transitional justice will be examined using a worldview lens, namely: reconciliation, accountability, and nation-building.

One of the challenges the Commission faced related to how the concept of reconciliation was interpreted (Wilson, 2001; Hamber, 2002; Evans, 2018). Within the TRC there were broadly two competing visions of what was meant by reconciliation, i.e. those who prioritised human rights and the rule of law, and those who prioritised the restoration of relationship. Reflecting the values within the Western liberal worldview, a human rights perspective saw reconciliation as possible only if social interactions were regulated through the rule of law. In contrast, for those coming from a relational perspective, reconciliation was only possibly on the basis of fostering positive interpersonal relationship and discovering the humanity in the 'other'. This speaks to an interconnected worldview in which the way to deal with the abuse of political power and prevent the recurrence of widespread human rights violations is to restore the humanity and relationship of the individuals involved (Shutte, 2009a; Kenyon, 2015). Significantly, this debate also raises the issue of human rights and how they are interpreted across different groups. As Kenyon (2015) points out, in a collective society human rights are interpreted in relation to belonging to the group and the wider collective. In contrast, a more individualised understanding of human rights tends to emphasise the autonomy of the individual. Nonetheless, by focusing on the interpersonal aspects of reconciliation, critics argue the TRC failed to deliver on victims' rights to justice (Chapman, 2008a, 2008b; Wilson, 2001).

This leads to a second discussion in relation to how transitional justice interprets the notion of nation-building. Those who interpreted the proceedings through the lens of human rights saw the TRC as a means to construct a new national identity on the basis of human rights as embedded in the South African Constitution (Wilson, 2001), whereas those following the logic of an interconnected worldview interpreted the reconstruction of a national identity from a more interpersonal level. In taking a relational approach, the Commission focused on the relationship between the victim and perpetrator, and emphasised their interconnectedness and common humanity (Tutu, 1999; Krog, 2008). In doing so, it was criticised for creating a victim identity that failed to hold perpetrators and beneficiaries accountable for the wrongs of the past and for failing to deliver on victims' rights to justice (Valji, 2004; Mamdani, 2000; Chapman, 2008a, 2008b; Wilson, 2001).

Further to this, Wilson (2001: 14–15) explains that by bringing victims and perpetrators together under a common humanity the nation was viewed as an organism in need of healing which, he argues, was the basis for creating a collective identity under the rubric of the Rainbow Nation.[1] However, this approach has received several critiques. First, Cockrell (1996) argues the metaphor the Rainbow Nation does not accommodate competing values, as it emphasises consensus-building while refraining from addressing what he refers to as the hard choices that a court of law is required to make (Wilson, 2001: 12). Second, whether or not nations can be healed in the same way individuals is the subject of strong debate

1 The Rainbow Nation was a term coined by Desmond Tutu, which served as a vision for national identity that united South Africans under a common identity while at the same time recognising the racial diversity of the nation (Wilson, 2001; Bornman, 2006; Ramsamy, 2007). In the early years of South Africa's transition the Rainbow Nation became a strong symbol of national pride which was seen as integral to the stability of the society (Isaacs-Martin, 2012).

(Ignatieff, 1998; Wilson, 2001; Hamber, 2002). The logic of applying interpersonal reconciliation to nations is seen to be flawed; only individuals, and not nations, can be reconciled (Cockrell, 1996; Borer, 2004). In turn, this also raises the question of how transitional justice interprets the notion of the community, i.e. a mechanical political construct as a means of organising a large number of individuals (as in the case of nationalism) or an interconnected collective.

One can argue that both approaches were concerned with restoring peace and stability to the country. Those emphasising human rights and who interpret the nation from an individualist and Western perspective emphasised the importance of applying the rule of law to individuals as means of securing the future stability of the country. Those interpreting the proceedings from an interconnected worldview emphasised the inter-relational relationship aspects for achieving the same ends. Given that the TRC was influenced by an interconnected worldview which prioritises relationship, such recourse would appear to be common sense. The difference lies in that one focuses on structural aspects of building a sustainable peace and the other on the relational aspects.

A further critique of the TRC relates to forgiveness and whether or not it was something that was imposed on victims (Chapman, 2008a, 2008b). If it is seen as a requirement, Evans (2018) argues that not only does it put the onus on victims to address the legacy of the conflict and secure a peaceful future for the society, but it also risks undermining the agency of victims to the extent that needs of the wider society are prioritised over their individual needs (see also Hamber and Wilson, 2002). However, Chapman (2008b) argues there is very little empirical evidence to suggest that forgiveness was something that was imposed, although there is evidence to show that people did think the Commission was about forgiveness. She argues that this could be due to the conflation of the terms 'reconciliation' and 'forgiveness', the emphasis placed by commissioners on restoring relationships between victims and perpetrators, and what was perceived as the TRC's Christian ethic (Krog, 2008). However, as Krog (2008) argues, the Commission's emphasis on forgiveness derives from the priority given to human interconnectedness and the understanding that one's humanity is caught up in the humanity of the other (see also Sooka, 2000; Truth and Reconciliation Commission, 1999b: 366). Moreover, interpreting this critique from the perspective of worldview would also account for why 'black' more so than 'white' South Africans saw forgiveness as a requisite for reconciliation (Chapman, 2008b).

The Commission has also been criticised for the way in which it individualised responsibility (Mamdani, 2000). This raises the question of how accountability in transitional justice is interpreted. As noted in the previous section, human rights and the rule of law are founded on an objectivist view of reality that is geared towards the individual (see also Hernández-Truyol, 2004; Kelsall, 2009; Kaschula and Ralarala, 2004). In contrast, in an interconnected worldview accountability is centred on maintaining the coherency of the society by restoring the dignity and humanity of the individuals (both victims and perpetrators) involved (Masina, 2000; Murithi, 2009; Tutu, 1999; Munyaka and Motlhabi, 2009). As Kenyon (2015) argues, in doing so, it gives or returns the right of the individual to belong to the group. Consequently, Tutu (1999) argues that truth commissions and restorative justice lend themselves more to African approaches to justice, while retributive justice and criminal courts represent a Western approach to justice (Tutu, 1999).

Related to this, Wilson (2001: 10, 164) asserts that through the TRC the concept of *ubuntu* became synonymous with 'justice proper', while retributive justice, criminal courts and punishment were interpreted as damaging to the well-being of the society. While noting this binary approach makes it difficult to engage in the role of retributive justice in promoting reconciliation, Wilson challenges the way in which this concept has been romanticised. He points out that despite *ubuntu*'s rejection of revenge, numerous such acts were carried out by people to whom this worldview was attributed (Wilson, 2001). However, Shutte (2009a) argues these acts of violent revenge were rather the result of being dehumanised, which an *ubuntu* approach to justice seeks to rectify in its endeavour to promote social peace.

For many people apartheid was interpreted as an evil that needed to be exorcised from the land (Tutu, 2008). Supporting the argument that the TRC needs to be interpreted from an interconnected worldview, Ashforth (2005) argues that part of the Commission's role should have been to expose the source of evil, which would have been achieved through full confession. This interpretation provides further insight into why Tutu emphasised the importance of confession and what was perceived as the religious aspects of reconciliation. However, Ashforth argues that by failing to persuade the leadership of the National Party to confess to their full activities, the source of evil that is perceived to account for the persisting levels of poverty and the continuing experience of oppression among 'black' South Africans remains hidden and alive (Ashforth, 2005).

The way in which an interconnected worldview was given primacy within the TRC also suggests an attempt at asserting an African identity and reclaiming an African way of being in the world that was overshadowed by apartheid. Balcomb (2014) argues that lying at the heart of African approaches to engaging with reality is the need to assert an African identity. Examples include the works of Frantz Fanon and his theories of decolonisation (Fanon, 1990), Steve Biko and the Black Consciousness Movement which promoted psychological liberation from apartheid and promoted the dignity of 'black' people (Biko, 1987), and, more recently, it is demonstrated in student protests in South Africa surrounding the 'Rhodes Must Fall' campaign calling for the removal of statues symbolising South Africa's colonial past and the need for a higher education curriculum that reflects African values and ways of being in the world (Rhodes Must Fall, n.d.; National Public Radio, 2015). The need to assert an African identity is also demonstrated in the attempt by (former president of South Africa) Thabo Mbeki at resurrecting the discourse on the African Renaissance, which is summarised in the slogan 'African solutions to African problems', that challenges Western approaches to addressing peace and security concerns on the African continent – as perceived to be embodied by the International Criminal Court (ICC) (for example Nathan, 2013; Reuters, 2015; IOL News, 2015). Indeed, African nations have agreed 'that sitting heads of state should not be put on trial by the International Criminal Court' (Mail and Guardian Online, 2013; Al Jazeera, 2014). The extent to which the African Union's criticisms of the ICC are genuinely grounded in a claim of African identity is debated. Notwithstanding these criticisms, the above examples point to different ways of being in the world and interpreting reality which are further complicated by histories of colonialism and Western hegemony.

Notwithstanding the criticisms of the ICC, competing worldviews can also be seen contributing to South Africa's decision, despite being signatories to the Rome Statute, not to arrest the Sudanese President Omar al-Bashir during his visit to South Africa (Al Jazeera, 2015; BBC News, 2015b). Defending the state's inaction, the (then) secretary-general of the ANC, Gwede Mantashe, argued that the decision was based on customary law which prohibits heads of state from being insulted, in this case through his arrest (Reuters, 2015). This raises serious concerns for the protection of human rights in Africa and brings into question how accountability in non-Western contexts is interpreted.

Conclusion

In conclusion, this chapter demonstrates how ontological disparities and different processes of meaning-making led to competing interpretations of South Africa's truth recovery process. Applying a worldview analysis to some of the criticisms directed to the TRC raises an important issue about how transitional justice deals with the past and interprets key concepts such as reconciliation, accountability and nation-building. It also suggests that a failure to understand different systems of meaning-making present within a peacebuilding process can contribute, alongside other complicating factors such as legacies of oppression, to the breakdown in reconciliation. When thinking about transitions, consideration needs to be given to how worldview impacts on protecting human rights and intergroup relations in culturally diverse societies and societies that may not share the same value system as those underpinning the human rights discourse.

Returning to the aims of transformative justice, in its quest to challenge structural and economic inequalities, it needs to also challenge the cultural inequalities and their associated power relations in conflict. Recognising different ways of being in the world not only contributes to restoring the dignity of formerly oppressed groups, it also contributes to strengthening local agency and promoting equality at an even deeper level. Moreover, by considering how different systems of meaning-making shape one's interpretation of transitions and building sustainable peace, transformative justice can correct the perceived imbalance in transitional justice which tends to take a more legal and structural approach to addressing the legacy of gross human rights violations and inculcate more relational approaches. However, it needs to be mindful of not prioritising the needs of the collective society at the expense of the agency of those most affected by the conflict (Evans, 2018). Nonetheless, by considering culture, more holistic approaches to transitional justice can be found, making it an imperative for the transformative justice agenda.

References

Al Jazeera. (2014) 'African Union Urges United Stand Against ICC', 1 February, www.aljazeera.com/news/africa/2014/02/african-union-urges-united-stand-against-icc-201421 11727645567.html [accessed 25 May 2018].

Al Jazeera. (2015) 'Why South Africa Let Bashir Get Away', 15 June, www.aljazeera.com/indepth/opinion/2015/06/south-africa-bashir-150615102211840.html [accessed 25 May 2018].

Anderson, Benedict. (1983) *Imagined Communities: Reflections on the Origin and Spread of Nationalism*. London: Verso.

Arthur, Paige. (2011) 'Introduction: Identities in Transition'. In Paige Arthur (ed.), *Identities in Transition: Challenges for Transitional Justice in Divided Societies*, 1–16. New York: Cambridge University Press.

Ashforth, Adam. (2005) *Witchcraft, Violence, and Democracy in South Africa*. Chicago, IL: The University of Chicago Press.

Asmal, Kader. (2000) 'Truth, Reconciliation and Justice: The South African Experience in Perspective'. *Modern Law Review* 63(1): 1–24.

Atran, Scott. (2010) *Talking to the Enemy: Violent Extremism, Sacred Values, and What it Means to be Human*. London and New York: Allen Lane/Harper Collins Publishers.

Avruch, Kevin and Peter W. Black. (1993) 'Conflict Resolution in Intercultural Settings: Problems and Prospects'. In Dennis J.D. Sandole and Hugo Van Der Merwe (eds), *Conflict Resolution Theory and Practice: Integration and Application*, 131–145. Manchester: Manchester University Press.

Balcomb, Anthony. (2014) *Journey into the African Sun: Soundings in Search of Another Way of Being in the World*. Pretoria: University of South Africa.

BBC News. (2015a) 'Paris Attacks: France Grapples with Freedom of Speech', 15 January, www.bbc.co.uk/news/blogs-eu-30829005 [accessed 25 May 2018].

BBC News. (2015b) 'South Africa may Leave ICC over Bashir Arrest Row', 25 June, www.bbc.co.uk/news/world-africa-33269126 [accessed 25 May 2018].

Bediako, Kwame. (2004) *Jesus and the Gospel in Africa: History and Experience*. Maryknoll, NY: Orbis Books.

Bendix, Reinhard. (1977) *Max Weber: An Intellectual Portrait*. Berkeley, CA and London: University of California Press.

Berger, Peter L. and Thomas Luckmann. (1966) *The Social Construction of Reality: A Treatise in the Sociology of Knowledge*. London: Allen Lane.

Biko, Steve. (1987) *I Write What I Like: Selected Writings* (edited by Aelred Stubbs). London: Heinemann Educational.

Blankenburgh, Marco. (2013) *Inter-cultural Intelligence: From Surviving to Thriving in the Global Space*. Dubai: KnowledgeWorkx.

Bond, Patrick. (2014) 'Marikana's Meaning for Crisis Management: An Instance of South Africa's Resource Curse'. In Ulrike Schuerkens (ed.), *Global Management, Local Resistances: Theoretical Discussion and Empirical Case Studies*, 192–219. Abingdon: Routledge.

Boraine, Alex. (2000) *A Country Unmasked: Inside South Africa's Truth and Reconciliation Commission*. Oxford: Oxford University Press.

Borer, Tristan Anne. (2004) 'Reconciling South Africa or South Africans? Cautionary Notes from the TRC'. *African Studies Quarterly* 8(1): 23–26.

Bornman, Elirea. (2006) 'National Symbols and National-building in the Post-Apartheid South Africa'. *International Journal of Intercultural Relations* 30: 383–399.

Bryan, Dominic. (2000) *Orange Parades: The Politics of Ritual, Tradition and Control.* London: Pluto Press.

Bryan, Dominic and Gillian McIntosh. (2005) 'Symbols: Sites of Creation and Contest in Northern Ireland'. *SAIS Review* 25(2): 127–138.

Bryan, Dominic and Clifford Stevenson. (2009) 'Struggles over Symbolic Landscape and the New Northern Ireland'. In Marc Howard Ross (ed.), *Culture and Belonging in Divided Societies: Contestation and Symbolic Landscapes*, 68–84. Philadelphia, PA: University of Philadelphia Press.

Chapman, Audrey R. (2008a) 'The TRC's Approach to Promoting Reconciliation in the Human Rights Violations Hearings'. In Audrey R. Chapman and Hugo Van Der Merwe (eds), *Truth and Reconciliation in South Africa: Did the TRC Deliver?*, 43–65. Philadelphia, PA: University of Pennsylvania Press.

Chapman, Audrey R. (2008b) 'Perspectives on the role of forgiveness in the Human Rights Violations Hearings'. In Audrey R. Chapman and Hugo Van Der Merwe (eds), *Truth and Reconciliation in South Africa: Did the TRC Deliver?*, 66–89. Philadelphia, PA: University of Pennsylvania Press.

Clark, Mary E. (1989) *Ariandne's Thread: The Search for New Modes of Thinking*. London: Macmillan Press.

Cockrell, Alfred. (1996) 'Rainbow Jurisprudence'. *South African Journal on Human Rights* 12(1): 1–38.

Daily Sun. (2015) 'Terror of the Muthi Bones!', 12 November, www.dailysun.co.za/News/National/terror-of-the-muthi-bones-20151112 [accessed 25 May 2018].

Docherty, Jayne S. (2001) *Learning Lessons from Waco: When the Parties Bring their Gods to the Negotiation Table*. Syracuse, NY: Syracuse University Press.

Dunne, Tim. (2006) 'Liberalism'. In John Baylis and Steve Smith (eds), *The Globalization of World Politics: An Introduction to International Relations*, 3rd edition, 185–201. Oxford: Oxford University Press.

ENCA. (2014) 'Marikana Commission: Cracks Begin to Show', 25 March, www.enca.com/south-africa/marikana-commission-cracks-begin-show [accessed 25 May 2018].

Eriksen, Thomas Hyland. (1997) 'Multiculturalism, Individualism and Human Rights: Romanticism, the Enlightenment and Lessons from Mauritius'. In Richard A. Wilson (ed.), *Human Rights, Culture and Context: Anthropological Perspectives*, 49–69. London and Sterling, VA: Pluto Press.

Eriksen, Thomas Hyland. (2001) 'Ethnic Identity, National Identity, and Intergroup Conflict'. In: Richard D. Ashmore, Lee Jussim and David Wilder (eds), *Social Identity, Intergroup Conflict, and Conflict Reduction*, 42–70. New York: Oxford University Press.

Evans, Matthew. (2018) 'A Future without Forgiveness: Beyond Reconciliation in Transitional Justice'. *International Politics* 55(5): 678–692.

Fanon, Frantz. (1990) *The Wretched of the Earth*. London: Penguin.

Gay, Peter. (1971) *Great Ages of Man: Age of the Enlightenment*. Amsterdam: Time-Life International.

Geertz, Clifford. (1973) *The Interpretation of Cultures: Selected Essays*. New York: Fontana Press.

Gelvin, James L. (2005) *The Israel-Palestine Conflict: One Hundred Years of War*. New York: Cambridge University Press.

Gibson, James L. (2004) *Overcoming Apartheid: Can Truth Reconcile a Divided Nation?* New York: Russel Sage Foundation.

Goffman, Erving. (1986) *Frame Analysis: An Essay on the Organization of Experience*. Boston, MA: Northeastern University Press.

Gready, Paul and Simon Robins. (2014) 'From Transitional to Transformative Justice: A New Agenda for Practice'. *International Journal of Transitional Justice* 8(3): 339–361.
The Guardian. (2015) 'Al-Jazeera Leak Reveals Staff Split over Response to Charlie Hebdo Killings', 11 January, www.theguardian.com/media/2015/jan/11/al-jazeera-leak-charlie-hebdo-emails [accessed 25 May 2018].
Guba, Egon G. and Yvanna S. Lincoln. (1998) 'Competing Paradigms in Qualitative Research'. In Norman K. Denzin and Yvonna S. Lincoln (eds), *The Landscape of Qualitative Research: Theories and Issues*, 195–220. Thousand Oaks, CA, London and New Delhi: SAGE Publications.
Halliday, Fred. (2006) 'Nationalism'. In John Baylis and Steve Smith (eds), *The Globalization of World Politics: An Introduction to International Relations*, 3rd edition, 521–538. Oxford: Oxford University Press.
Hamber, Brandon. (2002) '"Ere their Story Die": Truth, Justice and Reconciliation in South Africa'. *Race & Class* 44(1): 61–79.
Hamber, Brandon and Richard A. Wilson. (2002) 'Symbolic Closure through Memory, Reparation and Revenge in Post-conflict Societies'. *Journal of Human Rights* 1(1): 35–53.
Hernández-Truyol, Berta Esperanza. (2004) 'Panel V. Human Rights Commitments in the Americas: From the Global to the Local – The Rule of Law and Human Rights'. *Florida Journal of International Law* 16: 167–194.
Ignatieff, Michael. (1998) *The Warrior's Honour: Ethnic War and the Modern Conscience.* London: Chatto & Windus.
IOL News. (2015) 'ICC is Dangerous: Mantashe', 22 June, www.iol.co.za/news/politics/icc-is-dangerous-mantashe-1.1874842#.VZZxqBtVhHw [accessed 25 May 2018].
Isaacs-Martin, Wendy. (2012) 'National Identity and Distinctiveness: Developing a Common Identity in a Nation State (with reference to South Africa)'. *Africa Insight* 42 (2): 169–170.
Kaschula, Russell H. and Monwabisi K. Ralarala. (2004) 'Language Rights, Intercultural Communication and the Law in South Africa'. *South African Journal of African Languages* 24(4): 252–261.
Kelsall, Tim. (2009) *Culture Under Cross-examination: International Justice and the Special Court for Sierra Leone.* Cambridge: Cambridge University Press.
Kenyon, Kristi H. (2015) 'Localizing the Global/Globalizing the Local: Reconciling Botho and Human Rights in Botswana'. In Joel R. Pruce (ed.), *The Social Practice of Human Rights*, 101–119. New York: Palgrave Macmillan.
Koltko-Rivera, Mark E. (2004) 'The Psychology of Worldviews'. *Review of General Psychology* 8(1): 3–58.
Krog, Antjie. (2008) '"... if it Means he gets his Humanity Back ...": The Worldview Underpinning the South African Truth and Reconciliation Commission'. *Journal of Multicultural Discourses* 3(3): 204–220.
Krog, Antjie. (2015) 'Research into Reconciliation and Forgiveness at the South African Truth and Reconciliation Commission and Homi Bhabha's "Architecture of the New"'. *Canadian Journal of Law and Society* 30(2): 203–217.
Lawler, Steph. (2008) *Identity: Sociological Perspectives.* Cambridge: Polity Press.
Mail and Guardian Online. (2012) 'Gallery Refuses to Remove "Spear of the Nation" Artwork', 17 May, http://mg.co.za/article/2012-05-17-anc-irate-over-spear-of-the-nation-artwork [accessed 25 May 2018].
Mail and Guardian Online. (2013) 'Africans Tell ICC: Heads of State Should Not be Tried', 12 October, http://mg.co.za/article/2013-10-12-africans-tell-icc-heads-of-state-should-not-be-tried/ [accessed 25 May 2018].

Mail and Guardian Online. (2016) 'Desperate Lily Mine Families Seek Supernatural Help', 17 February, http://mg.co.za/article/2016-02-17-desperate-lily-mine-families-seek-supernatural-help [accessed 25 May 2018].

Malan, Jannie. (2011) *Being Similar, Different, and Coexistent*. Umhlanga Rocks: ACCORD.

Mamdani, Mahmood. (2000) 'The Truth According to the TRC'. In Ifi Amadiume and Abdullahi An-Na'im (eds), *The Politics of Memory: Truth, Healing and Social Justice*, 177–190. London and New York: Zed Books.

Masina, Nomonde. (2000) 'Xhosa Practices of *Ubuntu* for South Africa'. In William I. Zartman (ed.), *Traditional Cures for Modern Conflicts: African Conflict 'Medicine'*, 169–181. London: Lynne Rienner Publishers Inc.

Maslow, Abraham. (1954) *Motivation and Personality*. New York: Harper Bros.

Mbiti, John. (1969) *African Religions & Philosophy*. London: Heinemann.

McAuliffe, Pádraig. (2017) *Transformative Transitional Justice and the Malleability of Post-conflict States*. Cheltenham: Edward Elgar.

Merry, Sally Engle. (2006) *Human Rights and Gender Violence: Translating International Law into Local Justice*. Chicago, IL and London: The University of Chicago Press.

Metz, Thaddeus. (2011) 'Ubuntu as a Moral Theory and Human Rights in South Africa'. *African Human Rights Law Journal* 11: 532–559.

Munyaka, Mluleki and Mokgethi Motlhabi. (2009) 'Ubuntu and its Socio-moral Significance'. In Munyaradzi Felix Murove (ed.), *African Ethics: An Anthology of Comparative and Applied Ethics*, 63–84. Scottsville: University of KwaZulu-Natal Press.

Murithi, Tim. (2009) 'An African Perspective on Peace Education: Ubuntu Lessons in Reconciliation'. *International Review of Education* 55: 221–233.

Muvingi, Ismael. (2009) 'Sitting on Powder Kegs: Socioeconomic Rights in Transitional Societies'. *International Journal of Transitional Justice* 3(2): 163–182.

Nathan, Laurie. (2013) 'African Solutions to African Problems: South Africa's Foreign Policy'. *South African Foreign Policy Initiative Policy Brief* 51.

National Public Radio. (2015) 'Why South African Students Say the Statue of Rhodes Must Fall', 28 March, www.npr.org/sections/goatsandsoda/2015/03/28/395608605/why-south-african-students-say-the-statue-of-rhodes-must-fall [accessed 25 May 2018].

Naugle, David K. (2002) *Worldview: The History of a Concept*. Grand Rapids, MI and Cambridge: William B. Eerdmans Publishing Company.

Northrup, Terrell A. (1989) 'The Dynamic of Identity in Personal and Social Conflict'. In Louis Kriesberg, Terrell A. Northrup and Stuart J. Thorson (eds), *Intractable Conflicts and their Transformation*, 68–76. Syracuse, NY: Syracuse University Press.

Nürnberger, Klaus. (2007) *The Living Dead and the Living God: Christ and the Ancestors in a Changing Africa*. Pietermaritzburg: Cluster Publications.

Palmer, Nicola, Briony Jones and Julia Viebach (2015) 'Introduction – Ways of Knowing Atrocity: A Methodological Enquiry into the Formulation, Implementation, and Assessment of Transitional Justice'. *Canadian Journal of Law and Society* 30(2): 173–182.

Pepper, Stephen. (1942) *World Hypothesis: A Study in Evidence*. Berkeley, CA and London: University of California Press.

Ramsamy, Edward. (2007) 'Between Non-racialism and Multiculturalism: Indian Identity and Nation Building in South Africa'. *Tijdschrift voor Economische en Sociale Geografie* 98(4): 468–481.

Reuters. (2015) 'ICC asks South Africa to Explain Failure to Arrest Bashir', 9 September, www.africanindy.com/news/icc-asks-south-africa-to-explain-failure-to-arrest-bashir-1245388/ [accessed 25 May 2018].

Rhodes Must Fall. (n.d.) 'Rhodes Must Fall', http://rhodesmustfall.co.za/ [accessed 23 December 2015].

Richmond, Oliver P. (2011) *A Post-liberal Peace*. Abingdon and New York: Routledge.

Richmond, Oliver P. and Audra Mitchell. (2012) 'Introduction – Towards a Post-liberal Peace: Exploring Hybridity via Everyday Forms of Resistance, Agency and Autonomy'. In Oliver P. Richmond and Audra Mitchell (eds), *Hybrid Forms of Peace: From Everyday Agency to Post-liberalism*, 1–38. Basingstoke: Palgrave Macmillan.

Ross, Marc Howard. (2007) *Cultural Contestation in Ethnic Conflict*. Cambridge: Cambridge University Press.

Ross, Marc Howard. (2009) 'Cultural Contestation and the Symbolic Landscape: Politics by Other Means?'. In Marc Howard Ross (ed.), *Culture and Belonging in Societies: Contestation and Symbolic Landscapes*, 1–23. Philadelphia, PA: University of Pennsylvania Press.

Shutte, Augustine. (2009a) 'Politics and the Ethic of *Ubuntu*'. In Munyaradzi Felix Murove (ed.), *African Ethics: An Anthology of Comparative and Applied Ethics*, 375–390. Scottsville: University of KwaZulu-Natal Press.

Shutte, Augustine. (2009b) '*Ubuntu* as the African ethical vision'. In Munyaradzi Felix Murove (ed.), *African Ethics: An Anthology of Comparative and Applied Ethics*, 85–99. Scottsville: University of KwaZulu-Natal Press.

Smith, Anthony D. (1983) *Theories of Nationalism*, 2nd edition. London: Duckworth.

Smith, Anthony D. (2001) *Nationalism: Theory, Ideology, History*. Cambridge: Polity Press.

Sooka, Yasmin. (2000) 'South Africa's human spirit: an oral memoir of the truth and reconciliation commission – we should not forget', www.sabctruth.co.za/sabctruth/yasmin.htm [accessed 28 May 2018].

Sriram, Chandra Lekha. (2007) 'Justice as Peace? Liberal Peacebuilding and Strategies of Transitional Justice'. *Global Society* 21(4): 579–591.

Staub, Ervin. (1996) 'Cultural-societal roots of Violence: The Examples of Genocidal Violence and of Contemporary Youth Violence in the United States'. *American Psychologist* 51(2): 117–132.

Tarnas, Richard. (1991) *The Passion of the Western Mind: Understanding the Ideas that have Shaped our Worldview*. New York: Harmony Books.

Times Live. (2012) 'Ban the Spear, Stone its Maker', 22 May, www.timeslive.co.za/politics/2012/05/22/ban-the-spear-stone-its-maker [accessed 25 May 2018].

Truth and Reconciliation Commission. (1999a) *Truth and Reconciliation Commission of South Africa Report (Vol. 1)*. London: Macmillan.

Truth and Reconciliation Commission. (1999b) *Truth and Reconciliation Commission of South Africa Report (Vol. 5)*. London: Macmillan.

Turner, Harold W. (1977) 'The Primal Religions of the World and their Study'. In Victor C. Hayes (ed.), *Australian Essays in World Religions*, 27–37. Bedford Park: The Australian Association for the Study of Religions.

Tutu, Desmond M. (1999) *No Future without Forgiveness*. Rider: London.

Tutu, Desmond M. (2008) 'Interview'. In Institute of Justice and Reconciliation, *Truth, Justice, Memory: South Africa's Truth and Reconciliation Process*, DVD. Cape Town: Institute of Justice and Reconciliation.

Valji, Nahla. (2004) *Race and Reconciliation in a Post-TRC South Africa*. Paper presented at the conference 'Ten Years of Democracy in Southern Africa', Southern African Research Centre, Queen's University, Kingston, Canada, 2–5 May.

Weedon, Chris. (2004) *Identity and Culture*. Maidenhead: Open University Press.

Wilson, Richard A. (2001) *The Politics of Truth and Reconciliation in South Africa: Legitimizing the Post-Apartheid State*. Cambridge: Cambridge University Press.

Zulu, Melekias and Matthew Wilhelm-Solomon. (2015) 'Tormented by *Umnyama*: An Urban Cosmology of Migration and Misfortune in Inner-city Johannesburg'. In Ingrid Palmary, Brandon Hamber and Lorena Núñez (eds), *Healing and Change in the City of Gold: Case Studies of Coping and Support in Johannesburg*, 135–148. Cham: Springer.

7 Selective justice and constructions of victimhood at the Khmer Rouge Tribunal

Rachel Killean

Introduction[1]

Since World War II highlighted the grave harm so frequently inflicted on civilians during times of conflict, there has been a growing willingness to prosecute atrocities under international criminal law (ICL). This has been reflected in the proliferation of ICL mechanisms, including ad hoc tribunals, hybrid institutions and the permanent International Criminal Court (ICC). Such institutions have often been analysed for their ability to bring 'justice' to victims, and an ever-growing literature has developed in relation to victim-related issues, including reparations (Moffett, 2017; McCarthy, 2012), complex political victims (for example, Bernath, 2015; Meyers, 2011), the role of the victim within the courtroom (Trumbull, 2008; McGonigle Leyh, 2011), and victims' perceptions of justice (Stover, 2005; Hodžić, 2010). Parallel developments in victim-centric discourse and practice can be seen within ICL institutions. Victims have become a progressively more central figure in courts' legitimising practices,[2] while the inclusion of victim participation provisions in several courts have been heralded as signalling a move towards a more 'victim-orientated justice' (Vasiliev, 2009). Such developments have been accompanied by increased recognition within international human rights law of victims as holders of rights, including the rights to protection, participation, representation and reparation.[3]

Despite this nominal move towards 'victim-centrism', the extent to which victims are rendered visible within these processes remains contested (McEvoy and McConnachie, 2013; Kendall and Nouwen, 2013; Fletcher, 2015), and courts have found their ability to deliver justice subjected to criticism from victimised populations (Kutnjak Ivković and Hagan, 2011; Killean, 2016). This disjuncture between victim discourse and the delivery of 'justice' can in part be attributed to

1 This is an abridged version of Rachel Killean (2018) 'Constructing victimhood at the Khmer Rouge Tribunal: visibility, selectivity and participation', *International Review of Victimology* 24(3), 273–29 (DOI: 10.1177/0269758017747645). © 2018 by Rachel Killean. Reprinted by permission of SAGE Publications Ltd.

2 See for example, International Criminal Tribunal for the Former Yugoslavia (1995: paras 1, 198–199); International Criminal Tribunal for Rwanda (1998: para. 160).

3 See for example, UN (1985, 2005); UNOHCHR (1993, 2005).

the selective delivery of justice offered by legal institutions (Robins, 2017: 45). Only a small number of atrocities fall within the scope of ICL, and of those only some will be acknowledged as such by the international community (Cryer, 2005; Simpson, 1997). Even those victims whose atrocities fall within ICL may be excluded from recognition and redress (Robins, 2017), as prosecutorial strategies prioritise specific harms and perpetrators over others (Pritchett, 2008; Côte, 2005). These institutional choices create what Kendall and Nouwen (2013) have termed a 'pyramid' of victimhood, with victims of harm at the bottom, and those recognised by ICL institutions as worthy of redress at the top.

This chapter situates these institutional choices, the pyramid of victimhood they create and the selective justice they shape within broader criminological and victimological debates, drawing from critical victimology in particular. Rising out of a desire to critique definitions of symbolic or 'ideal' victims and perpetrators (Christie, 1986: 18), this branch of victimology is concerned with who has the power to apply the label 'victim' and what considerations influence that determination (Miers, 1989; Mawby and Walklate, 1994). Highlighting 'hierarchies of victimhood' (Carrabine et al., 2004: 117), which distinguish between those victims who are 'innocent' (McEvoy and McConnachie, 2012: 531–2), 'good' (Madlingozi, 2007), or 'worthy' (Tilly, 2008) and those who are not, victimologists have demonstrated that who acquires the label of victim depends not only on the victims' characteristics, but on the reactions of others (McAlinden, 2014). Thus, there is a political dimension to the hierarchy of victim legitimacy, with the very term 'victim' being open to manipulation by political and legal elites in the pursuit of other goals (Dignan, 2005; Walklate, 2011: 189). In response, critical victimologists have sought to uncover victimisations that may be rendered invisible due to the political climate, social factors, or the marginalised status of the victims (Holstein and Miller, 1990; McGarry and Walklate, 2015).

Although critical victimology developed in the context of Western domestic criminal justice, in recent years it has provided a framework for exploring the role of states in perpetrating crime (Kauzlarich, Matthews and Miller, 2001), international responses to atrocity (Letschert et al., 2011) and the emergence of victim hierarchies within transitional justice contexts (van Wijk, 2013; McEvoy and McConnachie, 2013). International criminal courts are increasingly acknowledged as having the power to produce and legitimise categories of victims, condemn perpetrators and shape understandings of conflicts (Mibenge, 2013). While the creation of such narratives is nominally based on issues of fact and law, hegemonic power relations contribute to the collation and interpretation of those issues (Mibenge, 2013: 4). Legal professionals, victor governments, other states, international organisations and donors all take part in the negotiating of law and fact, thus shaping which victims are legitimised within justice processes.

While the literature has acknowledged the political and legal construction of victimhood within both domestic and transitional contexts, the precise processes through which some victims are selected as worthy of recognition and redress is a relatively neglected dimension within current discourse. This chapter seeks to address this gap, providing a 'thicker' understanding of victim visibility within ICL

(Geertz, 1993; McEvoy, 2007) by exploring (a) how victim recognition is shaped by the specific political context within which a court operates, and (b) how victimhood continues to be 'produced, perceived and interpreted' by the various actors engaged in the work of the court (Geertz, 1993: 7). This actor-oriented approach allows for an exploration of the different stakeholders within ICL, their heterogeneous interests, and their influence over responses to victimisation. Institutions cannot think for themselves, but are shaped by the approaches of those engaged in their work (Douglas, 1987). Indeed, the new, evolving and often ad hoc nature of ICL grants its practitioners an influence beyond what would be found within domestic jurisdictions. Thus, an analysis of how the pyramid of victimhood has been shaped by various actors can highlight law 'as a dynamic and, in some ways, even contingent process' (Palmer, 2015: 15). As will be explored through this chapter, what is revealed through this analysis is a 'layered' process of victim selectivity, as political actors, lawyers, judges and civil society actors have constructed and interpreted responses to mass victimisation.

To conduct this analysis, this chapter focuses on the Extraordinary Chambers in the Courts of Cambodia (ECCC), or 'Khmer Rouge Tribunal' (KRT) as a case study. The KRT is a hybrid court (Raub, 2008–2009) established through an agreement between the United Nations (UN) and the Royal Government of Cambodia (RGC) to prosecute atrocities perpetrated during the Khmer Rouge regime (1975–1979). To date, two cases have been tried at the KRT. Case 001 concerned the former chairman of the S-21 detention centre, KAING Guek Eav, who was sentenced to life imprisonment in 2012.[4] Case 002 relates to crimes ranging across Cambodia, and the original accused were four former high-ranking Khmer Rouge: NUON Chea, KHIEU Samphan, IENG Sary, and IENG Thirith. However, IENG Thirith was found unfit to stand trial in 2011, and the case was terminated against both her and IENG Sary following their deaths in 2015 and 2013 respectively.[5] Due to fears about trial management and the advanced age of the remaining defendants, Case 002 was split into a series of sub-trials. The first concluded in 2016, finding the accused guilty of crimes against humanity,[6] and a judgment in the second was expected in 2018.

The KRT is expected to deliver somewhat broader social goals than are usually expected of a court. There is a high expectation that it will contribute to 'national reconciliation, stability, peace and security',[7] and the Court is therefore expected to be 'closer to the victims and the general population in Cambodia' (Zhang, 2016: 521). Yet, despite these expectations of long-term and general benefit,

4 Case 001, Appeal Judgment, 001/18-07-2007-KRT/SC, 3 February 2012.

5 Case 002, Decision on IENG Thirith's Fitness to Stand Trial, 002/19-09-2007/KRT/TC, 17 November 2011; Case 002, Termination of the Proceedings Against the Accused IENG Sary, KRT Trial Chamber, 002/19-09-2007/KRT/TC, 14 March 2013; Case 002, Termination of the Proceedings Against the Accused IENG Thirith, 002/19-09-2007/KRT/TC, 27 August 2015.

6 Case 002/01, Trial Judgment, 002/19-09-2007/KRT/TC, 7 August 2014; Case 002/01, Appeal Judgment, 002/19-09-2007/KRT/SC, 23 November 2016.

7 See UN Secretary-General (1998).

institutional choices with regards to jurisdictional limits, charges, and access to victim participation have inevitably produced Kendall and Nouwen's pyramid of victimhood, acknowledging but also excluding a range of victimisations.

This chapter proceeds as follows. The second section explores the role of political and legal elites in framing which victimisations are acknowledged as international crimes and subjected to prosecution within the KRT. To do so, it highlights the limits that have been placed on the Court's temporal and personal jurisdiction, the political contexts behind those limitations, and how prosecutorial discretion has further shaped the selective justice offered by the Tribunal. The third section then turns to the visibility of victims within the courtroom. The Court's creation of a civil party system gives victims the opportunity to participate in its work as parties with similar rights to the prosecution and defence. Thus, the question of who is recognised as a victim takes on significant practical relevance, as recognition may entitle individuals to a number of procedural and substantive rights. The analysis adopts a critical victimological lens throughout, while also drawing from broader transitional justice and socio-legal literature to enhance its analysis. It also draws from interviews conducted in Cambodia in 2013 and 2014 with court practitioners (18) and civil society actors (seven), who were asked to reflect on the mandate and practice of the Tribunal, as well as the role of victims within it. Through this analysis, it seeks to expose how heterogeneous actors pursuing a variety of (not necessarily aligned) goals, have contributed to a layered process of selectivity, with each layer shaping the pyramid of victims who are able to access recognition and redress, and determining the victimisations we 'see' as opposed to those which we do not 'see' (Mawby and Walklate, 1994: 19).

Selective justice and the construction of victimhood

Critical victimology acknowledges criminal law as something created and enforced on the basis of social convention and political considerations (Doak, 2008). Thus, while most of us will suffer harm of some kind throughout our life, only some of these harms will be defined as criminal (Hillyard et al., 2004), and only some of those who perpetrated criminal acts will find themselves prosecuted. While selective enforcement of law and prosecutorial discretion is established in many legal systems, issues arise when the selectivity is arbitrary or discriminatory (Gelsthorpe and Padfield, 2003: 5). From a victim-centric perspective, selective enforcement renders certain harms unrecognised and without redress (Cryer, 2005: 193).

This critique of selectivity in criminal law is mirrored within the transitional justice literature (Cryer, 2005; Damaska, 2008; McCormack, 1997, Simpson, 1997). As McCormack (1997: 683) has noted, selectivity can be 'found in relation to the acts the international community is prepared to characterise as "war crimes", and secondly, in relation to the particular alleged atrocities the international community is prepared to collectively prosecute'. Such critiques are linked to the concept of victors' justice, and the argument that only 'weak states' or the losers of a conflict will find themselves subjected to prosecution (Damaska, 2008: 361). While noting that the very definitions given to international crime naturally already exclude a multitude of grave harms (for example, harm caused by financial crises or poverty) (Kendall and Nouwen, 2013: 242), this section focuses on McCormack's definition of selectivity as limiting the acts that will be identified as falling within the definitions of international crimes, and the acts that will then be prosecuted. In doing so, it considers how the pyramid of victims has been shaped first by the limitations placed on the KRT's jurisdiction, and then by prosecutorial decisions around which suspects and crimes to prosecute.

The politics of victim recognition

The Khmer Rouge era in Cambodia perpetrated harm against millions of individuals, through a range of criminal acts. However, the years leading up to the Khmer Rouge regime also saw civilians suffer the brunt of armed struggle between a repressive monarchy and communist insurgents (Form, 2009), a four-year US bombing campaign (Kissinger, 1979; Owen and Kiernan, 2006), and the authoritarian violence of a US-backed right-wing military government (Chandler, 1991). While Vietnam's toppling of the Khmer Rouge in 1979 may have ended one violent regime, it was not until the 1990s that a tentative peace returned to Cambodia (Ciorciari and Heindel, 2014). This is in part attributable to the Cold War politics which saw the Khmer Rouge recognised as the legitimate government of Cambodia long after their defeat, while aid flowed in from states fearing a Vietnamese expansion (Fawthrop and Jarvis, 2005; Kunst, 2013). Thus, there has been a continuation of harm which cannot be attributed to the Khmer Rouge alone. Yet, while other acts of violence perpetrated against Cambodians arguably fall within the parameters of ICL (Owen and Kiernan, 2006; Fawthrop and Jarvis, 2005), they are not captured by the jurisdiction of the KRT, nor has legal accountability been pursued through other means.

This selectivity can in part be attributed to political interests. Although the new government prosecuted two Khmer Rouge leaders in the immediate aftermath of the regime (Gottesman, 2003), domestic policies developed to focus on encouraging the defection of Khmer Rouge cadres through amnesties, and reconciliation through 'burying the past' (Linton, 2004). Internationally, Cold War considerations prevented most states from engaging with Cambodia's violent past for many years (Fawthrop and Jarvis, 2005). With the thawing of the Cold War came new political agendas, and an increased international wish to hold the Khmer Rouge accountable. Domestically, trials were viewed by the newly formed government as a means of gaining foreign credibility, and threatening remaining Khmer Rouge into defecting (Ratner, 2007: 215; Strangio, 2014: 241). Yet a desire to limit the extent of this accountability was evident from early in this process. The initial idea of a truth commission received little support internationally or domestically, arguably due to fears about whether too much 'truth' might be revealed (Klosterman, 1998). A limited number of prosecutions suggested a means of both delimiting accountability and creating a politically acceptable narrative (Ciorciari and Heindel, 2014: 20–21), and negotiations commenced between the UN and the RGC in 1997, eventually culminating in the KRT.[8]

8 UN and Royal Government of Cambodia (2003).

The Tribunal's mandate is specifically limited to trying senior leaders of the Khmer Rouge and those most responsible for domestic and international crimes committed during the period from 17 April 1975 to 6 January 1979.[9] By restricting the time frame, and referencing the Khmer Rouge specifically, the drafters of the KRT's Law made a clear statement as to which victimisations would have their harm recognised through criminal proceedings. Despite the various harms perpetrated against the Cambodian population, these jurisdictional limits exclude atrocities perpetrated before and after the regime, as well as crimes perpetrated by foreign actors (Bates, 2007). Such a selective response to atrocity is in part a pragmatic move to avoid overburdening an institution with unmanageable caseloads (White, 2017: 138). However, in the case of the KRT it is also in part reflective of the agenda of political elites: for the RGC, the limited jurisdiction prevented a focus on crimes committed by those who overthrew the Khmer Rouge regime or during the war that followed (Heder, 2011), while the United States, which played a significant role in the KRT negotiations, avoided attention being drawn to their bombing campaign and support for the military government (Strangio, 2014: 243). Such jurisdictional restrictions reflect McCormack's first element of selectivity: the limiting of acts identified as international crimes. Indeed, they have been cited by members of the KRT's defence teams as impacting on the overall legitimacy of the process:

> The legitimacy of this tribunal can be questioned, first of all because of the temporal jurisdiction; nothing before 1975 or after '79 is subject of any debate, where it is obvious that crimes against humanity were committed.[10]

Mawby and Walklate's (1994) seminal work in critical victimology places state actors in a central role in contributing to the victims who are seen compared to those who are not, while subsequent critical work has continued to highlight the role of political motivations in what is deemed criminal (Doak, 2008: 23). Within transitional justice, critiques that international courts provide selective justice and are influenced by political considerations are not unique to the KRT, but are made throughout criminal courtrooms and the literature (Meernick, 2003; Cryer, 2005; Schabas, 2009–2010; Kramer and Killean, 2012). Indeed, 'each war crimes trial is an exercise in partial justice to the extent that it reminds that the majority of war crimes go unpunished' (Simpson, 1997: 8). Yet such critiques are worth reiterating. While the focus is often on the implications of selectivity for the legitimacy of the ICL project (Cryer, 2005; Brownlie, 2003; Wilkins, 2001; Damaska, 2008), such limitations also have very real implications for those most affected by mass atrocity: the victims themselves. In Cambodia, this has been demonstrated

9 *Law on the Establishment of Extraordinary Chambers in the Courts of Cambodia for the Prosecution of Crimes Committed during the Period of Democratic Kampuchea*, Law NS/RKM/0801/12, 10 August 2001.

10 Interview with lawyer (defence), 8 November 2013. See also Closing Statement of Co-Defence Counsel, Koppe, Trial Transcript Day 224, 002/19-09-2007-ECCC/TC, 31 October 2014, at 45.

through many years of impunity, through the explicit rejection of a truth recovery mechanism, and through the exclusion of judicial consideration of the harms perpetrated by foreign actors, by lower-level cadres, or pre-1975 and post-1979.

Prosecutorial selectivity and the visibility of harm

McCormack's (1997: 683) second element of selectivity, relating to 'the particular alleged atrocities the international community is prepared to collectively prosecute', also has resonance within the KRT. As with many domestic criminal systems, international criminal prosecutors are not under an obligation to investigate or prosecute every allegation of crime which falls within their mandate. Such an approach would overburden and potentially paralyse institutions, and the graver the crimes and higher the number of perpetrators and victims, the more selective they are expected to be (Jallow, 2005). This 'sordid paradox' (Aptel, 2012: 1360) has serious implications for the victimisations rendered visible by courts: prosecutions have significant weight in shaping accepted narratives of a conflict or regime, and thus determining which victims are acknowledged as worthy of redress, and which are 'symbolically rejected' (Aptel, 2012: 1372). However, despite the importance such decisions may have for victims, critical victimologists have noted that since the legal profession's 'theft of the conflict' from victims (Christie, 1977), victims' wishes are often considered a 'secondary topic' (Fattah, 1992: 198) in decisions around who and what to prosecute. In relation to *who*, there is a tendency within ICL to prioritise individuals who held positions of power (Damaska, 2008), while victims may also find their perpetrators excluded from prosecution due to political considerations (Gelsthorpe and Padfield, 2003: 5). In relation to *what*, prosecutors have normally focused on a few 'illustrative' or 'representative' events (Waldorf, 2011; Côte, 2005) due to factors such as jurisdictional limits, evidentiary sufficiency, resource constraints, legal principles, and the comparative gravity of different crimes (Jallow, 2005: 149–153). While such prosecutorial strategies may reflect legitimate concerns, they also reveal attitudes towards which harms should be condemned, and which victimisations should be included within the pyramid of victimhood.

In relation to *who* should be prosecuted, the influence of political considerations is highly visible within the KRT. During the Tribunal's negotiations, while the UN negotiators had hoped for between 20 and 30 prosecutions, the RGC consistently argued that too wide a net would 'invite social unrest' (Ciorciari, 2009: 72). As part of the government's 'reconciliation' process had involved offering former cadres informal amnesties, the negotiators may have initially had legitimate concerns about a reignition of civil war (Ciorciari, 2009: 72). However, this position has also been described by interviewees as 'designed to protect the present people in power'.[11] Certainly, several members of Cambodia's ruling party were Khmer Rouge cadres, and it is unlikely there was any wish to see liability stray too close to home (Strangio, 2014: 241). This perspective has arguably

11 Interview with lawyer (defence), 8 November 2013.

gained credence with the passage of time; while little evidence has emerged suggesting that prosecutions could cause social unrest, the RGC has continued to oppose any cases beyond Cases 001 and 002, resulting in tensions within and outside the KRT in relation to Cases 003 and 004.

These cases concern the actions of former Navy Commander MEAS Muth, and three former mid-level Khmer Rouge, Ao An, Yim Tith and Im Chaem (DeFalco, 2014). Although it is undisputed that all four were Khmer Rouge 'officials', and although researchers have linked them to the deaths of hundreds of thousands of people (Petit, 2010; Gillison, 2012), investigations in the two cases have been characterised by disagreements between national and international staff (KRT Website, 2012) as to whether the suspects should fall within the court's personal jurisdiction of 'senior leaders' and 'those most responsible' (Kunst, 2013: 17). Outside the court, Prime Minister Hun Sen has publicly stated that Case 002 should be the KRT's last (Se, 2010), leading to speculation that the RGC is actively opposing subsequent cases from progressing (DeFalco, 2014). Although official charges were eventually made, the case against Im Chaem was dismissed in February 2017, due to a finding that she was neither 'a senior leader [n]or one of those most responsible officials' of the Khmer Rouge regime (OCIJ, 2017). This has led commentators to critique the KRT for its failure to acknowledge the role of politics, describing the dismissal as a 'farce and pretence of justice' (Wallace, 2017). Concerns that the remaining cases will never make it to trial were raised again in May 2017, when a leaked document revealed that the co-investigating judges were considering a 'permanent stay on proceedings' due to 'lack of funding', and that such a move would 'prevent any re-opening of the investigations' (*Phnom Penh Post*, 2017). Funding has certainly been a consistent issue for the KRT, and one that has been interpreted by staff as a direct interference with the Tribunal's ability to deliver on its mandate.[12] As expressed by one interviewee, 'if the judges are dependent, if their work is frustrated by just lack of funding, there is no independence, there is no continuity, it impacts on many principles'.[13] However, some commentators have expressed scepticism that funding provides a full explanation for the co-investigating judges' position (*Phnom Penh Post*, 2017). As a result of these prosecutorial choices and challenges, the KRT's recognition of the victimisations which occurred under the Khmer Rouge are currently limited to those captured by Cases 001 and 002.

While Case 002 would seem to offer broad recognition of harm, due to its focus on the policies of the Khmer Rouge, and crimes perpetrated across the country, limitations on victim visibility result from strategies around *what* crimes to prosecute. This manifests both in the focus on specific crime sites, and specific categories of crime. As has been the case in previous tribunals (Waldorf, 2011), investigations at the KRT have focused on a limited number of specific crime sites. By way of example, the Case 002 Closing Order acknowledges that by the end of the regime approximately 200 security centres and countless execution sites had

12 Interview with Judge 1, 7 November 2013.
13 Interview with Lawyer 1 (Chambers), 11 November 2013.

been established throughout Cambodia, yet less than 10% are the focus of investigation.[14] As noted above, such choices may reflect legitimate issues around evidentiary sufficiency and resource constraints. However, the use of representative sites may go against the wishes of victims, who may seek a more exhaustive form of accountability, and who may have no other official mechanism from which to seek recognition and redress (Aptel, 2012: 1367). This was evidenced during Case 002's investigations, when a number of ethnic Vietnamese civil party applicants expressed consternation on learning that investigations into crimes committed against their ethnic group were limited to certain geographical areas (Nguyen and Sperfeldt, 2014). In response, their lawyers requested additional investigations, noting that 'it is critically important to our clients' that additional sites be investigated.[15] This request was rejected as being raised too late, and the applicants were initially excluded from participating as civil parties. As Nguyen and Sperfeldt (2014: 110) note, such exclusions demonstrate how prosecutorial selectivity can impact on the representativeness 'within and among the victim compositions participating in the judicial proceedings'. While the impact of this geographical selection has been mitigated to some extent by the broad definition given to civil parties (see below), decisions as to what *categories* of crime to prosecute have continued to have a significant impact on the visibility of victims at the KRT.

The visibility and prosecution of certain crimes over others has long featured in critical criminological and victimological analysis, which has sought to dissect why certain types of harm so frequently go unacknowledged and uncontrolled (Davies, Francis and Jupp, 1999; Davies, Francis and Wyatt, 2014). Although seeking to avoid a reduction of 'oppression to patriarchy' (Spencer and Walklate, 2016), critical victimology has drawn significantly from feminist scholarship in problematising the persistent invisibility of sexual and gender-based violence (SGBV) (Mawby and Walklate, 1994: 19). While feminist and critical interventions into ICL have succeeded in bringing about legal and policy developments enabling greater recognition of SGBV (Askin, 2003), efforts to acknowledge this type of harm continue to be critiqued as inconsistent and selective (Pritchett, 2008; SáCouto and Cleary, 2009). As has been the case in previous ICL courts (Askin, 2003; O'Rourke, 2013), the KRT has been criticised for its failure to adequately prosecute SGBV crimes (Williams and Palmer, 2015; Killean, 2015; Studzinsky, 2011). This failure has been attributed to a number of interlinked factors, including the prevalence of a myth that the regime prohibited and punished SGBV (Savorn, 2011; Anderson, 2005), resource constraints leading to a focus on those crimes most easily proven (Ciorciari and Heindel, 2014: 100–101; Williams and Palmer, 2015), a lack of female interpreters, analysts and investigators (Poluda, 2015), a lack of sufficient training to enable effective and sensitive interviewing of victims (Killean, 2015), and a lack of awareness of the stigmatisation that faced victims of SGBV (De Langis and Studzinsky, 2012). As a result of these interlinked factors,

14 Case 002, Closing Order, Co-Investigating Judges, Case No. 002/19-09-2007-ECCC-OCIJ, 15 September 2010, 48.
15 ECCC Civil Party Co-Lawyers (2009).

Case 001's indictment included only one incident of rape,[16] and the prosecutors' initial submissions in Case 002 contained no reference to SGBV at all.[17]

This initial invisibility was contested by civil society actors, who published reports documenting multiple incidents of rape, forced nudity, sexual mutilation, abuse of pregnant women, and forced marriage (for example, Natale, 2011; Jacobsen, 2008; Nakagawa, 2008), hosted student forums and radio shows (Ye, 2011), and organised 'women's hearings', at which victims of SGBV shared their experiences.[18] This work challenged the KRT's narrative of the past, and resonates with critical and feminist victimologies, which refute criminal law as the correct framework for identifying victimhood (Mawby and Walklate, 1994), and places victims' voices and experiences at the centre of their methodologies (McGarry and Walklate, 2015).

Within the KRT framework, victims and their advocates (Lilja, 2013) filed petitions and requested further investigations, with varied results.[19] In the context of forced marriage, civil party representatives successfully requested further investigations, leading to two charges being included in Case 002.[20] While this development has been applauded as a 'significant positive development' (Oosterveld, 2011), the KRT's legal framework has continued to act as a limitation on victims' ability to render themselves visible. Civil parties are unable to initiate investigations themselves,[21] and civil society organisations cannot compel the KRT to investigate specific crimes. This limitation was evidenced by the repeated exclusion of rape outside the context of forced marriage within Case 002, despite sustained advocacy.[22] Yet, investigations into SGBV both inside and outside forced marriage have been undertaken in Cases 003 and 004, with civil parties' evidence cited as a motivating factor.[23] This 'shift in attitude' (Palmer and Williams, 2017) demonstrates how engagement with diverse actors can combat 'elitist blind spots' (Rajagopal, 2003; Haslam, 2011; Haslam and Edmunds, 2013), and how victims and their advocates can contribute to the critical victimological goal of uncovering victimisations that may be rendered invisible due to the political climate, social factors, or the marginalised status of the victims (Holstein and Miller, 1990; McGarry and Walklate, 2015).

16 Case 001, Decision on Parties' Requests to Put Certain Matters before the Chamber Pursuant to Rule 87(2), 001/18-07-227/KRT/TC, 28 October 2009.
17 Case 002, Introductory Submission, Office of the Co-Prosecutor (confidential), 18 July 2007.
18 See Cambodian Defenders Project (2012a, 2012b, 2014).
19 Cited in Case 002, Forwarding Order to the Office of the Co-Prosecutors, 002/19-09-2007-KRT/OCIJ, 13 March 2009; Case 002, Closing Order, paras. 216–220.
20 Case 002, Closing Order, at 1430, 1442.
21 ECCC Internal Rules, Rule 49(1); Case 002, Order on the Admissibility of Civil Party Applicants from Current Residents of Svay Rieng Province, Case No. 002/19-09-2007- ECCC-OCIJ, 9 September 2010.
22 Case 001, Decision on Parties' Requests to Put Certain Matters before the Chamber Pursuant to Rule 87(2), 001/18-07-2007-ECCC-TC, 28 October 2009; Case 002, Closing Order, at para. 1426.
23 ECCC (2014a, 2014b).

The importance of this engagement has also been demonstrated in the context of minority rights. Civil parties and their advocates have successfully contributed to the inclusion in Case 002 of allegations of genocide, deportation and other crimes specific to the treatment of the Vietnamese (Nguyen and Sperfeldt, 2014),[24] while the advocacy of the Khmer Krom ethnic minority group and their representatives has drawn attention to the crimes perpetrated against that group (Mohan, 2010). As the crimes committed against the Khmer Krom appear most prominently within Case 004, that case's uncertain future risks excluding their harm from the KRT's jurisprudence. Indeed, as explored by Mohan (2010), much experienced by this group remains underexposed. It may be that the difficulties these groups have faced in comparison to the relative success of SGBV advocacy is in part reflective of international funding priorities. There is undoubtedly a current momentum behind initiatives that address conflict-related SGBV,[25] as noted by a former civil party lawyer:

> When you combine the words transitional justice and SGBV, doors are opened, funding is there from the UN, from everybody. These are the key words and it is a little bit unfortunate for victims of other harms.[26]

In contrast, staff from a minority rights nongovernmental organisation (NGO) spoke of difficulties in obtaining funding, and of trying to advocate on behalf of minorities who continue to face discrimination within Cambodia.[27] Thus, the popularity of the cause may also impact on the ability of victims and civil society actors to raise awareness of overlooked crimes, impacting on the visibility of such harms within transitional justice narratives.

Judicial selectivity and the civil party system

The analysis thus far has focused on the processes of selectivity which have shaped the victimisations that are rendered visible through their prosecution as crimes. This section moves to consider the role of the judiciary in determining which victims are able to have their victimhood acknowledged through civil party participation. The KRT features a unique civil party participation system, which in theory allows victims' rights similar to the prosecution and defence. Its introduction was heralded as an 'historical achievement in international criminal law' as victims would be 'fully involved in proceedings at the ECCC'.[28] However, an analysis of which victims are 'fully involved' reveals that even those victims whose harms are included within indictments will find their visibility shaped by professional elites

24 Case 002, Closing Order, at 778–814.
25 See for example, UN Security Council Resolutions 1325 (2000), 1820 (2008), 1888 (2009a), 1889 (2009b), 1960 (2010), 2106 (2013a), 2122 (2013b); Committee on the Elimination of Discrimination against Women (2013).
26 Interview with lawyer (former CP Team member), 11 September 2015.
27 Interview with legal assistant (CP Team), 10 December 2013.
28 ECCC (2008).

and legal frameworks. As a result, recognition of victimhood continues to be dependent on both the victims' own characteristics, and the reactions of others (McAlinden, 2014).

In analysing victim visibility through participation, this section focuses particularly on the Tribunal's judiciary. Civil party participation is not contained in either of the Court's founding documents. Instead, the civil party system's creation is a result of judicial policy-making (Rasmussen, 1986). This section therefore focuses on the role of judges in both creating and subsequently implementing civil party participation, drawing on theories of judicial behaviour to do so. While judicial behaviour within domestic contexts has been subjected to significant analysis, the role of ICL judges has received relatively little scholarly attention (exceptions include Jodoin, 2010; Wessel, 2006). Yet judicial discretion can be used to further a variety of political and legal agendas, with the developing nature of ICL arguably granting even greater space for judicial discretion and innovation (Jodoin, 2010). Dominant models of judicial behaviour include the strategic model, which perceives judges as motivated by specific political and legal goals (Epstein and Knight, 2000), and the attitudinal model, which views the ideas, attitudes and values of judges as key influencing factors (Tarr, 2003). While these models consider judicial motivations, Baum's (1995) hierarchical model notes that judges will also be constrained by legal rules, other participants, and their own political environments. Rather than committing to one specific model, I would argue that these factors are interlinked, and that consideration of the goals, attitudes and constraints that arguably shaped the KRT judiciary's attitude to victim participation assists in an analysis of the role legal elites play in shaping victim visibility.

In keeping with Baum's hierarchical model, it is arguable that the judges' initial decision to create a civil party system was influenced in part by their legal environment. Concerns around the appropriateness of using Cambodia's domestic criminal procedures led the judges to broadly interpret their right to seek guidance from international procedure, and draft their own Internal Rules (Acquaviva, 2008: 129). In doing so, they would have observed the growing international recognition of victims' rights, as evidenced by the ICC's Rome Statute and numerous international human rights declarations. Indeed, their drafting was accompanied by intense lobbying from victims' advocates, experts and NGOs, who cited such developments and promoted the creation of an expansive victim participation system (Saliba, 2009a). Wessel (2006) has noted that the role of a 'humanitarian technocrat' is often placed on international judges, who are encouraged to adopt professional customs and ethics which further humanitarian goals. Awareness of such expectations, when combined with the victim-centric developments in ICL, may have influenced the judges' approach.

Reflecting Tarr's attitudinal model, it has also been suggested that the judges' personal attitudes towards victim participation, as informed by their own domestic legal backgrounds, shaped their approach. Reportedly, most common-law judges favoured a lesser form of participation, while the French judge and his legal officer pressed for a French/Cambodian-styled model, and the national judges favoured the scheme as a way of incorporating Cambodian law (Ciorciari and Heindel,

2014: 204). The result was the creation of a system which drew from, but also differed from the Cambodian model (Boyle, 2006: 310), and which originally provided for some of the most expansive victims' rights granted by an ICL court (Mohan, 2009). However, the judges' determination that their Rules constitute the 'primary instrument ... in determining procedures'[29] and can be amended by the judges themselves, has allowed changing judicial strategies and attitudes to exert significant influence over who can be considered a victim entitled to participate as a civil party.

Recognising victimhood

Judicial attitudes towards who should be admitted as a civil party have differed as the KRT has proceeded with Cases 001 and 002. The Rules initially required applicants to demonstrate that they were 'victims of a crime coming *within the jurisdiction of the KRT*', and that their injuries were 'physical, material or psychological' and 'the direct consequence of the offence, personal and have actually come into being'.[30] Thus, applications could be submitted in relation to any crimes that fell under the Court's jurisdiction.[31] Applications were also allowed from indirect victims, and in certain cases the successors of a deceased applicant.[32] However, in 2010 the judges amended the Rules, requiring applicants to 'demonstrate as a direct consequence of at least one of the crimes *alleged against the Charged Person*, that he or she has in fact suffered physical, material or psychological injury'.[33] This amendment followed an announcement on the scope of Case 002, and with Case 002 encompassing complex crimes and multiple defendants, the judges were undoubtedly aware of the impact incorporating large numbers of victims might have on trial expediency (McGonigle Leyh, 2011). It is therefore arguable that the amendment was an attempt to limit applications to victims connected to Case 002's specific crimes and sites (Studzinsky, 2011), furthering a strategy of trial expediency, rather than victim inclusion.

The changes were made a few months before the Case 001 judgment, and after the deadline for Case 002 applications. However, they were retrospectively applied, contributing to 23 civil party applicants having their status revoked in the Case 001 trial judgment.[34] The applicants had participated throughout the trial, and had not been informed that their status was provisional. The decision caused extreme distress (Ciorciari and Heindel, 2014: 62), with the applicants perceiving the revocation of civil party status as a rejection of their experiences of harm (O'Toole, 2010). While the status of ten individuals was restored on appeal,[35]

29 Case 002, Decision on Nuon Chea's Appeal against Order Refusing Request for Annulment, 002/19-09-2007-ECCC/OCIJ, 26 August 2008.
30 Internal Rules, Revision 3, 6 March 2009, Rule 23(2)
31 KRT Law, Arts. 2, 4, 5, 6, 7 and 8.
32 Case 001, Trial Judgment.
33 Internal Rules, Revision 5, 9 February 2010.
34 Case 001, Trial Judgment, paras. 647–649.
35 Case 001, Appeal Judgment, at 252–280.

these strong reactions demonstrate the potentially harmful processes of exclusion that can result from linking victim recognition to legal institutions. The decision has since been critiqued by other judges as 'insensitive', and of being a reaction to the 'obscure' nature of the legal framework.[36] Certainly, the civil party system's unique and 'experimental' nature limited the external guidance available to judges,[37] which may also have influenced the changeable nature of its implementation.

The issue of civil party eligibility also proved divisive in Case 002. Applicants were initially required to show 'personal'[38] harm which resulted from material facts for which a judicial investigation had been opened.[39] This excluded applicants who had suffered from identical conduct at geographical sites not included within investigations. Of the 3,970 applications considered, 2,123 were admitted, and of the rejected applicants, 1,747 appealed.[40] The appeal decision revealed significantly different judicial attitudes, as the majority admitted applicants who claimed harm related to crimes alleged against the accused in locations excluded from investigations.[41] The majority further found that Cambodia's social and cultural context during the regime required a broader consideration of victimisation, allowing for injury to be caused through the death of members of the appellant's community, through the witnessing of direct victimisation, through the knowledge of a direct victim's fate, and through the fear of a similar fate that the policies instilled.[42] As a result, 1,728 appeals were granted, increasing the number of civil parties to 3,866.

In addition to highlighting the role legal institutions play in shaping victimhood through jurisdictional limits and substantive criteria (Robins, 2017; Kendall, 2015), these decisions demonstrate how victim recognition can fluctuate as a result of changing case law and judicial strategies (Kendall and Nouwen, 2013: 246). Interviews conducted with judges and judicial officers highlighted how divisive this issue had been. Reflecting the attitudinal model, interviewees appeared to be influenced by their own legal traditions, but also by their understandings of what the court's role should be in recognising and responding to victims. Thus, some interviewees from civil law backgrounds disagreed with the majority's expansive interpretation of victimisation, which shifts away from civil law's required link with the specific crimes charged.[43] Indeed, French Judge Marchi-Uhel issued a dissenting judgment, arguing that the inclusive approach would frustrate those who satisfied the original narrower criteria, while

36 Interview with Judge 1, 7 November 2013, and Judge 4, 13 January 2014.
37 Interview with Judge 1, 7 November 2013.
38 Case 002, Order on the Admissibility of Civil Party Applicants from Current Residents of Oddar Meanchey Province, 002/19-09-2007-KRT-OCIJ, 26 August 2010, at 13.
39 Case 002, Closing Order, at 10–12.
40 Case 002, Decision on Appeals against Orders of the Co-Investigating Judges on the Admissibility of Civil Party Applications, 002/19-09-2007-ECCC-PTC, 24 June 2011.
41 Ibid. at 76–77.
42 Ibid. at 83–92.
43 Interview with Judge 4, 13 January 2014; interview with Lawyer 2 (Chambers), 11 November 2013.

disappointing those who were admitted but did not subsequently see their specific harms reflected in the Court's work.[44] In contrast, those who supported the majority position spoke of the importance of acknowledging the nature of harm under the regime[45] and avoiding 'inappropriate re-victimization … by their exclusion'.[46]

While exclusions arise whenever legal institutions are used as the basis for recognising victimhood (Mawby and Walklate, 1994), the grave harms which form the subject matter of ICL courts render such exclusions particularly emotionally charged (McEvoy and McConnachie, 2013), as illustrated by the distress expressed by rejected applicants. However, even a broad policy of recognition will exclude some. This reality is demonstrated by Case 002, which focuses on criminal policies which arguably harmed the entire Cambodian population. While the majority decision eliminated the distinction drawn between those who had been harmed in one location from those harmed in another, the policy of broad recognition did not dispel arbitrary distinctions. Instead, the distinction became between those with the means to apply for civil party status, and those without. This distinction reflects what Rombouts and Vandeginste (2003: 114) term the 'public recognition selection process', in which only some have the 'power' to pursue recognition of their victimhood. Indeed, the argument has been made that justice is predominantly pursued by 'urban elites and high-profile victims, who have a strong moral voice and an ability to clearly articulate demands' but who may not be representative of all who have suffered harm (Van der Merwe, 2014: 200).

Access to assistance may also create distinctions. In addition to requiring the energy and time to engage with the Tribunal, which victims who are struggling to meet their basic needs may not have (Kendall and Nouwen, 2013), victims may face practical barriers, such as limited internet access or literacy skills (World Bank Website, 2017), which make them dependent on outside assistance. Indeed 84% of civil party applications were submitted through intermediary NGOs (Sperfeldt, 2012). Such statistics evidence the arbitrary distinctions between recognised and unrecognised victimhood: while evidence suggests that nearly all Cambodians who lived through the regime consider themselves victims (Pham et al., 2011), only a small fraction can pursue recognition and redress at the KRT (Ciorciari and Heindel, 2014: 207). As Robins (2017: 54) has noted, 'rights are mediated by the actors who articulate them', and 'become something that are largely claimed on behalf of victims rather than by victims themselves'. The result is that victim recognition within a legal institution is often dependent on expert assistance, enhancing the control elites exercise over victim recognition, and potentially excluding those victims who may be unable to access assistance due to geographical isolation, structural inequalities, or social marginalisation (Van der Merwe, 2014).

44 Case 002, Decision on Appeals Against Orders of the Co-Investigating Judges on the Admissibility of Civil Party Applications, Separate and Partially Dissenting Opinion of Judge Marchi-Uhel, 002/19-09-2007-ECCC/PTC, 24 June 2011.

45 Interview with Judge 2, 11 November 2013.

46 Interview with Judge 1, 7 November 2013.

Conclusion

As Miers (1989) has noted, many groups and individuals can claim the label of 'victim', but the key questions for a critical victimologist are who has the power to apply the label and what considerations are significant in that determination. Drawing from this critical starting point, this chapter has made the argument that in the context of the KRT in Cambodia, as in other contexts (Mawby and Walklate, 1994), recognition of victimhood has been narrowed by myriad heterogeneous actors pursuing a variety of political, legal and social goals. Applying the critical victimological argument that terms such as 'victim' and 'victimisation' are contested and open to manipulation (Dignan, 2005), it has explored how both the initial creation of the KRT and the way its practitioners have approached their work have excluded numerous individuals who have suffered harm from its remit, leaving many outside Kendall and Nouwen's pyramid of victimhood.

To conclude, I would argue that there is a need within ICL scholarship and practice to greater acknowledge the role of actors and contexts in shaping responses to victimisation. Such responses are sites of contestation (Haslam, 2007), in which the agendas of different transitional justice practitioners and other elites often play a significant role in demarcating the extent to which the real needs of victim populations in the aftermath of atrocity are addressed by transitional justice mechanisms. This can lead to restrictions being placed on the kind of victimisations which are rendered visible and worthy of redress, as evidenced by the compromises struck between the international community and RGC in creating and limiting the jurisdiction of the KRT. However, it can also lead to innovative processes which enhance victim visibility, for example through the creation of the civil party system and the work of civil society in expanding the Court's investigations and prosecutions to include greater acknowledgment of SGBV and crimes against minority groups. Acceptance of justice as a place of constraints and contest may contribute to greater honesty and humility in the discourse surrounding transitional justice (McEvoy, 2007). Such an increase in honesty and humility would provide welcome balance to the increased use of 'justice for victims' as legitimising rhetoric (McEvoy and McConnachie, 2013). By acknowledging the inherent limitations associated with using a criminal legal framework to define and recognise victimhood, trials can be more appropriately understood as one element of broader responses to grave victimisations. Unfortunately, when a small number of selective criminal trials form the only official response to atrocity, as has been the case in Cambodia, these layered processes of exclusion leave many harms invisible and many victims ultimately without redress.

References

Acquaviva, Guido. (2008) 'New Paths in International Criminal Justice? The Internal Rules of the Cambodian Extraordinary Chambers'. *Journal of International Criminal Justice* 6 (1): 129–151.

Anderson, Katrina. (2005) 'Turning Reconciliation on its Head: Responding to Sexual Violence under the Khmer Rouge'. *Seattle Journal for Social Justice* 3(2): 785–832.

Aptel, Cécile. (2012) 'Prosecutorial Discretion at the ICC and Victims' Right to Remedy'. *Journal of International Criminal Justice* 10: 1357–1375.

Askin, Kelly D. (2003) 'Prosecuting Wartime Rape and Other Gender-related Crimes under International Law: Extraordinary Advances, Enduring Obstacles'. *Berkeley Journal of International Law* 21(2): 288–349

Bates, Alex. (2007) 'Cambodia's Extraordinary Chamber: Is it the Most Effective and Appropriate Means of Addressing the Crimes of the Khmer Rouge?'. In Ralph Henham and Paul Behrens (eds), *The Criminal Law of Genocide: International, Comparative, and Contextual Aspects*, 185–197. Abingdon: Routledge.

Baum, Lawrence. (1995) 'Electing Judges'. In Lee Epstein (ed.), *Contemplating Courts.* Thousand Oaks, CA: SAGE.

Bernath, Julie. (2015) '"Complex Political Victims" in the Aftermath of Mass Atrocity: Reflections on the Khmer Rouge Tribunal in Cambodia'. *International Journal of Transitional Justice* 10(1): 46–66.

Boyle, David. (2006) 'The Rights of Victims: Participation, Representation, Protection, Reparation'. *Journal of International Criminal Justice* 4(2): 307–313.

Brownlie, Ian. (2003) *Principles of International Law.* Oxford: Oxford University Press.

Cambodian Defenders Project. (2012a) *Women's Hearing: True Voices of Women under the Khmer Rouge.* Report on the Proceedings of the 2011 Women's Hearing on Sexual Violence Under the Khmer Rouge Regime, May. Phnom Penh: Cambodian Defenders Project.

Cambodian Defenders Project. (2012b) *Asia-Pacific Regional Women's Hearing on Gender-based Violence in Conflict.* Report on the Proceedings, December. Phnom Penh: Cambodian Defenders Project.

Cambodian Defenders Project. (2014) *2013 Women's Hearing with the Young Generation on Gender-based Violence during the Khmer Rouge Regime.* Report on the Proceedings. Phnom Penh: Cambodian Defenders Project.

Carrabine, Eamonn, Paul Inganski, Maggy Lee, Ken Plummer and Nigel South (eds). (2004) *Criminology: A Sociological Introduction*, Abingdon: Routledge.

Chandler, David. (1991) *The Tragedy of Cambodian History.* New Haven, CT: Yale University Press.

Christie, Nils. (1977) 'Conflict as Property'. *British Journal of Criminology* 17(1): 1–15.

Christie, Nils. (1986) 'The ideal victim'. In Ezzat Fattah (ed.), *From Crime Policy to Victim Policy: Reorienting the Justice System*, 17–30. Basingstoke: Macmillan.

Ciorciari, John. (2009). 'History and Politics Behind the Khmer Rouge Trials'. In John Ciorciari and Anne Heindel (eds), *On Trial: The Khmer Rouge Accountability Process*, 33–84. Phnom Penh: DC-Cam.

Ciorciari, John and Anne Heindel (2014) *Hybrid Justice.* Ann Arbor, MI: University of Michigan Press.

Committee on the Elimination of Discrimination against Women. (2013) *CEDAW General Recommendation No. 30 on Women in Conflict Prevention, Conflict and Post-conflict Situations*, 18 October, UN Doc. CEDAW/C/GC/30.

Côte, Luc. (2005) 'Reflections on the Exercise of Prosecutorial Discretion in International Criminal Law'. *Journal of International Criminal Justice* 3(1): 162–186.

Cryer, Robert. (2005) *Prosecuting International Crimes: Selectivity and the International Criminal Law Regime.* Cambridge: Cambridge University Press.

Damaska, Mirjan R. (2008) 'What is the Point of International Criminal Justice?'. *Chicago-Kent Law Review* 83(1): 329–365.

Davies, Pamela, Peter Francis and Victor Jupp (eds). (1999) *Invisible Crimes: Their Victims and their Regulation.* London: Palgrave Macmillan.

Davies, Pamela, Peter Francis and Tanya Wyatt. (2014) *Invisible Crimes and Social Harms.* London: Palgrave Macmillan.

DeFalco, Randle. (2014) 'Cases 003 and 004 at the Khmer Rouge Tribunal: The Definition of "Most Responsible" Individuals According to International Criminal Law'. *Genocide Studies and Prevention: An International Journal* 8(2): 45–65.

De Langis, Theresa and Silke Studzinsky. (2012) *Briefing Paper on the ECCC, the Cambodian Women's Hearing, and Steps for Addressing Sexual Violence under the Khmer Rouge Regime.* Phnom Penh: Cambodian Defenders Project.

Dignan, James. (2005) *Understanding Victims and Restorative Justice.* Maidenhead and New York: Open University Press.

Doak, Jonathan. (2008) *Victims' Rights, Human Rights and Criminal Justice: Reconceiving the Role of Third Parties.* Oxford: Hart Publishing.

Douglas, Mary. (1987) *How Institutions Think.* London: Routledge and Kegan Paul Ltd.

ECCC. (2008) 'Historic Achievement in International Criminal Law: Victims of Khmer Rouge Crimes Fully Involved in Proceedings of the ECCC'. Statement by the Victims Unit, 4 February.

ECCC. (2014a) 'International co-prosecutor requests investigation of alleged sexual and gender-based violence in Case 004'. Press release, 24 April.

ECCC. (2014b) 'International Co-Prosecutor Files Supplementary Submission in Case 003'. ECCC Website, 4 November, www.eccc.gov.kh/en/articles/international-co-prosecutor-files-supplementary-submission-case-003 [accessed 12 July 2018].

ECCC Civil Party Co-Lawyers. (2009) 'Civil Parties' Request for Supplementary Investigations Regarding Genocide of the Khmer Krom and the Vietnamese'. Document D250/3, 3 December.

Epstein, Lee and Jack Knight. (2000) 'Towards a Strategic Revolution in Judicial Politics: A Look Back, A Look Ahead'. *Political Research Quarterly* 53(3): 625–661.

Fattah, Ezzat. (1992) *Towards a Critical Victimology.* London: Macmillan Press.

Fawthrop, Tom and Helen Jarvis. (2005) *Getting Away With Genocide?* London: Pluto Press.

Fletcher, Laurel. (2015) 'Refracted Justice: The Imagined Victim and the International Criminal Court'. In Christian De Vos, Sara Kendall and Carsten Stahn (eds), *Contested Justice: The Politics and Practice of International Criminal Court Interventions*, 302–326. Cambridge: Cambridge University Press.

Form, Wolfgang. (2009) 'Justice 30 years later? The Cambodian Special Tribunal for the Punishment of Crimes against Humanity by the Khmer Rouge'. *Nationalities Papers* 37 (6): 889–923.

Geertz, Clifford. (1993) 'Thick Descriptions: Toward an Interpretive Theory of Culture'. In Geertz, Clifford (ed.), *The Interpretation of Cultures: Selected Essays*, 3–32. London: Fontana Press.

Gelsthorpe, Loraine and Nicola Padfield. (2003) *Exercising Discretion: Decision Making in the Criminal Justice System and Beyond.* Portland, OR: Willan.

Gillison, Douglas. (2012) 'Crimes Scenes of the Khmer'. *The Investigative Fund*, 27 February.

Gottesman, Evan. (2003) *Cambodia After the Khmer Rouge: Inside the Politics of Nation Building.* New Haven, CT: Yale University Press.

Haslam, Emily (2007) 'Law, Civil Society and Contested Justice'. In Marie-Bénédicte Dembour and Tobias Kelly (eds), *Paths to International Justice: Social and Legal Perspectives*, 57–82. Cambridge: Cambridge University Press.

Haslam, Emily. (2011) 'Subjects and Objects: International Criminal Law and the Institutionalization of Civil Society'. *International Journal of Transitional Justice* 5(2): 221–240.

Haslam, Emily, and Rod Edmunds. (2013) 'Victim Participation, Politics and the Construction of Victims at the International Criminal Court: Reflections on Proceedings in Banda and Jerbo'. *Melbourne Journal of International Law* 14: 727–747.

Heder, Steve. (2011) 'A Review of the Negotiations Leading to the Establishment of the Personal Jurisdiction of the Extraordinary Chambers in the Courts of Cambodia'. *Cambodia Tribunal Monitor*, 1 August.

Hillyard, Paddy (ed.). (2004) *Beyond Criminology: Taking Harm Seriously.* London: Pluto Press.

Hodžić, Refik. (2010) 'Living the Legacy of Mass Atrocities: Victims' Perspectives on War Crimes Trials'. *Journal of International Criminal Justice* 8(1): 113–136.

Holstein, James and Gale Miller. (1990) 'Rethinking Victimisation: An Interactionist Approach to Victimology'. *Symbolic Interaction* 13(1): 103–122.

International Criminal Tribunal for the Former Yugoslavia. (1995) *Second Annual Report to the UN General Assembly*, UN Doc. A/50/365–S/1995/728.

International Criminal Tribunal for Rwanda. (1998) *Third Annual Report to the UN General Assembly*, UN Doc. A/53/429–S/1998/857.

Jacobsen, Trudy. (2008) *Lost Goddesses: The Denial of Female Power in Cambodian History.* Singapore: NIAS Press.

Jallow, Hassan. (2005) 'Prosecutorial Discretion and International Criminal Justice'. *Journal of International Criminal Justice* 3(1): 145–161.

Jodoin, Sébastien. (2010) 'Understanding the Behaviour of International Courts: An Examination of Decision-making at the ad hoc International Criminal Tribunals'. *Journal of International Law and International Relations* 6(1): 1–34.

Kauzlarich, David, Rick Matthews and William Miller. (2001) 'Towards a Victimology of State Crime'. *Critical Criminology* 10(3): 173–194.

Kendall, Sara. (2015) 'Beyond the Restorative Turn: The Limits of Legal Humanitarianism'. In Christian De Vos, Sara Kendall and Carsten Stahn (eds), *Contested Justice: The Politics and Practice of International Criminal Court Interventions*, 352–376. Cambridge: Cambridge University Press.

Kendall, Sara and Sarah Nouwen. (2013) 'Representational Practices at the International Criminal Court: The Gap between Juridified and Abstract Victimhood'. *Law and Contemporary Problems* 76: 235–262.

Killean, Rachel. (2015) 'An Incomplete Narrative: Prosecuting Sexual Violence Crimes at the Extraordinary Chambers in the Courts of Cambodia'. *Journal of International Criminal Justice* 13(2): 331–352.

Killean, Rachel. (2016) 'Procedural Justice in International Criminal Courts: Assessing Civil Parties' Perceptions of Justice at the Extraordinary Chambers in the Courts of Cambodia'. *International Criminal Law Review* 16: 1–38.

Kissinger, Henry (1979). *White House Years.* Boston, MA: Little Brown.

Klosterman, Theresa. (1998) 'The Feasibility and Propriety of a Truth Commission in Cambodia: Too Little? Too Late?'. *Arizona Journal of International and Comparative Law* 15(3): 833–870.

Kramer, Amanda and Rachel Killean (2012) 'Security Council Referrals to the ICC: A Politicised System'. *The Irish Yearbook of International Law* 8: 117–146.

KRT Website. (2012) 'Press Release from the International Reserve Co-Investigating Judge', March, www.eccc.gov.kh/en/articles/press-release-international-reserve-co-investigating-judge [accessed 30 April 2018].

Kunst, Christine. (2013) *The Protection of Victims and Witnesses at International and Internationalized Criminal Courts – the Example of the ECCC.* Nijmegen: Wolf Legal Publishers.

Kutnjak Ivković, Sandra and John Hagan. (2011) *Reclaiming Justice: The International Tribunal for the Former Yugoslavia and Local Courts.* Oxford: Oxford University Press.

Letschert, Rianne, Roelof Haveman, Anne-Marie De Brouwer and Antony Pemberton (eds). (2011) *Victimological Approaches to International Crimes: Africa.* Cambridge: Intersentia.

Lilja, Mona. (2013) *Resisting Gendered Norms: Civil Society, the Juridical and Political Space in Cambodia.* Aldershot: Ashgate.

Linton, Suzannah. (2004) *Reconciliation in Cambodia.* Phnom Penh: Documentation Centre of Cambodia.

Madlingozi, Tshepo. (2007) 'Good Victims, Bad Victims: Apartheid's Beneficiaries, Victims and the Struggle for Social Justice'. In Wessel Le Roux and Karin van Maerle (eds), *Law, Memory and the Legacy of Apartheid: Ten Years After AZAPO v President of South Africa*, 107–126. Pretoria: Pretoria University Law Press.

Madlingozi, Tshepo. (2010) 'On Transitional Justice Entrepreneurs and the Production of Victims'. *Journal of Human Rights Practice* 2(2): 208–228.

Mawby, Rob and Sandra Walklate. (1994) *Critical Victimology: International Perspectives.* London: SAGE.

McAlinden, Anne-Marie. (2014) 'Deconstructing Victim and Offender Identities in Discourses on Child Sexual Abuse: Hierarchies, Blame and the Good/Evil Dialectic'. *British Journal of Criminology* 54(2): 180–198.

McCarthy, Conor. (2012) *Reparations and Victim Support in the International Criminal Court.* Cambridge: Cambridge University Press.

McCormack, Timothy. (1997) 'Selective Reaction to Atrocity: War Crimes and the Development of International Criminal Law'. *Albany Law Review* 60: 681–733.

McEvoy, Kieran. (2007) 'Beyond Legalism: Towards a Thicker Understanding of Transitional Justice'. *Journal of Law and Society* 34(4): 411–440.

McEvoy, Kieran and Kirsten McConnachie. (2012) 'Victimology in Transitional Justice: Victimhood, Innocence and Hierarchy'. *European Journal of Criminology* 9(5): 527–538.

McEvoy, Kieran and Kirsten McConnachie. (2013) 'Victims and Transitional Justice: Voice, Agency and Blame'. *Social and Legal Studies* 22(4): 489–513.

McGarry, Ross and Sandra Walklate. (2015) *Victims: Trauma, Testimony and Justice.* Abingdon: Routledge.

McGonigle Leyh, Brianne. (2011) *Procedural Justice? Victim Participation in International Criminal Proceedings.* Leiden: Intersentia.

Meernick, James. (2003) 'Victors' Justice or the Law? Judging and Punishing at the International Criminal Tribunal for the Former Yugoslavia'. *Journal of Conflict Resolution* 47(2): 140–162.

Meyers, Diana. (2011) 'Two Victim Paradigms and the Problem of "Impure" Victims'. *Humanity: An International Journal of Human Rights, Humanitarianism, and Development* 2(2): 255–275.

Mibenge, Chiseche Salome. (2013) *Sex and International Tribunals.* Philadelphia, PA: University of Pennsylvania Press.

Miers, David. (1989) 'Positivist Victimology: A Critique Part 1'. *International Review of Victimology* 1: 3–22.

Moffet, Luke. (2014) *Justice for Victims before the International Criminal Court.* Abingdon: Routledge.

Moffett, Luke. (2017) 'Reparations for Victims at the International Criminal Court: A New Way Forward?'. *International Journal of Human Rights* 21(9): 1204–1222.

Mohan, Giles. (1999) 'Not so Distant, Not so Strange: The Personal and the Political in Participatory Research'. *Ethics, Place and the Environment* 2(1): 41–54.

Mohan, Mahdev. (2009) 'The Paradox of Victim-centrism: Victim Participation at the Khmer Rouge Tribunal'. *International Criminal Law Review* 9(5): 733–775.

Mohan, Mahdev. (2010) 'Reconstituting the "Un-Person": The Khmer Krom and the Khmer Rouge Tribunal'. *Singapore Yearbook of International Law* 12: 43–55.

Nakagawa, Kasumi. (2008) *Gender-based Violence during the Khmer Rouge Regime: Stories of Survivors from the Democratic Kampuchea (1975–1979)*. Phnom Penh: Cambodian Defenders Project.

Natale, Katrina. (2011) *'I Could Feel My Soul Flying Away From My Body': A Study on Gender-based Violence During Democratic Kampuchea in Battambang and Svay Rieng Provinces*. Phnom Penh: Cambodian Defenders Project.

Nguyen, Lyma and Christoph Sperfeldt. (2014) 'Victim Participation and Minorities: Ethnic Vietnamese Civil Parties at the Extraordinary Chambers in the Courts of Cambodia'. *Macquarie Law Journal* 14: 97–126.

Office of the Co-Investigating Judges (OCIJ). (2017) *Closing Order (Reasons), 004 07 09 2009 ECCC OCIJ*, 10 July.

Oosterveld, Valerie. (2011) 'Atrocity Crimes Litigation Year-in-Review (2010): A Gender Perspective'. *Northwestern Journal of International Human Rights* 9(3): 325–355.

O'Rourke, Catherine. (2013) *Gender Politics in Transitional Justice*. Abingdon: Routledge.

O'Toole, James. (2010) 'Reparations remain a key issue'. *The Phnom Penh Post*, 27 July.

Owen, Taylor and Ben Kiernan. (2006) 'Bombs over Cambodia'. *The Walrus Magazine*, October, 62–69.

Palmer, Emma and Sarah Williams. (2017) 'A "shift in attitude"? Institutional change and sexual and gender-based crimes at the Extraordinary Chambers in the Courts of Cambodia'. *International Feminist Journal of Politics* 19(1): 22–38.

Palmer, Nicola. (2015) *Courts in Conflict*. Oxford: Oxford University Press.

Petit, Robert. (2010) 'Lawfare and International Tribunals: A Question of Definition? A Reaction on the Creation of the "Khmer Rouge Tribunal"'. *Case Western Reserve Journal of International Law* 43(1): 189–199.

Pham, Phuong, Patrick Vinck, Mychelle Balthazard and Sokhom Hean. (2011) *After the First Trial: A Population-based Survey on Knowledge and Perception of Justice and the Extraordinary Chambers in the Courts of Cambodia*. Report by the Initiative for Vulnerable Populations, Human Rights Center, University of California, Berkeley, June. Berkeley, CA: University of California Press.

Phnom Penh Post. (2017) 'Staying Khmer Rouge tribunal cases mulled', 8 May, www.phnompenhpost.com/national/staying-khmer-rouge-tribunal-cases-mulled [accessed 30 April 2018].

Poluda, Julian. (2015) *Promoting Gender Equality and Improving Access to Justice for Female Survivors and Victims of Gender-Based Violence under the Khmer Rouge Regime: Final Evaluation Report*. Phnom Penh: Cambodian Defenders Project.

Pritchett, Suzan M. (2008) 'Entrenched Hegemony, Efficient Procedure, or Selective Justice?: An Inquiry into Charges for Gender-based Violence at the International Criminal Court'. *Transnational Law and Contemporary Problems* 17(1): 265–305.

Rajagopal, Balakrishnan. (2003) 'International Law and Social Movements: Challenges of Theorizing Resistance'. *Colombia Journal of Transnational Law* 41(2): 396–433.

Rasmussen, Hjalte. (1986) *On Law and Policy in the European Court of Justice: A Comparative Study in Judicial Policymaking*. Dordrecht: Martinus Nijhoff.

Ratner, Stephen. (2007) 'Justice for the Khmer Rouge? Sir Ninian Stephen and the United Nations Group of Experts for Cambodia'. In Timothy L.H. McCormack and Cheryl Saunders (eds), *Sir Ninian Stephen: A Tribute*, 206–219. Melbourne: Melbourne University Publishing.

Raub, Lindsey. (2008–2009) 'Positioning Hybrid Tribunals in International Criminal Justice'. *New York University Journal of International Law and Politics* 41: 1013–1053.

Robins, Simon. (2017) 'Failing Victims? The Limits of Transitional Justice in Addressing the Needs of Victims of Violations'. *Human Rights and International Legal Discourse* 9(1): 41–58.

Rombouts, Heidy and Stef Vandeginste. (2003) 'Reparation for Victims of Gross and Systematic Human Rights Violations: The Notion of Victim'. *Third World Legal Studies* 16: 89–114.

SáCouto, Susana and Katherine Cleary. (2009) 'The Importance of Effective Investigation of Sexual Violence and Gender-based Crimes at the International Criminal Court'. *American University Journal of Gender, Social Policy and the Law* 17(2): 337–359.

Saliba, Michael. (2009a) 'Civil Party Participation at ECCC: Overview'. *Cambodia Tribunal Monitor*, 6 November.

Saliba, Michael. (2009b) 'Civil Parties Boycott Start of Character Witness Testimony while Experts Offer Psychological Assessment of Duch'. *Cambodia Tribunal Monitor*, 31 August.

Savorn, Duong. (2011) *The Mystery of Sexual Violence under the Khmer Rouge Regime*. Phnom Penh: Cambodian Defenders Project.

Schabas, William. (2009–2010) 'Victor's Justice: Selecting "Situations" at the International Criminal Court'. *The John Marshall Law Review* 43: 535–552.

Se, Suy. (2010) 'Cambodian PM Says No Third Khmer Rouge Trial'. Agence France-Presse, 27 October.

Simpson, Gerry. (1997) 'War Crimes: A Critical Introduction'. In Timothy McCormack and Gerry Simpson (eds), *The Law of War Crimes: National and International Approaches*, 1–24. The Hague: Kluwer.

Spencer, Dale C. and Sandra Walklate (eds). (2016) *Reconceptualizing Critical Victimology: Interventions and Possibilities*. Lanham, MD: Lexington Books.

Sperfeldt, Christoph. (2012) 'Cambodian Civil Society and the Khmer Rouge Tribunal'. *International Journal of Transitional Justice* 6(1): 149–160.

Stover, Eric. (2005) *The Witnesses: War Crimes and the Promise of Justice in The Hague*. Philadelphia, PA: University of Pennsylvania Press.

Strangio, Sebastian. (2014) *Hun Sen's Cambodia*. New Haven, CT: Yale University Press.

Studzinsky, Silke. (2011) 'Victim's Participation before the ECCC'. *Zeitschrift für Internationale Strafrechtsdogmatik* 6: 887–891.

Tarr, G. Alan. (2003) *Judicial Process and Judicial Policy Making*. Boston, MA: Wadsworth.

Tilly, Charles. (2008) *Credit and Blame*. Princeton, NJ: Princeton University Press.

Trumbull, Charles (2008) 'The Victims of Victim Participation in International Criminal Proceedings'. *Michigan Journal of International Law* 29: 777–826.

UN. (1985) *UN Declaration of Basic Principles of Justice for Victims of Crime and Abuse of Power*, UNGA Res. 40/34, 29 November.

UN. (2005) *UN Basic Principles and Guidelines on the Right to a Remedy and Reparation for Victims of Gross Violations of International Human Rights Law and Serious Violations of International Humanitarian Law*, UNGA Res. 60/147, 16 December.

UN and Royal Government of Cambodia. (2003) *Agreement between the UN and the Royal Government of Cambodia Concerning the Prosecution under Cambodian Law of Crimes Committed during the Period of Democratic Kampuchea*, 6 June.

UNOHCHR. (1993) *The Right to Restitution, Compensation and Rehabilitation for Victims of Gross Violations of Human Rights and Fundamental Freedoms. Final Report of the Special Rapporteur, Mr M. Ch Bassiouni*, UN Doc. E/CN.4/2000/62, 5 March.

UNOHCHR. (2005) *Updated Set of Principles for the Protection and Promotion of Human Rights through Action to Combat Impunity*, UN Doc. E/CN.4/2005/102/Add.1, 18 February.

UN Secretary-General. (1998) *Letter addressed to the President of the General Assembly*, UN Doc. A/52/1007, 31 July.

UN Security Council. (2000) *Resolution 1325*, adopted by the Security Council at its 4,213th meeting, on 31 October, S/RES/1325.

UN Security Council. (2008) *Resolution 1820*, adopted by the Security Council at its 5,916th meeting, on 19 June, S/RES/1820.

UN Security Council. (2009a) *Resolution 1888*, adopted by the Security Council at its 6,195th meeting, on 30 September, S/RES/1888.

UN Security Council. (2009b) *Resolution 1889*, adopted by the Security Council at its 6,196th meeting, on 5 October, S/RES/1889.

UN Security Council. (2010) *Resolution 1960*, adopted by the Security Council at its 6,453rd meeting, on 16 December, S/RES/1960.

UN Security Council. (2013a) *Resolution 2106*, adopted by the Security Council at its 6,984th meeting, on 24 June, S/RES/2106.

UN Security Council. (2013b) *Resolution 2122*, adopted by the Security Council at its 7,044th meeting, on 18 October, S/RES/2122.

Van der Merwe, Hugo. (2014) 'Reparations through different lenses: the culture, rights and politics of healing and empowerment after mass atrocities'. In Jo-Anne M. Wemmers (ed.), *Reparation for Victims of Crimes against Humanity*, 200–218. Abingdon: Routledge.

Van Wijk, Joris. (2013) 'Who is the "Little Old Lady" of International Crimes? Nils Christie's Concept of the Ideal Victim Reinterpreted'. *International Review of Victimology* 19(2): 159–179.

Vasiliev, Sergey. (2009) 'Article 68(3) and the Personal Interests of Victims in the Emerging Practice of the ICC'. In Carsten Stahn and Göran Sluiter (eds), *The Emerging Practice of the International Criminal Court*, 635–691. Leiden: Martinus Nijhoff.

Waldorf, Lars. (2011) '"A Mere Pretense of Justice": Complementarity, Sham Trials and Victor's Justice at the Rwanda Tribunal'. *Fordham International Law Journal* 33(4): 1220–1277.

Walklate, Sandra. (2011) 'Reframing Criminal Victimization: Finding a Place for Vulnerability and Resilience'. *Theoretical Criminology* 15(2): 179–194.

Wallace, Julia. (2017) 'The Bucolic Life of a Cambodian Grandmother Accused of Mass Killings'. *New York Times*, 24 February.

Wessel, Jared. (2006) 'Judicial Policy-making at the International Criminal Court: An Institutional Guide to Analyzing International Adjudication'. *Columbia Journal of Transnational Law* 44(2): 377–452.

White, Cheryl S. (2017) *Bridging Divides in Transitional Justice*. Cambridge: Intersentia.

Wilkins, Burleigh T. (2001) 'Whose Trials? Whose Reconciliation?'. In Aleksandr Jokic (ed.), *War Crimes and Collective Responsibility: A Reader*, 85–96. Maiden, MA: Blackwell.

Williams, Sarah and Emma Palmer. (2015) 'The Extraordinary Chambers in the Courts of Cambodia: Developing the Law on Sexual Violence?'. *International Criminal Law Review* 15(3): 452–484.

World Bank Website. (2017) 'Cambodia Statistics', data.worldbank.org/country/Cambodia [accessed 30 April 2018].
Ye, Beini. (2011) 'Forced Marriages as Mirrors of Cambodia Conflict Transformation'. *Peace Review: A Journal of Social Justice* 23(4): 469–475.
Zhang, Binxin. (2016) 'Recognising the Limits of Victims Participation: A Comparative Examination of the Victim Participation Schemes at the ECCC and ICC'. In Simon Meisenberg and Ignaz Stegmiller (eds), *The Extraordinary Chambers in the Courts of Cambodia: Assessing their Contribution to International Criminal Law*, 515–535. Berlin: Asser Press.

8 Distant historical wrongs, truth telling and restorative justice

Exploring schools and museums as potential vehicles for repairing historical wrongs

David Wilkins

Introduction

This desire for recognition of wrongdoing and for acts of contrition or reparations for historical injustices are increasingly common, often inspired by reparations for the Holocaust (Gibney, Howard-Hassmann, Coicaud and Steiner, 2008: 44). One of the most developed calls for reparations for historical injustice concerns transatlantic slavery. Calls have been issued for reparations to African Americans from the US government and from Western countries to African and Caribbean countries, the most recent example being the case developed by the Caribbean Community (CARICOM) against Britain, France, Spain, Portugal, the Netherlands, Sweden and Denmark.[1] This claim, however, has been rebuffed by those subject to it (Wilkinson, 2017; Weaver, 2015), as was the case with claims for reparations presented at the 2001 United Nations (UN) Conference Against Racism and Xenophobia, where Western nations recognised 'slavery and the slave trade are a crime against humanity and should always have been so', both signalling disapproval of slavery but asserting that past values were different and therefore reparations not a legitimate request (UN, 2001: 6; Howard-Hassmann, 2008; Beckles, 2013). But this does not mean that there are not legacies of transatlantic slavery that are deserving of redress and that there are no other avenues open to repair.

This chapter does not concern itself directly with the case for and against reparations for slavery. Like David Miller (2007), the chapter is predicated on the position that historic injustices which have not been addressed deserve repair and, as Janna Thompson (2002) argues, citizens of countries and members of communities, as intergenerational collectives, have a duty to contribute to the repair of harm that arises from past actions of members of their collective. However, it also takes the position that claims for financial reparations and apology for transatlantic slavery often oversimplify the history and legacy of transatlantic slavery and offer a repair that is too blunt to satisfactorily address the attitudinal and relational legacy of slavery (see also Evans and Wilkins, 2017). Echoing criticisms of the processes of transitional justice that have informed and shaped demands for reparations for transatlantic slavery (Gready and Robins, 2014), the chapter instead

1 See for example: Biondi (2007: 255–256); Howard-Hassmann (2004: 86); Gifford (2000: 16–18); Leigh Day (2014); Beckles (2013).

seeks to explore how this history can be learnt from in a way that facilitates relational and attitudinal changes that enable a transformation that delivers a just future.

This chapter argues that schools and museums can act as sites for historical truth telling, dialogue and relational repair. The revision of historical curricula and museum representations of slavery and abolition has long been called for by advocates of reparations who identify such revision as both a form of symbolic redress for slavery and its legacy and as needed to reform historical consciousness rooted in racial prejudice and the exclusion of African contributions to Western development that prevents the economic legacies of slavery from being recognised and addressed (see, for example Robinson, 2000: 7–10, 47–96; Brooks, 2004: 38; Lowen, 2007: 135–171). CARICOM's Ten Point Plan for Reparations calls for the funding of museums and for the revision of Eurocentric historiography, and for the funding of projects to raise awareness of Caribbean African heritage and history (Leigh Day, 2014). However, this chapter differs from the CARICOM approach. First, it does not suggest that the historical narrative is completely decided but rather that the truth is yet to be fully established and that this process can be achieved through collaboration. Second, whilst it is likely that international collaboration would be predominantly funded by the wealthier nations that are also subject to claims for reparations, such funding should not be considered as reparation, nor should repair be considered as monetarily quantifiable (see also Evans and Wilkins, 2017). Rather, processes of dialogue and relational repair should not be timebound, but should constitute a collaborative, critical reflection on transatlantic slavery and its legacy, including regarding how this history has been (mis)remembered, and the impact of historical memory on present-day attitudes, relationships and socioeconomic justice. In further outlining how this process could work, this chapter draws upon the strengths of transitional justice processes, notably the values of Socratic citizenship identified by David Thelen (2003) in the South African Truth and Reconciliation Commission's (TRC) process of public testimony, and how this could facilitate attitudinal changes and relational repair which could result in support for policies to realise transformational change.

By envisioning a process of historical truth telling via schools and museums which seeks to facilitate dialogue and a transformative attitudinal and relational repair, this chapter offers a model of repair for the legacies of transatlantic slavery that is superior to financial reparations. Financial reparations oversimplify the legacies of transatlantic slavery by failing to address the attitudinal and relational harms which perpetuate economic inequalities. Attitudinal and relational repair instead can create the political climate in which financial inequalities that are, in part, a legacy of transatlantic slavery, are addressed, but for forward-looking reasons and not (only) as reparation for past action. This is important as it is not only less divisive than calls for financial reparations based on legal principles, but it is also more progressive. John Torpey (2006, 2009) argued that the reparations movement is not only divisive but potentially regressive as it situates the duty to address present-day inequalities and injustices in justice for historical wrongdoing and not in the meeting of present-day and future need. As Pamina Firchow

(2013) has demonstrated regarding Colombia, such concerns are not unfounded as governments will seek to downplay their duty to address present-day need by arguing that if there is no identifiable historical wrong-doing that caused a specific suffering, then there is no wrong to address. But inequality always deserves to be addressed because it is wrong and because it creates future inequality and injustice (see Evans and Wilkins, 2017). Learning from the past in order to create a better justice should therefore be the primary motivation. Whilst calls for financial reparations help to demonstrate the historical causes of present-day inequality and thereby help emphasise that they are unjust rather than natural, by framing the need for justice as backward looking, they ultimately undermine the present-day and future case for justice and equality of descendants of enslaved and colonised individuals and the lessons that can be learnt from this history in building a more just future for all.

To advance its argument, the chapter develops in two stages. First, it examines why relational and attitudinal repair is so important for repairing legacies of transatlantic slavery. Second, it explores the idea of relational repair and truth telling, commencing with the basic principles of restorative justice, transitional justice and truth commissions, before considering how such ideas have been adapted in museum exhibitions and educational curricula. The chapter then considers how such ideas can also be identified by referring to museum and educational developments in the UK, USA and transnationally with the UNESCO Slave Route Project, and how processes of reconciliation can be furthered by following restorative justice-inspired programmes of the organisations Coming to the Table and Traces of the Trade.

The importance of attitudinal and relational repair to overcoming the legacies of transatlantic slavery

Instead of being the primary legacy of transatlantic slavery, economic inequality between nations and racially defined socioeconomic inequality within states are symptoms of the attitudinal and relational legacies of transatlantic slavery and it is these that first and foremost need to be addressed. Significantly, these relational and attitudinal differences reflect the way that the history of transatlantic slavery has been remembered by those on all sides of the reparations debate. On the one hand, transatlantic slavery helped to develop and entrench ideas of racial hierarchy and racism which have shaped the way this history has been remembered. Even abolitionism did not challenge the overall racist thinking of transatlantic slavery. Instead, abolitionism was celebrated as an enlightened gift by European nations, particularly Britain, and came to be incorporated into a narrative of colonialism as a civilising mission (Blackburn, 2011: 440–444). In the French Caribbean, freed slaves were urged to forget slavery and to thank the French government for their liberty whilst in France itself slavery was forgotten as the French Revolution and its ideas of liberty, fraternity and equality came to form the basis of national historical consciousness and identity (Gross, 2011). In the USA, reconciliation between the North and South following the Civil War was rooted in the exclusion of African

Americans (Blight, 2002: 120–152; Kaufman, 2006; McElya, 2007: 8–9; Foner, 1988). The Confederate apologist narrative of 'The Lost Cause' which presented Southern slavery as paternalistic and benign alongside the erasure of African American resistance to slavery, service in the Union forces and a whitewashing of the Underground Railroad distorted US historical memory and denied African Americans their role in their own struggle (McElya, 2007: 130–143; Blight, 2002: 191–210, Kachun, 2003: 155). In a country whose founding myth rooted the rights of citizenship in the Revolutionary War, the erasure of African Americans' resistance to enslavement helped white Americans legitimate their denial of African American equality and civil rights (Blight, 2002: 120–152).

Whilst dominant understanding of slavery and abolition across Western countries was entwined with Eurocentric prejudices and hierarchies reflective of slavery, the perspective of those once enslaved and their descendants nevertheless survived. In the USA, historians such as Frederick Douglass and W.E.B. du Bois led the fight to preserve their community's memories and perspectives on American history (Blight, 2002: 93–113). African American colleges were important to this intellectual resistance and, by welcoming African and African Caribbean scholars, helped to foster a wider pan-African consciousness (Parker, 2008). Pan-African historiography, notably the work of C.L.R. James (2001), Eric Williams (1944) and Walter Rodney (1973) (which promoted slave resistance as precipitating abolition, demonstrated how the profits of transatlantic slavery drove industrialisation in the global North and how the slave trade under-developed Africa, leaving it vulnerable to European colonialisation), has come to underpin the historical perspective of reparations advocates (Beckles, 1987). Whilst some aspects of their arguments have been criticised by historians,[2] the premise that transatlantic slavery benefitted European and American states at the expense of Africa and that resistance to slavery was an important factor in abolition's triumph is generally accepted (Davis, 2006: 157–174, 205–230, 240–249). However, whether this amounts to a case for reparations remains both politically subjective and divisive, as there is a great deal of mistrust over the evidence as well as the political motivations of different interpretations. As Manfred Berg (2009: 73–74) writes concerning the US debate for reparations:

> arguments made by both sides are often based on flawed history. Many reparations activists, for example, grossly inflate the mortality of the slave ships to an alleged 25 million victims, which, they claim, dwarfs the Nazi genocide of the Jews of Europe. Virtually all historians of the transatlantic slave trade agree, however, that the total volume of the trade ranged from 10 million to

2 For example, Seymour Drescher in *Econocide* (1977) undermined Williams's argument that abolitionism was economically motivated. Historians of industrialisation have also questioned the extent to which the profits of slavery were responsible for industrialisation, pointing to technological innovation and the exploitation of the working class (Mokyr, 1993: 76–78). Supporters of Williams, such as Joseph Inikori (1987, 2002), denounce analysis which discounts such perspectives as 'inward looking' (1987: 783). See also Eltis and Engerman (2000) and Lovejoy (1989).

> 13 million between 1500 and the late nineteenth century and that roughly 2 million Africans died during the infamous 'middle passage' from Africa to the Americas. Reparations critics, on the other hand, tend to warm up outdated notions of North American slavery as a benevolent and paternalistic system in which slaves had 'rights' and enjoyed the protection of the laws.

As Berg (2009: 74) notes, it is therefore necessary 'to set the historical record straight'. However, it is also necessary to 'analyze the historical discourse' (Berg, 2009: 74) and, I would add, to seek to repair the relationships and attitudes which both perpetuate the harms of slavery and prevent the building of consensus between those divided by this history over its present-day ramifications.

Legalised approaches to reparations which prioritise financial reparations are intrinsically ill-suited to repairing the attitudinal and relational harms of transatlantic slavery's legacy due to their combative nature (and this is before considering legal obstacles including statutes of limitations and determining what court has the jurisdiction to hear such a case; see, for example, Berg and Schaffer, 2009: 2; Brooks, 2004: 123; Brophy, 2006: 3). Rhoda Howard-Hassmann argued in *Reparations to Africa* (2008: 166) that a truth commission for Africa concerning the lasting impact of the transatlantic slave trade and colonialism on present-day African under-development could be beneficial. The idea of a truth commission can also be seen in Congressman John Conyers's bill HR40 (see Brophy, 2006: 50). Introduced each year since 1989, HR40 has called for an investigation into the legacy of slavery in the USA and whether reparations are needed. Due to public opposition to reparations in the USA, the bill has never passed. Opposition from Western nations to even the concept of reparations, exhibited at the 2001 Durban Conference, similarly suggests that it is highly unlikely that an international truth commission concerning the case for reparations could ever be established. But the ideas of truth telling still have much to offer in conceptualising how to repair the attitudinal and relational legacies of transatlantic slavery outside of the confines of a formal truth commission.

Facilitating relational repair

Restorative justice avoids punitive measures and instead seeks to facilitate reconciliation between individuals and communities (Minnow, 1998: 9–24). It often prioritises personal testimony and dialogue between victims and offenders in which the victim can articulate their perspective and attain 'closure', and the offender hopefully learns the impact of their actions and becomes rehabilitated (Hudson and Galloway, 1996: 9–10). At its most advanced, restorative justice seeks to identify and repair the structural inequalities and prejudices, 'such as racism, sexism and classism', which 'prevent society from living in whole, harmonious and healthy relationships' (Van Ness and Heetberks Strong, 2006: 42).

The role of truth telling in both individual and societal healing is underlined by the four types of truth identified by South African truth and reconciliation commissioners (Posel, 1999: 11–12). The first was 'forensic or factual truth', a form of truth which could be established in a court of law and which might include, in the case of South Africa, the location of the body of a victim of political violence. The second form of truth was 'personal or narrative truth', a concept which acknowledges subjective understandings individuals hold regarding their direct experiences and the emotional and psychological impact of past wrongdoing. Creating space for the telling of personal truths serves to affirm the innate worth of those victimised and offers a reminder of the personal tragedies involved in mass injustices. The third truth, 'social truth', refers to how different communities hold collective understandings of history and society due to shared experiences and 'interaction, discussion and debate' about these events (Posel, 1999: 12). Telling social truths both acknowledges the validity of differing perspectives whilst also enabling the critical deconstruction of collective memory and the ways it can constitute an obstacle to relational repair. By telling and discussing these three truths it is hoped that 'healing truth' is created whereby differing opinions are understood and respected, where contentious disagreements over past events are minimised, and mutual empathy and respect are fostered (Posel, 1999: 12).

Truth commissions, therefore, seek to provide a process of 'social memory making' in which 'social, political and collective identities can be revised and relationships based upon these identities can be repaired' (de Brito, Aguilar and Gonzaléz-Enríquez, 2001: 25). This repair of identities and relationships is hoped to provide a platform for the socioeconomic transformation of society. However, this has often not occurred. Commenting on the TRC, Alfred Brophy (2006: 47) concluded that it 'offered little more than truth and precious little reconciliation'. As transformation over the first two and a half decades of democracy has been slow, critics of the TRC have increasingly identified its circumscribed focus (only on gross human rights violations and the post-1948 period) as having downplayed the everyday economic violence of apartheid and the need for economic as well as political transformation (Christodoulidis and Veitch, 2008: 13; du Bois, 2008: 128–33; Waldorf, 2012: 177). Other truth commissions have similarly been criticised for too narrow a focus (such as the failure to include the activities of the USA in Latin American truth commissions), and for failing to facilitate transformation (Parodi, 2008; Gready and Robins, 2014). These shortcomings, however, reflect limitations of the design of the commissions and of political action to capitalise on their impact. As Fullard and Rousseau (2008) have argued, the personal testimonies provided during the TRC's Committee on Human Rights Violations hearings were highly impactful. Witnessed on television around the country, personal testimonies brought home to many South Africans (particularly those white South Africans who were sheltered from the direct violence of apartheid) the gross violence and suffering of many victims and provided a unifying effect upon the country.

David Thelen (2003: 161) argues that the TRC's process of public testimony created the conditions of Collingwoodian 're-enactment' and Socratic citizenship. In using the term re-enactment, Collingwood did not refer to the acting out of past actions but rather the attempt to critically think through historical events, to try to understand not only what happened but why. Collingwoodian re-enactment necessitates an engagement with and understanding of how people thought in the past, and why they thought the way they did (personal and social truths) (Thelen, 2003: 151–165, 169–170). Observers of testimony were, therefore, induced to critically reflect upon apartheid and ask difficult questions concerning historical agency and choice, including how they might have acted in the past if they happened to be in the position of a perpetrator, victim or bystander. Consequently, Thelen argues, the TRC emphasised everyone's 'responsibility for creating a culture of human rights' (Thelen, 2003: 161). The TRC did, therefore, provide a platform for attitudinal change and relational repair but this was arguably not fully captured for transformation. The reasons for the failure of the TRC to facilitate transformation reflect that focus of the TRC was curtailed by focusing on gross human rights violations and the impact on specific individuals as 'the Commission paid little attention to gross violations suffered by the vast majority of the South African population, violations that took the form of pass laws, forced removals, convict labor for farms, detentions without trial, and so forth' (Mamdani, 2002: 58). As such, the TRC perpetuated the political compromise which enabled political transition and failed to deliver societal reconciliation and economic transformation, the latter being illustrated by the Commission's focus on individual victims and advocacy of individual reparations, not communal reparations (Mamdani, 2002: 54–56).

The constraints of a formal commission process also apply for truth commissions for more distant historical wrongs, such as the lack of exploration of the wider history of Canada's colonisation in the Canadian Truth and Reconciliation Commission into the abuse suffered by children in Indian residential homes (Nagy, 2013). Mauritius's Truth and Justice Commission into the lasting impact of the island's history of colonisation, slavery and indentured labour under Dutch, French and British rule was similarly undermined by the constraints of a formal truth commission. As Rosabelle Boswell (2014) notes, like South Africa's TRC, the commission's short period of operation and its legalised approach contributed to the homogenisation and essentialisation of descendants of enslaved persons and oversimplified the evolution and operation of racism within society, whilst also downplaying the role of recent economic development in shaping inequality. Nevertheless, Boswell (2014: 179) argues, the commission 'opened the door' for further processes which seek to advance equality and transform Mauritian society by learning from its past. The commission itself recommends using commemorational and educational initiatives to increase awareness of the history and legacy of slavery and indentured labour, for instance: a '"Museum of Slavery" to be created in the capital city of Port Louis' and a memorial at 'the islet where infected slaves were disembarked on the Ilot du Morne/Pointe Marron, forming today part of Hotel Paradis' (Truth and Justice Commission, 2011: 395).

The strengths and weaknesses of truth commissions demonstrate the potential reparative impact of truth-telling processes but also that these processes need to extend beyond the confines of official commissions. In the words of Margaret Urban Walker (2006: 144), 'repair is in the history we make and make sure is told'. She adds that this is a 'process we should expect to be intergenerational' (Walker, 2006: 144). It is, therefore, not enough just to hold truth commissions. The truths told must keep being retold and the wider injustices and flaws within society that they illuminate must be explored and addressed. Significantly, the findings of truth commissions often form a central role in heritage and educational initiatives in post-transitional countries, such as Sierra Leone's Peace Museum (established following the Sierra Leone Truth and Reconciliation Commission). By retelling the truths of the commissions, such commemorative institutions can help to maintain a focus on past injustice that helps present-day society identify potential legacies and remnants of this past injustice in itself and, therefore, help motivate and inform political pressure for further political, social and economic transformations. Like Sierra Leone's Peace Museum, South Africa's Apartheid Museum was also heavily influenced by the findings of the TRC, although this arguably contributes to the narrative of apartheid presented in the museum reflecting the TRC's weaknesses, specifically in its lack of attention to the everyday economic violence of apartheid (Bremner, 2007; Verbeeck, 2007). Again, this demonstrates that truth commissions should only be considered the start of the truth-telling process which creates a platform for wider societal engagement in processes of truth telling, critical reflection on the past (and how it has shaped the present), and the role of memory in creating and perpetuating social divisions and injustices. As 'contact zones' (Purkis, 2013), museums and schools are ideal sites in which factual, personal and social truth telling and dialogue can occur.

When first coined, the term 'contact zone' described how museums could be sites in which visitors were introduced to new research, ideas and historical narratives which differ to those they hold (Purkis, 2013). The term has since developed to refer to safe spaces in which individuals from diverse backgrounds can meet and learn about one another, aiding community cohesion by tackling issues of prejudice and mistrust which often arise from lack of knowledge about and understanding of people from different communities (Purkis, 2013). Similarly, Alan McCully (2010, 2012) has argued, with reference to Northern Ireland, that if history is taught as a subject of investigation rather than as an imposed and fixed narrative to learn, the school classroom can act as a place in which students are able to step away from communal understandings of the past in order to critically and dispassionately engage with history and issues of legacy. In outlining this potential of school history, McCully (2010) refers to the work of Peter Seixas (2004), who has argued for the teaching of critical historical thinking in modern, diverse societies. Whilst history in schools has typically promoted a patriotic narrative that has celebrated essentialist understandings of the nation and its people, teaching *historical thinking* breaks away from the top-down imposition of historical narrative and instead teaches students to critically engage with history, how it has been represented and how it has been remembered. Critical historical thinking reflects the Socratic citizenship of the TRC identified by Thelen, further underlining the importance of exploring not only what happened in the past but why. This necessitates seeking to understand: the motives and fears of those in the past; how history has been catalogued and remembered, and the reasons behind divergent communal memories; how these factors shape, and relate to, present-day political interests and socioeconomic relationships. Exploring the concept of truth telling, McCully (2012) has also suggested that storytelling can help with enabling students to empathise with historical victims from different backgrounds to them. The utilisation of schools – and museums – as sites for historical truth telling need not be limited to individual museums and classrooms but can be transnational projects, as illustrated by the Foundation for German Polish Reconciliation. Established in 1990, this foundation has seen collaboration between Germany and Poland in the development of school textbooks and touring museum exhibitions (Hofhansel, 2005). Whilst there is still criticism of how many in Germany have struggled to come to terms with familial complicity in Nazi crimes (see, for example, Bachman, 2013), this project has sought to share perspectives and voices from Germany and Poland and to create a shared understanding of the shared history of the Second World War.[3] Despite imperfections and limitations, such projects offer an insight into how historical truth telling can be developed concerning the history and legacy of transatlantic slavery. As we shall now see, some existing projects can also be identified as potential contributors to processes of historical truth telling to be built upon and expanded.

Developing a truth-telling framework to repair the legacies of transatlantic slavery

In recent years, transatlantic slavery and its legacy has become increasingly discussed and commemorated across the Atlantic world with many of these developments fulfilling aspects of historical truth telling. The following paragraphs will consider how historical research and archaeological investigations can fulfil the role of factual truth telling, and how museums, schools and memorials can facilitate and reflect processes of personal and social truth telling. The chapter will then explore how processes of personal and social truth telling, dialogue and relational repair can be further expanded.

As noted above, the most basic conceptualisation of truth by the TRC was factual truth. Also, as Manfred Berg (2009: 74) noted of the divisive reparation debate, it is necessary to set the historical record straight. It is, therefore, important to explore how this could be facilitated. An example of how historians can contribute to processes of factual historical truth telling comes from *Voyages: The*

3 There is a wider criticism of how Eastern European countries have confronted their complicity in Nazi-era crimes, including the Holocaust. Part of this problem has been located in how the Soviet Union did not see Jewish people as exceptional victims of the Nazis but as part of the Soviet victims of the Nazis. This both denied Jewish people's exceptional victimhood of the Holocaust and enabled a deliberate failure to explore how Eastern Europeans had been complicit in the extermination of Jewish communities and how this reflected a wider and deeper history of anti-Semitism. The consequences of this failure to confront past anti-Semitism and complicity in the Holocaust is arguably contributing to worrying developments in countries such as Poland and Hungary (see for example Tobias, 2018; Gunter, 2018).

Trans-Atlantic Slave Trade Database. [4] Culminating decades of research into the archives of shipping companies involved in the transatlantic slave trade, the database has enabled authoritative estimates of the numbers involved in the slave trade, including numbers and regions of embarkation, disembarkation and death rates.[5] Available online for members of the public to search and utilise, the database demonstrates how academic research can both reveal information about the past and be made available for public consumption in innovative ways so that the information can be assessed and explored by all with internet access. Similarly, the Legacies of British Slavery Project by University College London (UCL) has explored the archival records of compensation payments paid by the British state for loss of rightful 'property' due to the Abolition of Slavery in the British Empire Act 1833.[6] The project's research has traced not only who the payments were made to but also sought to explore how these payments were used, further expanding understanding of how slavery helped finance British industrialisation, the building of stately homes, the capitalisation of banks, and the wealth of the British establishment and state (Draper, 2010; Hall et al., 2014). Like *Voyages*, the Legacies of British Slavery Project has created a database from its research material, enabling members of the public to conduct their own analysis and make their own interpretations.

Archaeological research can also provide a form of factual truth telling to shape wider dialogues about the history, nature and legacy of slavery. For example, the unearthing of the African Burial Ground in Manhattan, New York, during the excavation of foundations for a new federal government office building in 1991 has helped to stimulate research into the history of slavery in New York and the Northern US states (National Parks Service, n.d.). Further research into the city's history of slavery and the lives of enslaved Africans in early New Amsterdam (later New York) formed the basis of a permanent museum at the African Burial Ground, which catalogues the process of archaeological research for visitors. There is also a permanent memorial which honours and reimposes the presence of those once forgotten (National Parks Service, n.d.). This helped challenge the popular idea, associated with the Civil War, that slavery was only ever practised in the Southern states. The discovery precipitated further research by the New York Historical Society into slavery, race and the Civil War in New York City's history, including the links between New York bankers and slavery which almost led to New York seceding to join the Confederacy (Berlin and Harris, 2005; New York Historical Society, n.d.).

The developments in New York reflect wider developments in how slavery has been represented in institutions across the USA, including sites such as Virginia's Colonial Williamsburg, Washington DC's African American Civil War Museum and Memorial, and Cincinnati's National Underground Railroad Freedom Center, and even sites which were originally established to promote neo-Confederate

4 Voyages: The Trans-Atlantic Slave Trade Database (2008).
5 Voyages: The Trans-Atlantic Slave Trade Database (2008).
6 UCL Department of History (2018).

historiography, such as the Museum of the Confederacy and Virginia Historical Society, both situated in Richmond, Virginia (see Tyler-McGraw, 2006; Campbell and Rice, 1991; Horton, 2006; The African American Civil War Museum, n.d.; National Underground Railroad Freedom Center, n.d.). Federal institutions have been at the forefront of the battle to revise how the history of slavery is remembered and understood. Notably, the National Parks Service no longer presents the Civil War as being about 'states' rights' and has developed new sites to memorialise the Civil Rights Movement and the Underground Railroad, particularly from African American perspectives (Nash, 2006; Pitcaithley, 2006; Glass-Avery, 2011). Revisions of narrative at sites such as Philadelphia's Liberty Bell Museum to include the role of slavery and the experience of slaves in the building and city's history have also served to reverse past silences concerning the deeper and more extensive history of slavery in the Northern US states (Nash, 2006). Whilst the USA does not have a national curriculum, federally supported curriculum guidelines were devised during the 1990s by Gary Nash and University of California, Los Angeles's National Center for History in the Schools (Nash and Crabtree, 1996), which sought to challenge past Confederate sympathies and to promote an historical curriculum reflective of the experiences and perspectives of all Americans. Like many of the wider developments mentioned above, this provoked a backlash with conservative politicians labelling the curriculum 'Cultural Marxism', although the curriculum won the support of the American Historical Association (Levine, 2006: 194).[7] Of symbolic significance, the Smithsonian Institute opened the National Museum of African American History and Culture in Washington DC in September 2016 following federal funding assistance from a 2004 Act of Congress (Horton, 2006: 54; see also National Museum of African American History and Culture, n.d.). These developments demonstrate how academic historical and archaeological research, and the greater space for African American voices, is reshaping how America represents its history to its children, to its public and to visitors. These changes acknowledge that America's past has not always been just, that lasting damage may have been caused and that this should be addressed going forward. Similar changes to the English National Curriculum following the 2007 Bicentenary of the Abolition of the British Slave Trade also attest to the power of museums, commemoration and public dialogue to change how a nation understands and seeks to represent its past to its children and the potential impact that this could have in the future (Hall, 2010).

Within the USA, there are also groups which are more closely following the ideal of restorative justice and seeking to create healing dialogue between those divided by the history and legacy of slavery. *Traces of the Trade: A Story From the Deep North* (2008) is a film by Katrina Browne (and Alla Kovgan) in which she and

7 Debates over history, particularly that of slavery and the Confederacy, remain highly contentious, as the recent violence in Charlottesville, Virginia, involving extreme right-wing groups who had ostensibly rallied to protest the removal of a statue of Confederate General Robert E. Lee attest (Astor et al., 2017; Wright, 2017; Little, 2017). For further insight into the strength of neo-Confederate historiography and its cultural role see Kaufman (2006); Horwitz (1999); Coski (2005); Blight (2002).

relatives discuss their ancestors, the DeWolf family's role as the leading slave traders in Rhode Island, and how this history and legacy is manifest in racial injustice across the USA today. The organisation Traces of the Trade now produces discussion guides for schools, churches and other groups to discuss these themes following a viewing of the film and has been supported in further promoting such resources by the Public Broadcasting Service (PBS) (Traces of the Trade, n.d.; PBS, n.d.). Coming to the Table is a project that commenced in:

> January 2006, [when] black and white descendants of ancestors linked by a slave/slave-owner relationship, a blood connection, or both came together in a small retreat which took place at Eastern Mennonite University in Harrisonburg, Virginia, to explore the history of slavery – its legacy and impact on their lives today.
>
> (Coming to the Table, n.d.)

Gather at the Table (2012) sees Thomas DeWolf, a participant featured in *Traces of the Trade* and executive director of Coming to the Table, travel on a series of journeys over a three-year period with Sharon Leslie Morgan, to visit historic sites of slavery and racial injustices, and to discuss this history and its legacies, their hope being to 'inspire a national dialogue about the legacies of slavery and racism, and offer practical guidance for individuals and groups dedicated to healing America' (see Gather at the Table, 2012; DeWolf, 2008; DeWolf and Morgan, 2012). Such conversations can and should be seen as something that museums could facilitate as part of public engagement and criticism of their exhibits and past practice. In preparation for the development of galleries to mark the 2007 Bicentenary of the Abolition of the British Slave Trade, for instance, museums in Britain did prioritise community engagement (Fouseki, 2010; Wilson, 2010; Museum of London Docklands, 2008). However, such processes should not be timebound with a limited number of participants but expanded and seen as a central part of the museum's operation.

The abovementioned developments in US museums, schools and memorials are reflected by developments across the Atlantic world (see Araujo, 2012; Hamilton, Hodgson and Quirk, 2012; Lovejoy and Bowser, 2012). As in the USA, changing political environments have influenced these developments, reshaping whose voices influence historical debate and memorialisation. Indicative of the international trend for the increased memorialisation of transatlantic slavery is the Arc of Return memorial to the victims of transatlantic slavery at the UN headquarters in New York (see UN, n.d.). This memorial reflects how UNESCO has sought to aid the processes of decolonising history, which started in the 1970s with the UNESCO General History of Africa series (later followed by general histories of the Caribbean, Central Asia, Latin America and Islamic Culture) (see UNESCO, n.d.). The subsequent UNESCO Slave Route Project, established in 1994, has sought to further collate international research on the history and legacy of transatlantic slavery, and to promote African and Caribbean perspectives within five areas of specific interest: '1. Documentary sources, archives and data banks. 2.

Research. 3. Education and publications. 4. Physical heritage, museums and cultural tourism. 5. Artistic activities and information' (UNESCO, 1994: 1–2). With a limited budget, the Slave Route Project primarily operates as a co-ordinating body. For example, it worked with Anti-Slavery International in the promotion of the 1998 website *Breaking the Silence*, which formed part of its Breaking the Silence: Transatlantic Slave Trade Education Project funded by Norway (see UNESCO ASPnet, 2004; Beckles, 2002). In partnership with the UN World Tourism Organization, the Slave Route Project has also promoted the preservation and status of historical sites associated with transatlantic slavery through the project *Cultural Tourism – Tourism of Memory* (UNESCO, 2000). The Slave Route Project has also increasingly come to support reparations for slavery, declaring support for 'Ethical Reparations', 'Historical Reparations', 'Educational Reparations' and 'Socio-economic Reparations' (Quirk and Landers, 2015). These reparations would reflect a symbolic acknowledgement of historical wrongdoing, call for education and memorialisation, and policies to address the social and economic harms of slavery going forward. In many ways, these calls reflect the idea of historical truth telling outlined in this chapter and how such truth telling could be transformative, although it is not clear that the Slave Route Project views itself as an historical truth-telling vehicle of repair.

The UNESCO Slave Route Project does, however, encapsulate many of the concepts of truth telling. Its organisational structure, with its leadership and direction shaped by an International Scientific Committee of academic experts, could also be likened to the role of the commissioners in a formal truth commission. It empowers previously suppressed historical sources and perspectives (social truths), and disseminates materials to reshape dialogue over this history and its legacy (UNESCO, 2010). The International Committee also acts as a contact zone for individuals from different national backgrounds and perspectives, whilst the production of new research, educational resources and museums also sees UNESCO use these sites as contact zones in which individuals are introduced to new information and perspectives. By sponsoring international teacher institutes and school twinning, the Slave Route Project further acts as a contact zone as it enables contact, dialogue and interaction between individuals from different backgrounds and sides of this history (UNESCO ASPnet, 2011). In such situations, UNESCO helps create the conditions for personal restorative dialogue to occur in the manner that Coming to the Table aspires, and there is a potential transformative outcome if such processes are both successful and expanded.

Conclusion

This chapter has explored the potential insights that processes of restorative justice utilised in transitional justice settings can offer to the repair of legacies of transatlantic slavery. It has done so because calls for financial reparations based upon legal arguments oversimplify the history and legacy of transatlantic slavery and do not offer to satisfactorily repair the attitudinal and relational harms which perpetuate the socioeconomic injustices reparations are called upon to address. By drawing upon the strengths of truth-telling processes in transitional justice settings, historians and archaeologists, schools and museums can help facilitate necessary repair of attitudes and relationships. Not only is such attitudinal and relational repair necessary, but such repair is also superior to financial reparations alone, as it can help create a platform for transformational repair.

Attitudinal and relational repair is not easy to accomplish and the shortcomings of official truth commissions in transitional justice settings illustrate the need not to artificially circumscribe the scope or the period of operation of historical truth-telling processes. Indeed, this chapter has advocated not for an official commission but for the work of historians and archaeologists, schools and museums to be seen as potential contributors to a broad process of historical truth telling which both reveals how history has shaped present-day inequalities and prejudices, and where the discussion of this can help repair these harms. Across the Atlantic world, historians and archaeologists are working to increase understanding of the scope, nature and impact of transatlantic slavery. Their work contributes to a form of factual truth telling which can help to stimulate wider dialogue about the history and its legacy. The revision of museum galleries, educational curricula and memorial landscapes is also contributing to widen public debates. However, the stimulation of direct, interpersonal dialogue is rarely facilitated outside of restorative justice-inspired organisations such as Coming to the Table. Museums and schools, as contact zones, have the potential to stimulate such dialogue by being sites in which historical evidence is presented dispassionately, where critical engagement is encouraged and where different perspectives can be voiced – but also critically explored. Transnational school twinning projects, such as that facilitated by the UNESCO Slave Route Project, can contribute to processes of transnational contact, dialogue and reconciliation. By highlighting developments already underway, this chapter hopes to illustrate how such processes of discussion can be potentially reparative. Whilst this process of repair may seem to lack the substance of financial reparations, it potentially offers more, as greater understanding about the foundations of present-day injustices and the repair of relationships can provide the foundation for policies which transform society.

References

The African American Civil War Museum. (n.d.) 'The African American Civil War Museum', www.afroamcivilwar.org/ [accessed 10 August 2017].

Araujo, Ana. (2012) *Politics of Memory: Making Slavery Visible in the Public Space*. New York: Routledge.

Astor, Maggie, Christian Caron and Daniel Victor. (2017) 'A Guide to the Violence in Charlottesville'. *New York Times*, 13 August, www.nytimes.com/2017/08/13/us/charlottesville-virginia-overview.html [accessed 14 August 2017].

Bachman, Klaus. (2013) 'Conflict Avoidance, Forgetting, and Distorted Memories by Media Influence on Family Memories: Grandpa Was No Nazi and No Communist'. In Michael Linden and Krysztof Rutkowski (eds), *Hurting Memories and Beneficial Forgetting: Posttraumatic Stress Disorders, Biographical Developments, and Social Conflicts*, 203–216. London: Elsevier.

Beckles, Hilary. (1987) '"The Williams Effect": Eric Williams's Capitalism and Slavery and the Growth of West Indian Political Economy'. In Barbara Solow and Stanley Engerman (eds), *British Capitalism and Caribbean Slavery: The Legacy of Eric Williams*, 303–316. Cambridge: Cambridge University Press.

Beckles, Hilary. (2002) *Slave Voyages: The Transatlantic Slave Trade in Enslaved Africans*. Paris: UNESCO.

Beckles, Hilary. (2013) *Britain's Black Debt: Reparations for Caribbean Slavery and Native Genocide*. Kingston: University of West Indies Press.

Berg, Manfred. (2009) 'Historical Continuity and Counterfactual History in the Debate Over Reparations for Slavery'. In Manfred Berg and Bernd Schaffer (eds), *Historical Justice in International Perspective*, 69–91. Cambridge: Cambridge University Press.

Berg, Manfred and Bernd Schaffer. (2009) 'Introduction'. In Manfred Berg and Bernd Schaffer (eds), *Historical Justice in International Perspective*, 1–17. Cambridge: Cambridge University Press.

Berlin, Ira and Leslie Harris. (2005) 'Uncovering, Discovering and Recovering: Digging in New York's Slave Past Beyond the African Burial Ground'. In Ira Berlin and Leslie Harris (eds), *Slavery in New York*, 1–27. New York: New Press.

Biondi, Martha. (2007) 'The Rise of the Reparations Movement'. In Michael Martin and Marilyn Yaquinto (eds), *Redress for Historical Injustices in the United States: On Reparations for Slavery, Jim Crow, and their Legacies*, 255–269. Durham, NC: Duke University Press.

Blackburn, Robin. (2011) *The American Crucible: Slavery, Emancipation and Human Rights*. London: Verso.

Blight, David. (2002) *Beyond the Battlefield: Race, Memory and the American Civil War*. Amherst and Boston, MA: University of Massachusetts Press.

Boswell, Rosabelle. (2014) 'Can Justice Be Achieved for Slave Descendants in Mauritius?'. *International Journal of Law, Crime and Justice* 42: 146–161.

Bremner, Lindsay Jill. (2007) 'Memory, Nation Building and the Post-Apartheid City: The Apartheid Museum in Johannesburg'. In Noëleen Murray, Nick Shepherd and Martin Hall (eds), *Desire Lines: Space, Memory and Identity in the Post-Apartheid City*, 140–169. Abingdon: Routledge.

Brooks, Roy. (2004) *Atonement and Forgiveness: A New Model for Black Reparations*. London: University of California Press.

Brophy, Alfred. (2006) *Reparations: Pro and Con*. Oxford: Oxford University Press.

Browne, Katrina and Alla Kovgan. (2008) *Traces of the Trade: A Story from the Deep North*. New York: American Documentary.

Campbell, Edward D.C. and Kym S. Rice (eds). (1991) *Before Freedom Came: African American Life in the Antebellum South*. Charlottesville, VA: The Museum of the Confederacy and the University Press of Virginia.

Christodoulidis, Emilios and Scott Veitch. (2008) 'Reconciliation as surrender: configurations of responsibility and memory'. In Francois du Bois and Antje du Bois-Pedain (eds), *Justice and Reconciliation in Post-Apartheid South Africa*, 9–36. Cambridge: Cambridge University Press.

Coming to the Table. (n.d.) 'Coming to the Table', http://comingtothetable.org/ [accessed 16 August 2017].

Coski, John. (2005) *The Confederate Battle Flag: America's Most Embattled Emblem*. Cambridge, MA: The Belknap Press of Harvard University Press.

Davis, David Brion. (2006) *Inhuman Bondage: The Rise and Fall of Slavery in the New World*. Oxford: Oxford University Press.

de Brito, Alexandra Barahona, Paloma Aguilar and Carmen Gonzaléz-Enríquez (2001) 'Introduction'. In Alexandra Barahona de Brito, Carmen Gonzaléz-Enríquez and Paloma Aguilar (eds), *The Politics of Memory: Transitional Justice in Democratizing Societies*, 1–39. Oxford: Oxford University Press.
DeWolf, Thomas. (2008) *Inheriting the Trade: A Northern Family Confronts its Legacy as the Largest Slave-trading Dynasty in US History*. Boston, MA: Beacon Press.
DeWolf, Thomas and Sharon Leslie Morgan. (2012) *Gather at the Table: The Healing Journey of a Daughter of Slavery and a Son of the Slave Trade*. Boston, MA: Beacon Press.
Draper, Nicholas. (2010) *The Price of Emancipation: Slave-ownership, Compensation and British Society at the End of Slavery*. Cambridge: Cambridge University Press.
Drescher, Seymour. (1977) *Econocide: British Slavery in the Era of Abolition*. Pittsburgh, PA: University of Pittsburgh Press.
du Bois, Francois. (2008) 'Reparations and the forms of justice'. In Francois du Bois and Antje du Bois-Pedain (eds), *Justice and Reconciliation in Post-Apartheid South Africa*, 116–143. Cambridge: Cambridge University Press.
Eltis, David and Stanley Engerman. (2000) 'The Importance of Slavery and the Slave Trade to Industrializing Britain'. *The Journal of Economic History* 60(1): 123–144.
Evans, Matthew and David Wilkins. (2017) 'Transformative justice, reparations and transatlantic slavery'. *Social and Legal Studies*. DOI: 10.1177/0964663917746490.
Firchow, Pamina. (2013) 'Must Our Communities Bleed to Receive Social Services? Development Projects and Collective Reparations Schemes in Colombia'. *Journal of Peacebuilding and Development* 8(3): 50–63.
Foner, Eric. (1988) *Reconstruction: 1863–1877*. New York: Harper Row.
Fouseki, Kalliopi. (2010) '"Community voices, curatorial choices": community consultation for the 1807 exhibitions'. *Museum and Society* 8(3): 180–192.
Fullard, Madeleine and Nicky Rousseau. (2008) 'Uncertain borders: the TRC and the (un) making of public myths'. *Kronos* 34(1): 215–239.
Gather at the Table. (2012) 'Gather at the Table', http://gatheratthetable.net/ [accessed 16 August 2017].
Gibney, Mark, Rhoda Howard-Hassmann, Jean-Marc Coicaud and Niklaus Steiner. (2008) 'Introduction: Apologies and the West'. In Mark Gibney, Rhoda Howard-Hassmann, Jean-Marc Coicaud and Niklaus Steiner (eds), *The Age of Apology: Facing Up to the Past*, 1–9. Philadelphia, PA: University of Pennsylvania Press.
Gifford, Anthony. (2000) 'The Legal Basis of the Claim for Slavery Reparations'. *Human Rights: Journal of the Section of Individual Rights and Responsibilities* 27(2): 16–18.
Glass-Avery, Hermina. (2011) *Assessing African American Attitudes Towards the Civil War: The War of Jubilee: Tell Our Story and We Will Come*, Final Group Report. Washington, DC: National Parks Service.
Gready, Paul and Simon Robins. (2014) 'From Transitional to Transformative Justice: A New Agenda for Practice'. *International Journal of Transitional Justice* 8(3): 339–361.
Gross, Ariela J. (2011) 'All Born to Freedom? Comparing the Law and Politics of Race and the Memory of Slavery in the US and France Today'. University of Southern California Legal Studies Working Paper Series 82.
Gunter, Joel. (2018) 'Holocaust law wields a "blunt instrument" against Poland's past'. *BBC News*, 3 February, www.bbc.co.uk/news/world-europe-42920934 [accessed 12 July 2018].
Hall, Catherine. (2010) 'Afterword'. In Cora Kaplan and John Oldfield (eds), *Imagining Transatlantic Slavery*, 191–201. Basingstoke: Palgrave Macmillan.

Hall, Catherine, Nicholas Draper, Keith McClelland, Katie Donnington and Rachel Lang. (2014) *Legacies of British Slave-ownership: Colonial Slavery and the Formation of Victorian Britain*. Cambridge: Cambridge University Press.

Hamilton, Douglas, Kate Hodgson and Joel Quirk (eds). (2012) *Slavery, Memory and Identity: National Representations and Global Legacies*. London: Pickering and Chatto.

Hofhansel, Claus. (2005) *Multilateralism, German Foreign Policy and Central Europe*. Abingdon: Routledge.

Horton, John Oliver. (2006) 'Slavery in American History: An Uncomfortable National Dialogue'. In John Oliver Horton and Lois E. Horton (eds), *Slavery and Public History: The Tough Stuff of American History* , 35–55. New York: The New Press.

Horwitz, Tony. (1999) *Confederates in the Attic: Dispatches from the Unfinished Civil War*. New York: Vintage.

Howard-Hassmann, Rhoda E. (2004) 'Reparations to Africa and the Group of Eminent Persons'. *Cahiers d'Études Africaines* XLIV (1/2), 173–174: 81–97.

Howard-Hassmann, Rhoda E. (2008) *Reparations to Africa*. Philadelphia, PA: University of Pennsylvania Press.

Hudson, Joe and Burt Galloway. (1996) 'Introduction'. In Joe Hudson and Burt Galloway (eds), *Restorative Justice: International Perspectives*, 1–14. Monsey, NY: Criminal Justice Press.

Inikori, Joseph E. (1977) 'The Import of Firearms into West Africa 1750–1807: A Quantitative Analysis'. *The Journal of African History* 18(3): 339–368.

Inikori, Joseph E. (1987) 'Slavery and the development of industrial capitalism in England'. *Journal of Interdisciplinary History* 27(4): 771–793.

Inikori, Joseph E. (2002) *Africans and the Industrial Revolution in England: A Study in International Trade and Economic Development*. Cambridge: Cambridge University Press.

James, C.L.R. (2001) *The Black Jacobins: Toussaint L'Ouverture and the San Domingo Revolution*. London: Penguin Books.

Kachun, Mitch. (2003) *Festivals of Freedom: Memory and Meaning in African American Emancipation Celebrations, 1808–1915*. Amherst and Boston, MA: University of Massachusetts Press.

Kaufman, Will. (2006) *The Civil War in American Culture*. Edinburgh: Edinburgh University Press.

Leigh Day. (2014) 'CARICOM nations unanimously approve 10 point plan for slavery reparations', 14 March, www.leighday.co.uk/News/2014/March-2014/CARICOM-nations-unanimously-approve-10-point-plan [accessed 17 August 2017].

Levine, Bruce. (2006) 'In Search of a Usable Past: Neo-Confederates and Black Confederates'. In John Oliver Horton and Lois E. Horton (eds), *Slavery and Public History: The Tough Stuff of American History*, 187–211. New York: The New Press.

Little, Becky. (2017) 'How the Cult of Robert E. Lee Was Born'. *History.com*, 14 August, www.history.com/news/how-the-cult-of-robert-e-lee-was-born [accessed 16 August 2017].

Lovejoy, Paul E. (1989) 'The Impact of the Atlantic Slave Trade on Africa: A Review of the Literature'. *The Journal of African History* 30(3): 365–394.

Lovejoy, Paul E. and Benjamin P. Bowser (eds). (2012) *The Transatlantic Slave Trade and Slavery: New Directions in Teaching and Learning*. Trenton, NJ: Africa World Press.

Lowen, James W. (2007) *Lies My Teacher Told Me: Everything Your American History Textbook Got Wrong*. London: The New Press.

Mamdani, Mahmood. (2002) 'Amnesty or Impunity? A Preliminary Critique of the Report of the Truth and Reconciliation Commission of South Africa (TRC)'. *Diacritics* 32(3/4): 33–59.

McCully, Alan. (2010) 'What Role for History Teaching in the Transitional Justice Process in Deeply Divided Societies?'. In Irene Nakou and Isabel Barca (eds), *Contemporary Public Debates Over History Education*, 169–184. Charlotte, NC: Information Age Publishing.

McCully, Alan. (2012) 'History Teaching, Conflict and the Legacy of the Past'. *Education, Citizenship and Social Justice* 7(2): 145–159.

McElya, Micki. (2007) *Clinging to Mammy: The Faithful Slave in Twentieth-century America*. Cambridge, MA: Harvard University Press.

Miller, David. (2007) *National Responsibility and Global Justice*. Oxford: Oxford University Press.

Minnow, Martha. (1998) *Between Vengeance and Forgiveness: Facing History after Genocide and Mass Violence*. Boston, MA: Beacon Press.

Mokyr, Joel. (1993) 'Editor's Introduction'. In Joel Mokyr (ed.), *The British Industrial Revolution: An Economic Perspective*, 1–131. Oxford: Westview Press.

Museum of London Docklands. (2008) *The Making of London, Sugar and Slavery: A Toolkit for Community Participation*. London: Museum of London.

Nagy, Rosemary L. (2013) 'The Scope and Bounds of Transitional Justice and the Canadian Truth and Reconciliation Commission'. *International Journal of Transitional Justice* 7(1): 52–73.

Nash, Gary B. (2006) 'For Whom Will the Liberty Bell Toll? From Controversy to Cooperation'. In John Oliver Horton and Lois E. Horton (eds), *Slavery and Public History: The Tough Stuff of American History*, 75–101. New York: The New Press.

Nash, Gary and Charlotte Crabtree (eds). (1996) *National Standards for History: Basic Edition*. Los Angeles, CA: National Center for History in the Schools.

National Museum of African American History and Culture. (n.d.) 'National Museum of African American History and Culture', https://nmaahc.si.edu/about/museum [accessed 17 August 2017].

National Parks Service. (n.d.) *African Burial Ground: National Monument*, www.nps.gov/afbg/index.htm [accessed 18 October 2012].

National Underground Railroad Freedom Center. (n.d.) 'National Underground Railroad Freedom Center', www.freedomcenter.org/ [accessed 10 August 2017].

New York Historical Society. (n.d.) 'Slavery in New York', www.slaveryinnewyork.org [accessed 17 July 2011].

Parker, Jason C. (2008) *Brother's Keeper: The United States, Race, and Empire in the British Caribbean, 1937-1962*. Oxford: Oxford University Press.

Parodi, Carlos A. (2008) 'State Apologies Under U.S. Hegemony'. In Mark Gibney, Rhoda Howard-Hassmann, Jean-Marc Coicaud and Niklaus Steiner (eds), *The Age of Apology: Facing Up to the Past*, 171–186. Philadelphia, PA: University of Pennsylvania Press.

PBS. (n.d.) *Traces of the Trade*, www.pbs.org/pov/tracesofthetrade/ [accessed 16 August 2017].

Pitcaithley, Dwight T. (2006) '"A Cosmic Threat": The National Park Service and the Causes of the American Civil War'. In John Oliver Horton and Lois E. Horton (eds), *Slavery and Public History: The Tough Stuff of American History*, 169–186. New York: The New Press.

Posel, Deborah. (1999) *The TRC Report: What Kind of History? What Kind of Truth? A Preliminary Exploration*. Paper presented at the workshop 'The TRC: Commissioning the Past', Wits History Workshop, University of the Witwatersrand, Johannesburg, South Africa, 11–14 June, http://wiredspace.wits.ac.za/bitstream/handle/10539/8046/HWS-341.pdf [accessed 5 April 2018].

Purkis, Harriet. (2013) 'Making Contact in an Exhibition Zone: Displaying Contemporary Cultural Diversity in Donegal, Ireland, Through an Installation of Visual and Material Portraits'. *Museum and Society* 11(1): 50–67.

Quirk, Joel and Jane Landers. (2015) *UNESCO Slave Route Project: Resistance, Liberty, Heritage*. Meeting of the International Scientific Committee (ISC) Cabo Verde, 26–29 October 2015, Final Report. Cidade Velha: UNESCO.

Robinson, Randall. (2000) *The Debt: What America Owes to Blacks*. London: Plume.

Rodney, Walter. (1973) *How Europe Underdeveloped Africa*. London: Bogel-L'Ouverture Publications.

Sierra Leone Truth and Reconciliation Commission. (n.d.) 'Peace Museum', www.sierraleonetrc.org/index.php/sierra-leone-peace-museum [accessed 17 August 2017].

Thelen, David. (2003) 'Learning from the Past: Individual Experience and Re-enactment'. *Indiana Magazine of History* 99(2): 155–171.

Thompson, Janna. (2002) *Taking Responsibility for the Past: Reparation and Historical Justice*. Cambridge: Polity Press.

Tobias, Manuela. (2018) 'Understanding Poland's "Holocaust law"'. *Politifact*, 9 March, www.politifact.com/truth-o-meter/article/2018/mar/09/understanding-polish-holocaust-law/ [accessed 12 July 2018].

Torpey, John. (2006) *'Making Whole What Has Been Smashed': On Reparations Politics*. Cambridge, MA: Harvard University Press.

Torpey, John. (2009) 'An Avalanche of History: The "Collapse of the Future" and the Rise of Reparations Politics'. In Manfred Berg and Bernd Schaffer (eds), *Historical Justice in International Perspective*, 21–38. Cambridge: Cambridge University Press.

Traces of the Trade. (n.d.) *Traces of the Trade*, www.tracesofthetrade.org/ [accessed 16 August 2017].

Truth and Justice Commission. (2011) *Report of the Truth and Justice Commission: Volume One*. Pointe aux Sables: Government Printing.

Tyler-McGraw, Marie. (2006) 'Southern Comfort Levels: Race, Heritage Tourism, and the Civil War in Richmond'. In John Oliver Horton and Lois E. Horton (eds), *Slavery and Public History: The Tough Stuff of American History*, 151–167. New York: The New Press.

UCL Department of History. (2018) *Legacies of British Slave-ownership*, www.ucl.ac.uk/lbs/ [accessed 4 April 2018].

UN. (n.d.) *Remember Slavery*, www.un.org/en/events/slaveryremembranceday/memorial.shtml [accessed 11 August 2017].

UN. (2001) *World Conference against Racism, Racial Discrimination, Xenophobia and Related Intolerance: Declaration*, www.un.org/WCAR/durban.pdf [accessed 17 August 2017].

UNESCO. (n.d.) *Learning to Live Together: General and Regional Histories*, www.unesco.org/new/en/social-and-human-sciences/themes/general-and-regional-histories/ [accessed 11 August 2017].

UNESCO. (1994) *First Session of the International Scientific Committee for the 'Slave Route' project*. Ouidah: UNESCO.

UNESCO. (2000) *Report on the 2nd Caribbean Workshop on the UNESCO/WTO Cultural Tourism Programme of the Slave Route Project*. Paris: UNESCO.

UNESCO. (2010) *Slave Routes: A Global Vision*. DVD. Paris: UNESCO.

UNESCO ASPnet. (2004) *'Breaking the Silence': The Transatlantic Slave Trade (TST) Education Project, All Equal in Diversity: International Campaign Mobilising Schools Against Racism, Discrimination and Exclusion*. Paris: UNESCO.

UNESCO ASPnet. (2011) *Teaching the Transatlantic Slave Trade: Achievements, Challenges and Perspectives, Final Report of the Interregional Online Consultation of the UNESCO Associated Schools (ASPnet), 30 November to 16 December 2010*. Paris: UNESCO.

Van Ness, Daniel W. and Karen Heetberks Strong. (2006) *Restoring Justice: An Introduction to Restorative Justice*. Cincinnati, OH: LexisNexis.

Verbeeck, Georgi. (2007) 'Structure of memory: Apartheid in the museum'. In Hans Erik Stolten (ed.), *History Making and Present Day Politics: The Meaning of Collective Memory in South Africa*, 217–226. Stockholm: Elanders Gotab AB.

Voyages: The Trans-Atlantic Slave Trade Database. (2008) www.slavevoyages.org/tast/index.faces [accessed 17 August 2017].

Waldorf, Lars. (2012) 'Anticipating the Past: Transitional Justice and Socio-economic Wrongs'. *Social and Legal Studies* 21(2): 171–186.

Walker, Margaret Urban. (2006) *Moral Repair: Reconstructing Moral Relations after Wrongdoing*. Cambridge: Cambridge University Press.

Weaver, Matthew. (2015) 'British slavery reparations Q&A'. *The Guardian*, 30 September, www.theguardian.com/world/2015/sep/30/british-slavery-reparations-qa [accessed 7 April 2018].

Wilkinson, Bert. (2017) 'Europe replies to demand for reparations'. *Amsterdam News*, 20 July, http://amsterdamnews.com/news/2017/jul/20/europe-replies-demand-reparations/ [accessed 7 April 2018].

Williams, Eric. (1944) *Capitalism and Antislavery*. Chapel Hill, NC: University of North Carolina Press.

Wilson, Ross. (2010) 'Rethinking 1807: museums, knowledge and expertise'. *Museum and Society* 8(3): 165–179.

Wright, Robin. (2017) 'Is America Headed for a New Kind of Civil War?'. *The New Yorker*, 14 August, www.newyorker.com/news/news-desk/is-america-headed-for-a-new-kind-of-civil-war [accessed 16 August 2017].

Afterwords on aftermaths

Lars Waldorf

Introduction

Transitional justice is beginning to look less like a field and more like kudzu. It has spread from authoritarian transitions to conflict transitions to non-transitions to post-transitions. It has encroached into adjacent fields: development, humanitarianism, and peacebuilding. It has grown in ambition, from combating impunity to transforming society. This expansionism is fuelled not by success but rather by disappointment with earlier experiments in transitional justice.

There are two principal groups promoting expansion. One, rallying under the banner of 'transformative justice', argues that transitional justice should challenge structural violence (including gender inequalities) through bottom-up, participatory, and victim-centric processes (for example Gready and Robins, 2014).[1] The other group, which includes former UN Special Rapporteur Pablo de Greiff, uses 'guarantees of non-recurrence' to 'help navigate between the insufficiency of current [transitional justice] measures and the risks of over-expansion and continued overpromising that accompany a "transformative" agenda' (Roht-Arriaza, 2016: 4). Both groups are influencing debates over policy and practice, including those over transformative reparations in Colombia and guarantees of non-recurrence in Sri Lanka.

I have serious reservations about both these efforts to expand transitional justice. Elsewhere, I have called for 'good enough' transitional justice (Waldorf, forthcoming), and for linking transitional justice to sustainable development through legal empowerment (Waldorf, 2019). At a time when populist authoritarianism threatens the modest but real achievements of the liberal-legalist human rights framework (Alston, 2017; see also Vinjamuri, 2017), what's needed is less hubristic overreaching and more principled pragmatism.[2]

1 Evans (Chapter 3, this volume) makes the more persuasive argument that transformative justice should be conceptualised and implemented separately from transitional justice. But that remains very much a minority position among those espousing transformative justice.

2 I have borrowed the term 'principled pragmatism' from a conversation with Pablo de Greiff.

Transformative justice: a litany of doubts

While this volume makes a useful contribution to the debates over transitional and transformative justice, it does not allay my concerns about transformative justice. If anything, it helpfully highlights some of the ongoing problems with both the concept and its application.

First, several of the chapters spend more time critiquing transitional justice or international criminal justice than they do making a positive case for transformative justice. As a result, transformative justice remains vaguely defined and weakly conceptualized. Indeed, McGill admits that '[t]he meaning of transformative justice is still rather nebulous, with no commonly agreed definition or components'. Similarly, Evans recognises that 'transformative justice' risks becoming an empty signifier, rather like 'reconciliation'. While such acknowledgment is welcome, it remains unclear exactly what transformative justice is seeking to transform: political structures, social relations, economic relations, or individuals? If the first two, then transformative justice needs to engage with the literature on how to change formal – and especially informal – institutions (see Waldorf, 2017; Chappell, 2014). If the latter two, then transformative justice might usefully look to the capability approach (for example Nussbaum, 2011).

Second, advocates of transformative justice tend to privilege process over outcomes (for example Gready and Robins, 2014). Their assumption is that participatory processes will either be transformative in themselves (Evans, Chapter 3, this volume) or produce transformative outcomes. There are several problems with this assumption. For one thing, as Lai and Bonora's chapter on the former Yugoslavia reminds us, participatory victims' processes may actually promote ethnic exclusion. For another, it's difficult to see how localised, participatory processes (when progressive) can lead to structural transformation on a wider level. Finally, it's also harder to have faith in scaled-up participatory processes after Colombia's 2016 referendum on the peace agreement, as well as recent evidence of how social media and disinformation have combined to undermine deliberative democracy.

Third, transformative justice advocates largely ignore 'scope conditions': that is, what are the political, economic, and social factors that make transformative justice endeavours and outcomes more likely (Vinjamuri and Snyder, 2015)? In his chapter, McAuliffe rightly observes that transformative justice overlooks the political economy of transition and transformation. By contrast, transitional justice scholars and policymakers have (belatedly) begun to look at how to encourage more inclusive political settlements or elite bargains (Bell and Pospisil, 2017).

Finally, transformative justice advocates have a tough time pointing to any real-world examples of how it has been, or can be, applied. Evans (Chapter 3, this volume) forthrightly states that transformative justice is more useful as an analytical lens than as an explicit way of shaping policy and practice. McGill (Chapter 2, this volume) seems to concur: he applies his model of transformative justice to two rural policy initiatives in Colombia, the Peasant Reserve Zones and the Land Restitution Program. His observations are equivocal: while the Peasant Reserve Zones were more transformative in terms of diagnosis and process, he admits that the Land Restitution Program 'may prove to have more transformative effects … primarily because it is the best-resourced mechanism in the country and was symbolically important for the Santos administration'.[3] Similarly, Lai and Bonora argue that the 2014 economic protest movement in Bosnia had more 'transformative *potential*' (emphasis added) than the Regional Commission (RECOM), but acknowledge that, 'in the long run, the more institutionalised RECOM initiative might have a more prominent legacy'. Indeed, they admit that the 2014 protests did not lead to changes in Bosnia's economic structures or policies, and did not lead to more lasting social mobilisation. These examples from Colombia and Bosnia only serve to reinforce McAuliffe's critique of transformative justice: 'a discourse premised around the twin poles of rejecting liberal-legalist models and celebrating the emancipatory potential of localised justice projects cannot identify the political levers or economic tools that might catalyse the desired broader agenda for change'.

Conclusion

I have been writing this piece in an ill-conceived hotel in Vavuniya that feels like it was built for a post-war boom which never arrived. For many years, this was a border town: the Sri Lankan government's last stronghold on the A9 highway before one reached the Tamil Tigers' shadow state. Vavuniya still bears the imprint of war with large military garrisons flanking the town and families of the disappeared holding an 18-month protest vigil outside the main Hindu temple (Fernando, 2018). When I made a 'solidarity visit' last year with a group studying transitional justice and reconciliation, one of the women broke ranks and angrily questioned in a shout whether our presence would make any difference while her colleagues tried to quieten her. For me, that outburst underscored how the government's unfulfilled promises of transitional justice had created further suffering. More than a year on, there is now an Office of Missing Persons but the families still don't know what happened to their loved ones and so are maintaining their vigil. Given the limited prospects for meaningful transitional justice in the current political context (see Fonseka, 2017; International Crisis Group, 2017), it's hard to see what transformative justice has to offer – other than more raised expectations and bitter frustrations.

References

Alston, Philip. (2017) 'The Populist Challenge to Human Rights'. *Journal of Human Rights Practice* 9(1): 1–15.

Bell, Christine and Jan Pospisil. (2017) 'Navigating Inclusion in Transitions from Conflict: The Formalised Political Unsettlement'. *Journal of International Development* 29(5): 576–593.

3 McGill points to the need for further empirical work to determine which program actually reduces structural violence.

Chappell, Louise (2014) '"New," "Old," and "Nested" Institutions and Gender Justice Outcomes: A View from the International Criminal Court'. *Politics and Gender* 10(4): 572–594.

Fernando, Ruki. (2018) '366 Days – Roadside Protests in Kilinochchi'. *Groundviews*, 22 February, https://groundviews.org/2018/02/22/366-days-roadside-protests-in-kilinochchi/ [accessed 15 August 2018].

Fonseka, Bhavani (ed.). (2017) *Transitional Justice in Sri Lanka: Moving beyond Promises.* Colombo: Centre for Policy Alternatives.

Gready, Paul and Simon Robins. (2014) 'From Transitional to Transformative Justice: A New Agenda for Practice'. *International Journal of Transitional Justice* 8(3): 339–361.

International Crisis Group. (2017) *Sri Lanka's Transition to Nowhere.* Brussels: International Crisis Group.

Nussbaum, Martha. (2011) *Creating Capabilities: The Human Development Approach.* Cambridge, MA: Harvard University Press.

Roht-Arriaza, Naomi. (2016) *Measures of Non-repetition in Transitional Justice: The Missing Link?* Research Paper No. 160, University of California Hastings College of the Law Legal Studies Research Paper Series. San Francisco, CA: UC Hastings.

Vinjamuri, Leslie. (2017) 'Human Rights Backlash'. In Stephen Hopgood, Jack Snyder, and Leslie Vinjamuri (eds), *Human Rights Futures*, 114–134. Cambridge: Cambridge University Press.

Vinjamuri, Leslie and Jack Snyder. (2015) 'Law and Politics in Transitional Justice'. *Annual Review of Political Science* 18: 303–327.

Waldorf, Lars. (2017) 'Institutional Gardening in Unsettled Times: Transitional Justice and Institutional Contexts'. In Roger Duthie and Paul Seils (eds), *Justice Mosaics: How Context Shapes Transitional Justice in Fractured Societies*, 40–83. New York: International Center for Transitional Justice.

Waldorf, Lars. (2019) 'Between transition and transformation: legal empowerment as collective reparation'. In Paul Gready and Simon Robins (eds), *From Transitional to Transformative Justice.* New York: Cambridge University Press.

Waldorf, Lars. (forthcoming) '"Good Enough" Transitional Justice'. Unpublished manuscript.

Index

For Product Safety Concerns and Information please contact our EU representative GPSR@taylorandfrancis.com Taylor & Francis Verlag GmbH, Kaufingerstraße 24, 80331 München, Germany